**NORTH DAKOTA
STATE UNIVERSITY**

MAY 9 1985

LIBRARY

The African Political Dictionary

THE AFRICAN POLITICAL DICTIONARY

Claude S. Phillips
Western Michigan University

ABC-CLIO Information Services
Santa Barbara, California
Oxford, England

© 1984 by Claude S. Phillips

All rights reserved. No part of this publication may be reproduced, stored in a retrieval system, or transmitted, in any form or by any means, electronic, mechanical, photocopying, recording, or otherwise, except for the inclusion of brief quotations in a review, without prior permission in writing from the publishers.

Maps in Appendix A have been adapted from *Africa Report* 27 (1): 58 (January–February 1982).

Cartography by Alyson Nethery

Library of Congress Cataloging in Publication Data

Phillips, Claude S.
    The African political dictionary.

    (Clio dictionaries in political science; #6)
    Includes index.
    1. Africa—Politics and government—1960– —Dictionaries. I. Title. II. Series.
DT30.5.P47   1983   960'.03'21   82-24353
ISBN 0–87436–036–6
ISBN 0–87436–040–4 (pbk.)

10 9 8 7 6 5 4 3 2

ABC-Clio Information Services
2040 Alameda Padre Serra, Box 4397
Santa Barbara, California 93103

Clio Press Ltd.
55 St. Thomas Street
Oxford, OX1 1JG, England

Manufactured in the United States of America

Clio Dictionaries in Political Science

#1 *The Latin American Political Dictionary*
Ernest E. Rossi and Jack C. Plano

#2 *The International Relations Dictionary,* third edition
Jack C. Plano and Roy Olton

#3 *The Dictionary of Political Analysis,* second edition
Jack C. Plano, Robert E. Riggs, and Helenan S. Robin

#4 *The Soviet and East European Political Dictionary*
Barbara P. McCrea, Jack C. Plano, and George Klein

#5 *The Middle East Political Dictionary*
Lawrence Ziring

#6 *The African Political Dictionary*
Claude S. Phillips

Forthcoming

#7 *The European Political Dictionary*
Ernest E. Rossi and Barbara P. McCrea

#8 *The Constitutional Law Dictionary*
Ralph C. Chandler, Richard A. Enslen, and Peter G. Renstrom

#9 *The Presidential-Congressional Political Dictionary*
Jeffrey M. Elliot and Sheikh R. Ali

#10 *The Asian Political Dictionary*
Lawrence Ziring and C. I. Eugene Kim

SERIES STATEMENT

Language precision is the primary tool of every scientific discipline. That aphorism serves as the guideline for this series of political dictionaries. Although each book in the series relates to a specific topical or regional area in the discipline of political science, entries in the dictionaries also emphasize history, geography, economics, sociology, philosophy, and religion.

This dictionary series incorporates special features designed to help the reader overcome any language barriers that may impede a full understanding of the subject matter. For example, the concepts included in each volume were selected to complement the subject matter found in existing texts and other books. All but one volume utilize a subject-matter chapter arrangement that is most useful for classroom and study purposes.

Entries in all volumes include an up-to-date definition plus a paragraph of *significance* in which the authors discuss and analyze each term's historical and current relevance. Most entries are also cross-referenced, providing the reader an opportunity to seek additional information related to the subject of inquiry. A comprehensive index, found in both hardcover and paperback editions, allows the reader to locate major entries and other concepts, events, and institutions discussed within these entries.

The political and social sciences suffer more than most disciplines from semantic confusion. This is attributable, *inter alia*, to the popularization of the language, and to the focus on many diverse foreign political and social systems. This dictionary series is dedicated to overcoming some of this confusion through careful writing of thorough, accurate definitions for the central concepts, institutions, and events that comprise the basic knowledge of each of the subject fields. New titles in the series will be issued periodically, including some in related social science disciplines.

— Jack C. Plano
Series Editor

CONTENTS

A Note on How to Use This Book, **xi**
Frequently Used Abbreviations, **xiii**
Preface, **xv**
Guide to Countries, **xvii**

1. Land and People, **3**
2. Culture and Tradition, **19**
3. Colonial Perspectives, **35**
4. African Resistance to Colonialism, **53**
5. Political Culture and Ideology, **67**
6. Governmental Institutions and Processes, **85**
7. Political Development and Modernization, **103**
8. Revolutionary and Counterrevolutionary Forces, **121**
9. Intra-African Law, Organization, and Relations, **139**
10. Africa and the World, **169**

Appendix A: Maps, **193**
Appendix B: Tables, **199**
Selected Bibliography, **219**
Index, **227**

A NOTE ON HOW TO USE THIS BOOK

The African Political Dictionary is organized so that entries and supplementary data can be located in either of two ways. First, items are arranged alphabetically within subject-matter chapters. Terms relating to political activities like elections or indigenization, for example, can be found in the chapter titled Governmental Institutions and Processes. When doubtful about which chapter to look up, consult the general index. Page numbers for entries appear in the index in heavy black type; subsidiary concepts discussed within entries can be found in the index identified by page numbers in regular type. For study purposes, numerous entries have also been subsumed under major topical headings in the index, giving the student access to broad classes of related information.

The student can also more fully explore a topic by using the extensive cross-references provided in most entries. These may lead to materials included in the same chapter or may refer the student to other chapters. Page numbers have been included in all cross-references. A few concepts can be found as entries in more than one chapter; in each case the definition and significance of the item is related to the subject matter of each chapter in which the entry appears.

The author has designed the unique format of this book to offer the student a variety of useful applications in the quest for information. These include its use as (1) a *dictionary* and *reference guide* to the language of African political systems; (2) a *study guide* for the books, articles, and lectures used in introductory courses on African politics; (3) a *source of review material* for the political science major enrolled in advanced courses; and (4) a *social science aid* for use in courses in cognate fields that deal with the cultures, economics, geography, history, and social institutions of Africa.

FREQUENTLY USED ABBREVIATIONS

ACP	African, Caribbean, and Pacific States
ADB	African Development Bank
ALC	African Liberation Committee (Organization of African Unity)
ANC	African National Congress
BADEA	Arab Bank for Economic Development in Africa
CEAO	West African Economic Community
EAC	East African Community
ECA	Economic Commission for Africa
ECOWAS	Economic Community of West African States
EEC	European Economic Community
FAO	Food and Agricultural Organization (United Nations)
FLN	National Liberation Front (Algeria)
FNLA	National Front for the Liberation of Angola
FNLC	National Front for the Liberation of the Congo
FRELIMO	Front for the Liberation of Mozambique
IBRD	International Bank for Reconstruction and Development
IDA	International Development Association
IFC	International Finance Corporation
LDC	Less Developed Country
LLDC	Least Developed Country
MNC	Multinational Corporation
MPLA	Popular Movement for the Liberation of Angola
NIEO	New International Economic Order
OAPEC	Organization of Arab Petroleum Exporting Countries
OAU	Organization of African Unity
OCAM	African and Mauritanian Common Organization
OPEC	Organization of Petroleum Exporting Countries
PAC	Pan-Africanist Congress
SADCC	Southern African Development Coordination Conference
SADR	Saharan Arab Democratic Republic
SWAPO	South West African People's Organization

UDEAC	Customs and Economic Union of Central Africa
UDI	Unilateral Declaration of Independence
UN	United Nations
UNDP	United Nations Development Program
UNESCO	United Nations Educational, Scientific and Cultural Organization
UNHCR	United Nations High Commissioner for Refugees
UNITA	National Union for the Total Independence of Angola
WHO	World Health Organization

PREFACE

The African Political Dictionary is the fruit of my frustration in teaching African politics to students who had no historical, economic, geographic, or cultural context in which to cultivate such knowledge. I was encouraged to prepare this dictionary by my friend and colleague Jack C. Plano, series editor of the Clio Dictionaries in Political Science, and successful author or coauthor of ten such books. In 1980, I came to believe that it was possible to compile an African political dictionary that would complement general texts, introduce students to the basic information significant to the study of African politics, and be easily updated in subsequent editions. Whether or not I have succeeded is, of course, for both students and professors to decide.

The Clio Dictionaries in Political Science are designed to solve two problems related to dictionaries intended for regular classroom use. One problem is that of making dictionary terms directly applicable to the classroom topic at hand. To this end, Plano organized the dictionaries into a chapter format paralleling topics most often used in the classroom. Each chapter lists alphabetically the terms most appropriate for the subject. The terms are generally defined in six to ten sentences, but up to a page or more is used if necessary. The second major problem regards entry selection—the process of electing to include one dictionary term over another. Plano stipulated that each dictionary entry must be meaningful for the study of politics in the context of the major interest; in this particular volume, Africa. Each definition is followed by a significance paragraph for that entry, which may also range from a few sentences to a page or more in length. In this manner, major terms are delineated and their significance for African politics interpreted. Terms of secondary importance are defined and discussed within the main entries. The resulting book encompasses more topics than are usually found in most textbooks. Each definition includes references to parallel terms, and a cross-referenced index enables the reader to follow concepts through numerous chapters.

In preparing this volume, I have frequently relied on the following works: *Africa Research Bulletin,* Vol. 18 (Exeter, England: African Research Ltd., 1981); *Africa South of the Sahara,* Tenth Edition (London:

Europa Publications, 1981); Colin Legum, ed., *Africa Contemporary Record*, Volumes 1–13 (New York: Africana Publishing Co., 1969–1981); and Roland Oliver and Michael Crowder, eds., *Cambridge Encyclopedia of Africa* (Cambridge: Cambridge University Press, 1981). I have also benefited greatly from the works cited in the Selected Bibliography. Professor Earl Phillips, through ABC-Clio Information Services, provided a valuable critique of the entire manuscript. My colleagues Alan Jacobs and William Garland (both in Anthropology), and William Ritchie (Political Science), contributed their comments on certain terms in Chapters 2 and 5 respectively. Jack Plano saved me from numerous stylistic errors. Despite the debt I owe to these scholars and resources, I alone am responsible for the selection of terms, their definitions, and the statements of significance. I hope, however, that Africanists and students will point out errors of commission and omission. Finally, I owe much to my wife, Nancy, for her patience during certain very demanding months.

— Claude S. Phillips
Western Michigan University

GUIDE TO COUNTRIES

Algeria
African Liberation Committee (ALC) and, 142
Arab League and, 153, 169
border clash with Morocco, 155
Casablanca Group and, 157
Communist party, 70
competitive "one-party" elections, 72, 89, 113
customs union with Morocco and Tunisia, 164
economic viability of, 115
embassies abroad, 144, 214
French colony, 45
GNP/PC, 200
guerrilla warfare, 142
location, 8
military rule, 133
OPEC and, 111
petroleum in, 106, 115
Polisario and, 8, 160
political data, 177, 204, 208
population, 200–201
relations with China, 177
relations with Soviet Union, 161
relations with United States, 189, 190
social development, 113
socialism, 70, 83

Angola
agriculture, 106
civil war, 123, 177
Clark Amendment and, 177
Cuban troops in, 156, 178, 188
economic viability of, 115
embassies abroad, 214
Front for the National Liberation of Angola (FNLA), 127, 176, 177, 178
Front-Line State, 149
guerrilla warfare, 126, 158
location, 15
Lusophone, 181–182
Marxist state, 75
National Union for the Total Independence of Angola (UNITA), 128, 129, 142, 178
Neto, Agostinho, 143
petroleum in, 115
political data, 204, 208
Popular Movement for the Liberation of Angola (MPLA), 127, 128, 142, 159, 178
population, 201
Portuguese colony, 49, 142, 181
refugees, 162, 165
relations with United States, 188, 189
social development, 113
South African incursions into, 151
Southern African Development Coordination Conference (SADCC), 166
Soviet-Chinese rivalry in, 176
Soviet intervention, 186
urbanism, 33

Benin
African and Mauritian Common Organization (OCAM), 153
China and, 177
embassies abroad, 214
Entente Council and, 154, 180
Executive Council, 95
Francophone, 180–181
Franc Zone and, 153
French colony, 45
invaded, 130
least developed countries (LLDC), 106
location, 17
Marxist state, 75
mercenaries in, 130
militarism, 133
nationalization, 98

xvii

Niger Basin Authority and, 154
political data, 204, 208
population, 9, 201

Botswana
Anglophone, 173–174
British colony, 41, 173
Commonwealth and, 153, 174
constitutionalism, 71, 85, 87
elections, 89, 113
embassies abroad, 214
Front-Line State, 149
GNP/PC, 200
House of Chiefs, 94
least developed countries (LLDC), 106
legislature, 93, 94
location, 15
majoritarian democracy, 72
PAC guerrillas, 134
political data, 100, 204
population, 201
relations with South Africa, 141, 148
relations with United States, 189
Southern African customs union, 164
Southern African Development Coordination Conference (SADCC), 166

Burundi
Belgian mandate, 38
Black-minority government, 162
civil war, 123
constitution suspended, 86
embassies abroad, 214
Francophone, 180–181
genocide of Hutu, 84, 146
guerrilla warfare, 126
history, 38, 46
least developed countries (LLDC), 106
location, 3
military rule, 133
political data, 204, 208
population, 9, 201
refugees, 84, 162
relations with China, 177
relations with Israel, 170
terrorism, 84

Cameroon
Anglophone, 173–174
British mandate, 41
Customs and Economic Union of Central Africa (UDEAC) and, 153–154, 164
embassies abroad, 214
federalism abandoned, 102
Francophone, 180–181
Franc Zone and, 153

French mandate, 45
German colony, 46
GNP/PC, 200
location, 3
nationalization, 98
Niger Basin Authority and, 154
origin of Bantu, 22
political data, 204, 208
political prisoners, 135
population, 201
refugees, 162

Cape Verde
embassies abroad, 214
entrenched leadership, 112
least developed countries (LLDC), 106
location, 17
Lusophone, 181
political data, 204
population, 9, 201
Portuguese colony, 49
relations with France, 181
socialism in, 83

Central African Republic
African and Mauritian Common Organization (OCAM) and, 153
constitution status unclear, 86
embassies abroad, 214
Francophone, 180–181
Franc Zone and, 153
French colony, 45
guerrilla warfare, 126
least developed countries (LLDC), 106
location, 3
ministry for women's affairs, 88
monarchy abolished, 96
"no-party" system, 97
political data, 204, 208
political prisoners, 135
population, 201
refugees, 84
slaughter of citizens, 146
'terrorism, 84

Chad
civil war, 123
constitution status unclear, 86
Customs and Economic Union of Central Africa (UDEAC) and, 154, 164
embassies abroad, 214
Francophone, 180–181
Franc Zone and, 153
French colony, 45
French troops in, 180
guerrilla warfare, 126
Habré, Hissene, 160

least developed countries (LLDC), 106
Libyan intervention in, 156, 159
location, 3
Niger Basin Authority and, 154
political data, 204, 208
population, 201
refugees, 162
relations with Israel, 170

Comoro Islands
embassies abroad, 144, 214
Franc Zone and, 153
French colony, 45
least developed countries (LLDC), 106
location, 7
mercenaries in, 130
political data, 204, 208
political systems, 92, 97, 167
population, 9, 201

Congo
Customs and Economic Union of
    Central Africa (UDEAC) and, 154,
    164
embassies abroad, 214
Francophone, 180-181
Franc Zone and, 153
French colony, 45
guerrilla warfare, 126
location, 3
Marxist state, 75
military rule, 133
nationalization, 98
political data, 204, 209
population, 201
relations with Israel, 170

Djibouti
Arab League and, 153, 169
constitution delayed, 86
embassies abroad, 214
entrenched leadership, 112
French colony, 45
guerrilla warfare, 126
location, 3
political data, 204, 209
population, 9, 201
refugees, 162
relations with China, 177
relations with United States, 189

Egypt
African Liberation Committee (ALC)
    and, 142
agriculture, 106
Anglophone, 173-174
Aswan Dam, 116-117, 186
British colony, 41

Casablanca Group and, 157
Communist party, 70
constitutionalism, 71, 87
Coptic Christianity, 29
democracy, 72, 87, 93
elections, 85, 89, 100, 113
embassies abroad, 144, 214
expulsion from Arab League, 169, 171
GNP/PC, 200
guerrilla warfare, 126
location, 8
militarism, 133
military coup (1952), 126
monarchy abolished, 96
Muhammad Ali, 60
Nasser, Gamel Abdul, 185
peace treaty with Israel, 184
political data, 204, 209
population, 12, 115, 200-201
relations with China, 128
relations with Soviet Union, 117, 186
relations with United States, 189
war with Libya, 155

Equatorial Guinea
border clash with Gabon, 155
constitution suspended, 86
Cuban troops in, 178
embassies abroad, 144, 214
guerrilla warfare, 126
Hispanophone, 181
location, 3
military rule, 133
Nguema, Francisco, 84
Nguema, Macias, 146
political data, 204, 209
political prisoners, 135
population, 201
refugees, 84
slaughter of citizens, 146
Spanish colony, 52
Supreme Military Council, 95
terrorism, 84

Ethiopia
African Liberation Committee (ALC)
    and, 142
agriculture, 21, 106
Black African support in war, 143, 151,
    159
civil war, 77, 123, 136
class society, 82
communism and, 70
constitution suspended, 86
Coptic Christianity, 28
Cuban troops in, 156, 178, 184, 186
drought, 15
economic viability of, 115

embassies abroad, 144, 214
Eritrea, 48, 77, 136
escaped colonial domination (pre-1936), 42, 49
guerrilla warfare, 126
iron use, 26
least developed countries (LLDC), 106
location, 3
Marxist state, 75
Mengistu, Haile Miriam, and "red terror," 84
military rule, 133
monarchy abolished, 96
nationalization, 98
Ogaden secession attempt, 136
political data, 205, 209
political prisoners, 135
population, 12, 115, 200–201
refugees, 84, 162
relations with Israel, 170
relations with Soviet Union, 184, 186
Sahel, 14–15
Somalia military intervention in, 124, 151, 155, 156
Somali irredentism, 77, 136, 155
Soviet intervention in, 186
terrorism, 84
urbanism, 33
war with Somalia, 124, 155

Gabon
border clash with Equatorial Guinea, 155
Customs and Economic Union of Central Africa (UDEAC) and, 154, 164
embassies abroad, 214
Francophone, 180–181
Franc Zone and, 153
French colony, 45
French-speaking, 180
GNP/PC, 200
location, 3
mercenaries in, 130
ministry for women's affairs, 88
nationalization, 98
OPEC and, 111
petroleum in, 106, 116
political data, 205, 209
population, 10–11, 201
refugees, 162
social development, 113
U.S. aid to, 189

Gambia
Anglophone, 173–174
British colony, 41
Commonwealth and, 153, 174

constitutionalism, 71, 87
democracy, 72, 87, 93
elections, 85, 89, 100, 113
embassies abroad, 214
entrenched leadership, 112
least developed countries (LLDC), 106
location, 17
political data, 205, 209
population, 9, 201

Ghana
Anglophone, 173–174
Ashanti resistance, 54–55
Ashanti vs. Fante, 65
British colony, 41
Casablanca Group and, 157
Commonwealth and, 153, 174
conflict with Togo, 155
constitution suspended, 86
Convention People's Party, 127
Council of State, 95
criticism of Arab aid, 170
Danquah, J. B., 68
early resistance to colonialism, 65
embassies abroad, 144, 214
Ewé secessionist attempt, 136
Fante, 65
guerrilla warfare, 126
indigenization, 93
Limann, Hilla, 95
location, 17
military coup (1966), 125
military rule, 133
ministries, 95
nationalization, 98
Nkrumah, Kwame, 67, 73, 77–78, 107, 139, 142, 157, 169
political data, 205, 209
population, 12, 115, 200–201
proto-nationalism in, 61–62
relations with Israel, 171
relations with Soviet Union, 185
restoration of civilian rule, 134
Tallensi, 82
urbanism, 33

Guinea
African Liberation Committee (ALC) and, 142
Casablanca Group and, 157
Cubans in, 178
embassies abroad, 214
entrenched leadership, 112
Francophone, 180–181
French colony, 45
guerrilla warfare, 126
least developed countries (LLDC), 106
location, 17

Guide To Countries xxi

mercenaries in, 130
mining in, 106
nationalization, 98
Niger Basin Authority and, 154
political data, 205, 209
political prisoners, 84, 135
population, 201
private investment in, 109
refugees, 84
rejects French community, 44, 45
relations with Israel, 170
relations with Soviet Union, 185, 186
relations with United States, 190
Samori Touré, 62
self-reliance, 109
socialism in, 83
terrorism, 84
Touré, Sekou, 73, 77, 109, 169

Guinea-Bissau
constitution suspended, 86
Cuban troops in, 178
embassies abroad, 214
least developed countries (LLDC), 106
location, 17
Lusophone, 181–182
political data, 205, 209
population, 201
Portuguese colony, 49, 142
relations with France, 181
socialism in, 83
unilateral declaration of independence, 167

Ivory Coast
African Development Bank (ADB) and, 140
Agni secessionist attempt, 136
capitalism in, 99
civil war, 123
competitive "one-party" system, 72, 89, 113
economic affiliations, 153, 154, 180
economic growth, 105
embassies abroad, 214
Francophone, 180–181
Franc Zone and, 153
French colony, 45
GNP/PC, 200
Houphouet-Boigny, Felix, 37, 44, 72
location, 17
mercenaries in, 130
Niger Basin Authority and, 154
political data, 205, 209
population, 201
relations with Israel, 170, 171
social development, 113

status quo power, 112, 136
troops to Zaire, 166

Kenya
Anglophone, 173–174
British colony, 41
capitalism in, 146
Commonwealth and, 153, 174
competitive "one-party" system, 72, 89, 113
East African Community (EAC) and, 146, 164
embassies abroad, 214
Indians in, 64
indigenization, 93
Kenyatta, Jomo, 77
location, 3
Maasai, 26, 82
Mau Mau, 59
Mboya, Tom, 142
Moi, Daniel Arap, 160
nationalization, 98
political data, 205, 209
political prisoners, 135
population, 11–12, 115, 200–201
relations with China, 177
relations with Israel, 170
relations with United States, 189
settlers, 51
Somali irredentism, 155
Somali secessionist attempt, 136
Swahili, 28
Tiriki, 30
urbanism, 33

Lesotho
Anglophone, 173–174
British colony, 41
constitution status unclear, 86
economic affiliations, 153, 164, 166, 174
embassies abroad, 214
Jonathan, Leabua, 96
least developed countries (LLDC), 106
location, 15
monarchy, 96
Moshoeshoe II (King), 96
palace coup (1970), 126
parliamentary executive, 90
political data, 205, 210
population, 201
refugees, 163
relations with South Africa, 141

Liberia
Anglophone, 173–174
colonial domination avoided, 42, 49
constitution suspended, 86
embassies abroad, 214

freed slaves, 29
Kpelle, 30
location, 17
military rule, 131, 133
mining in, 106
Niger Basin Authority and, 154
"no-party" system, 97
People's Redemption Council, 95
political data, 205, 210
political prisoners, 135
population, 9, 201
relations with Israel, 170, 171
relations with United States, 188, 189

Libya
Arab Bank for Economic Development of Africa (BADEA) and, 175
Arab League and, 153, 169
Arab unity, 79
economic viability of, 115, 200
embassies abroad, 214
General Popular Committee, 95
guerrilla warfare, 126
Italian colony, 63
location, 8
military rule, 133
monarchy abolished, 96
petroleum and, 106, 111, 115
political data, 205, 210
political prisoners, 135
population, 201
Qaddafy, Muammar, 73, 133, 134
relations with United States, 189
Sanusiyya resistance, 63
social development, 113
socialism in, 83
supports Eritrea and Somalia, 159
troops in Chad, 156
war with Egypt, 155

Madagascar
Communist party, 70
embassies abroad, 214
French colony, 45
languages, 27
location, 7
Marxist state, 75
military rule, 133
Mongoloid gene pool, 12
nationalization, 98
political data, 205, 210
population, 201
relations with China, 177
Supreme Revolutionary Council, 96

Malawi
agriculture, 106
Anglophone, 173–174

British colony, 41
Central African Federation and, 55–56
Chilembwe, John, 56
economic affiliations, 41, 153, 166, 174
embassies abroad, 214
entrenched leadership, 112
guerrilla warfare, 126
least developed countries (LLDC), 106
location, 15
nationalization, 98
political data, 205, 210
population, 9, 201
relations with Israel, 170
relations with South Africa, 141, 144, 155, 156
Watch Tower Movement and, 66
World War I battles in, 56

Mali
Casablanca Group and, 157
economic affiliations, 154
embassies abroad, 214
Francophone, 180–181
Franc Zone and, 153
French colony, 45
least developed countries (LLDC), 106
location, 17
military rule, 133
nationalization, 98
Niger Basin Authority and, 154
political data, 206, 210
political prisoners, 135
population, 201
relations with Israel, 170
seeks increased trade with United States, 190
urbanism, 33

Mauritania
Arab League and, 153, 169
claimed by Morocco, 158
constitution suspended, 86
economic affiliations, 154, 180
embassies abroad, 214
Francophone, 180–181
French colony, 45
location, 17
Military Committee for National Salvation, 96
military rule, 133
nationalization, 98
"no-party" system, 97
Polisario, Western Sahara and, 160–161
political data, 206, 210
population, 201
relations with China, 177
Sahel, 14

Guide To Countries

Mauritius
African and Mauritian Common Organization (OCAM) and, 153
Anglophone, 173–174
British colony, 41
Commonwealth and, 153, 174
constitutionalism, 71
democracy, 72, 87
Diego Garcia, 175
elections, 83, 85, 89, 112, 113
embassies abroad, 214
GNP/PC, 200
language, 27, 174
location, 7
political data, 206
political system, 87, 90, 93, 96, 100
population, 9, 201
Queen of England and, 96
relations with China, 177
relations with France, 181
relations with South Africa, 141
socialism in, 83

Morocco
Arab League and, 153, 169
border clash with Algeria, 155
Casablanca Group and, 157
claims Mauritania, 158
constitutionalism, 71, 87
customs union with Algeria and Tunisia, 164
democracy, 72, 87, 93
elections, 89, 113
embassies abroad, 214
French colony, 45
GNP/PC, 200
guerrilla warfare, 126
location, 8
Maghreb independence, 169–170
mercenaries in, 130
monarchy, 90, 96
Organization of African Unity (OAU) and, 158, 160
Polisario and, 8, 124, 143, 151, 155, 160
political data, 206, 210
political parties, 85, 100
political prisoners, 135
population, 12, 115, 200–201
relations with China, 177
relations with United States, 189
sends troops to Zaire, 166
Spanish colonialism, 52
war with Polisario, 124
Western Sahara and, 77, 160

Mozambique
agriculture, 106
Cubans in, 178
early independence movements, 127
embassies abroad, 214
entrenched leadership, 112
Front-Line State, 149
guerrilla warfare, 126, 158
Islam in, 16
location, 15
Lusophone, 181
Marxist state, 75
political data, 206
population, 12, 115, 200–201
Portuguese colony, 49, 142
relations with South Africa, 141
relations with United States, 177, 189, 190
South African Development Coordination Conference (SADCC), 166

Namibia
African Group and, 141, 173
Class C mandate of South Africa, 182
Cuban troops in Angola and, 186
economic viability of, 115
formerly South West Africa, 182
German colony, 46
GNP/PC, 200
Great Britain and, 174
guerrilla warfare, 158
independence movement, 15, 127
International Court of Justice and, 183
last remaining colony in Africa, 42
location, 15
political data, 206
population, 201
relations with United States, 188
South West African People's Organization (SWAPO) and, 143, 183
White settlers, 51

Niger
constitution suspended, 86
economic affiliations, 153, 154, 180
embassies abroad, 214
Francophone, 180–181
French colony, 45
least developed countries (LLDC), 106
location, 17
military rule, 133
"no-party" system, 97
political data, 206, 211
population, 201
relations with Israel, 170

Nigeria
Aba Women's Riots, 53

African Liberation Committee (ALC) and, 142
agriculture, 106
aid to and from, 116
Anglican Church and, 54
Anglophone, 173–174
Awolowo, Obafemi, 77
Azikiwe, Nnamdi, 77
ban on "dash," 80
Bantu origins, 22
battle of Burmi, 57
Benin City destroyed by British, 64
Biafra and, 77, 136
bilateral declaration of independence, 167
British colony, 41, 57
civil war, 92, 123, 159
Commonwealth and, 153, 174
constitutionalism, 71
democracy, 72, 87
Economic Commission of West African States (ECOWAS), 116, 147
economic viability of, 115
elections, 85, 89, 100, 113
embassies abroad, 144, 214
Fulani, 57
GNP/PC, 200
government structure, 87, 90, 92, 93, 94
great power, 149
Hausa, 30, 33
Igbo, 19, 30, 33, 82, 123
independent policies, 108
indigenization, 93
indirect rule, 47
location, 17
military coup (1975), 125
military rule, 133
Namibia and, 183, 188
nationalization, 98
Niger Basin Authority and, 154
Okpara, Michael, 68
OPEC and, 111
Order of Seraphim and Cherubim, 54
petroleum in, 106, 116
political data, 206, 211
population, 9, 11–12, 115, 200–201
refugees, 162
relations with Israel, 170, 171
relations with Soviet Union, 185
relations with United States, 189, 190
restoration of civilian rule, 134
social development, 113
special Presidential advisors and, 95
Tiv, 19, 30
United Native African Church and, 54
urbanism, 33
Yoruba, 30, 33

Réunion
French colony, 45
GNP/PC, 200
location, 7
political data, 206
population, 9, 201

Rwanda
African and Mauritian Common Organization (OCAM) and, 153
Belgian mandate, 38
civil war, 123
embassies abroad, 214
formerly Ruanda, 38
Francophone, 180–181
German colony, 46
least developed countries (LLDC), 106
location, 3
military rule, 133
political data, 206, 211
population, 9, 201
refugees, 84, 162
relations with United States, 189
terrorism, 84

São Tomé and Príncipe
embassies abroad, 144, 214
location, 3
Lusophone, 181
political data, 206, 211
population, 9, 201
Portuguese colony, 49
relations with France, 181
socialism in, 83

Senegal
African Liberation Committee (ALC) and, 142
Communist party, 70
democracy, 72, 87
economic affiliations, 147, 153, 154, 180
elections, 83, 85, 89, 100, 113
embassies abroad, 214
Francophone, 180–181
French base in, 181
Fench colony, 45, 63
government system, 71, 72, 87, 93
Islam in, 16
location, 17
mercenaries in, 130
nationalization, 98
political data, 206, 211
population, 201
relations with China, 177
relations with United States, 189
Senghor, Leopold, 68, 77
socialism in, 83
troops to Zaire, 166

Seychelles
Anglophone, 173-174
British colony, 41
Commonwealth and, 153, 174
embassies abroad, 214
GNP/PC, 200
location, 7
mercenaries in, 129
palace coup (1977), 126
political data, 206, 211
population, 9, 201
relations with China, 177
socialism in, 83

Sierra Leone
Anglophone, 173-174
Bai Bureh, 64
British colony, 41
Commonwealth and, 153, 174
embassies abroad, 214
freed slaves, 29
location, 17
Mende-Temne clashes, 124
military intervention in, 112
nationalization, 98
Niger Basin Authority and, 154
political data, 206, 211
political prisoners, 135
population, 9, 201
Poro Society, 31
relations with France, 181
restoration of civilian rule, 134
Sande Society, 31

Somalia
aggression toward Ethiopia, 151, 156
Anglophone, 173-174
Arab League and, 153, 169
British colony, 41
embassies abroad, 214
irredentism, 124, 155
Italian colony, 48
least developed countries (LLDC), 106
location, 3
Marxist state, 75
military rule, 133
nationalization, 98
Politburo, 96
political data, 206, 211
political prisoners, 135
population, 201
refugees, 162
relations with China, 176
relations with Cuba, 178
relations with France, 181
relations with Soviet Union, 176, 186
relations with United States, 189

urbanism, 33
war with Ethiopia, 124, 155

South Africa
Afrikaans, 35
Afrikaner cultural nationalism, 35, 40
aid for UNITA and FNLA, 128, 178
African National Congress (ANC) and, 61, 121
Anglophone, 173-174
apartheid, 35, 40, 73
Arab states and, 173
arms embargo, 148, 159
Asian settlers, 51
bannings, 123
Bantu Affairs Department, 39
"Bantus," 23, 39
Black African states and, 36
Blacks in, 39, 121
Boers in, 39
boycott of, 141, 165
British colony, 41
Broederbond, 41
Chinese policy toward, 177
coloreds, 42-43
Commonwealth and, 174
Communist party, 70
democracy, 87
Department of Plural Relations and Development, 39
divestiture, 179-180
Dutch Reformed Church and, 35
economic growth, 105
economic viability of, 115
elections, 85, 89, 100
embassies abroad, 144, 148, 215
excluded from ECA and UNESCO, 159
Executive Council, 95
Front for the National Liberation of Angola (FNLA) and, 143
GNP/PC, 200
government system, 40, 87, 90, 93
Great Trek, 46
guerrilla warfare, 36, 52, 126
Homelands for Black South Africans, 149-150
identification passes, 121
Industrial and Commercial Workers' Union (1918) and, 65
International Court of Justice and, 182
intervention in Angola, 151, 177, 188
Kadalie, Clements, 65
legitimacy, 74
location, 15
Malan, D. F., 40
migrant labor, 65
miscegenation prohibited, 43

opposes Popular Movement for the
   Liberation of Angola (MPLA), 159
Namibia and, 15, 182
National Party, 35, 40
non-White churches, 55
non-White majority, 35
Organization of African Unity (OAU)
   and, 158, 170, 185
Pan-Africanist Congress (PAC) and, 134
parastatals, 99
plural economic activities, 106
political data, 206, 211
political prisoners, 135
political rights in, 35
population, 12, 115, 200–201
possibility of racial war, 36, 121
racism in, 13, 35
rejects liberalism, 47
relations with Israel, 170
relations with Malawi, 155, 156
relations with Zaire, 165
republic (1961), 40
slavery in, 42
social development, 113
Southern African Customs Union and,
   164
Southern African Development
   Coordination Conference
   (SADCC) and, 166
Sullivan principles, 187
terrorism, 84
Tile, Nehemiah, 55
trade with African states, 141
UN Security Council arms embargo,
   148
Watch Tower Movement and, 66
White settlers, 51
Zulu and, 64

Sudan
agriculture, 106
Anglophone, 173–174
Arab Bank for Economic Development
   of Africa (BADEA) and, 175
Arab League and, 153, 169
British colony, 41
civil war, 123
Communist party, 70
economic viability of, 115
embassies abroad, 215
guerrilla warfare, 126
iron use in, 26
least developed countries (LLDC), 106
location, 8
Mahdi, Muhammad Ahmad al-, 64
mass instability in, 129
military rule, 133
Muhammad Ali, 60

Nuer, 19, 82
political data, 207, 212
population, 12, 115, 200–201
quasi-federal system, 92
refugees, 162
relations with Soviet Union, 186
relations with United States, 189
secessionist movements, 136
socialism in, 83
southern provinces, 123

Swaziland
Anglophone, 173–174
British colony, 41
Commonwealth and, 153, 174
constitution status unclear, 86
embassies abroad, 215
GNP/PC, 200
location, 15
monarchy, 90, 96
"no-party" system, 97
palace coup (1973), 96, 126
political data, 207, 212
population, 201
refugees, 163
relations with Israel, 170
relations with South Africa, 141
Southern African Customs Union and,
   164
Southern African Development
   Coordination Conference
   (SADCC) and, 166

Tanzania
African Liberation Committee (ALC)
   and, 142
African socialism and, 68
African unity and, 79
aggression against Uganda, 146, 151,
   156
agricultural collectives, 68–69
Anglophone, 173–174
Arusha Declaration, 68–69
Asian settlers, 51
British mandate, 41
Commonwealth and, 153, 174
criticizes Arabs, 170–171
East African Community (EAC) and,
   146, 164
economic growth, 105
embassies abroad, 215
entrenched leadership, 112
equality, 104
Front for the Liberation of
   Mozambique (FRELIMO) and, 142
Front-Line State, 149
German colony, 46
government system, 68, 72, 89, 113

guerrilla warfare, 126
least developed countries (LLDC), 106
location, 3
Maasai, 26, 82
Maji Maji Rebellion, 59
nationalization, 98
Nyerere, Julius, 68, 77, 136, 146, 169
political data, 207
political prisoners, 135
population, 12, 115, 200–201
refugees, 162
rejection of aid "strings," 117
relations with China, 177
relations with Israel, 170, 171
self-reliance, 104, 109
socialist, 83, 146
Southern African Development
 Coordination Conference
 (SADCC) and, 166
Swahili, 28
Tan-Zam railroad, 128
village cooperatives, 68
war with Uganda, 156

Togo
British mandate, 41
conflict with Ghana, 155
embassies abroad, 215
economic affiliations, 153, 154, 158, 180
Francophone, 180–181
French mandate, 45
German colony, 46
Kodjo, Edem, 160
location, 17
mercenaries in, 130
military rule, 133
ministry for women's affairs, 88
nationalization, 98
Niger Basin Authority and, 154
political data, 207, 212
population, 9, 201
relations with China, 177
relations with Ghana, 158
troops to Zaire, 166

Tunisia
Arab League and, 153, 169
Communist party, 70
competitive "one-party" system, 89, 113
customs union with Morocco and
 Algeria, 164
embassies abroad, 144, 215
entrenched leadership, 112
French colony, 45
GNP/PC, 200
guerrilla warfare, 126
location, 8
political data, 207

population, 201
relations with China, 177
socialism in, 83

Uganda
African Liberation Committee (ALC)
 and, 142
Amin, Idi, 84, 129, 146, 170, 185
Anglophone, 173–174
British colony, 41
Commonwealth and, 153, 174
constitution status unclear, 86
East African Community (EAC) and,
 146, 164
embassies abroad, 215
expulsion of Asians, 51
federalism abandoned, 102
guerrilla warfare, 126
invasion by Tanzania, 151, 156
Kabaka of Baganda, 64
least developed countries (LLDC), 106
location, 3
mercenaries in, 129
military coup (1971), 125
military rule, 133
nationalization, 98
palace coup (1966), 126
political data, 207, 212
population, 9, 12, 115, 200–201
refugees, 84, 162
relations with Israel, 170
rescue at Entebbe, 185
secessionists in, 136
terrorism, 84
war with Tanzania, 156

Upper Volta
economic affiliations, 153, 154, 180
embassies abroad, 215
Francophone, 180–181
French colony, 45, 64
least developed countries (LLDC), 106
location, 17
military rule, 133
ministry for women's affairs, 88
Niger Basin Authority and, 154
palace coup (1974), 126
political data, 207, 212
population, 201

Western Sahara
Arabic, 169
Hispanophone, 181
location, 8
Organization of African Unity (OAU)
 and, 155
Polisario, 160
political data, 207

population, 201
Spanish colony, 52

Zaire
African Liberation Committee (ALC) and, 142
Belgian colony, 37
civil war, 123
Congo crisis (1960–65), 185, 188
economic viability of, 115
embassies abroad, 215
federalism abandoned, 102
former Congo Free State, 37
Francophone, 180–181
guerrilla warfare, 126
independence movement, 127
indigenization, 93
Kimbanguism, 57
Kitawala movement, 57–58
Leopold II (King of Belgium), 64
location, 3
mercenaries in, 130
military coup (1960), 126
military rule, 133
mining, 106
National Executive Council, 95
nationalization, 98
political data, 207, 213
political prisoners, 135
population, 12, 115, 200–201
refugees, 84, 162
refuge of Lumpa Church members, 124
relations with Israel, 170, 171
relations with South Africa, 141
secessionists in, 136
secret societies, 31
Shaba invasions, 159, 165
terrorism, 84
Watch Tower Movement in, 66

Zambia
agriculture, 106
Anglophone, 173–174
British colony, 41
Commonwealth and, 153, 174
competitive "one-party" system, 72, 89, 113
embassies abroad, 215
entrenched leadership, 112
Front-Line State, 149
GNP/PC, 200
indigenization, 93
Kaunda, Kenneth, 68
location, 15
Lumpa Church in, 124

mining, 65, 106
multinational corporations in, 119
nationalization, 98
political data, 207, 213
political prisoners, 135
population, 201
refugees, 162, 166
relations with China, 177
relations with South Africa, 141
socialism in, 83
Southern African Development Coordination Conference (SADCC) and, 166
strikes by Blacks, 65
Watch Tower Movement in, 66

Zimbabwe
African-Caribbean-Pacific Community (ACP) and, 172
Anglophone, 173–174
boycotts, 165
British colony, 41
Commonwealth and, 153, 174
democracy, 72, 87
economic viability of, 115
elections, 85, 89, 94, 113
embassies abroad, 215
Front-Line State, 149
GNP/PC, 200
government system, 71, 87, 90, 93, 94
guerrilla warfare, 55, 126, 149, 158
iron use in, 26
location, 15
ministry for women's affairs, 88
Mugabe, Robert, 86, 128
Muzerewa, Abel, 176
Ndebele-Shona Rebellion, 61
Nkomo, Joshua, 128
Patriotic Front, 159
plural economic activities, 106
political data, 207
political parties, 100
population, 9, 201
refugees, 162
relations with China, 176, 177
relations with United States, 189
social development, 113
Southern African Development Coordination Conference (SADCC) and, 166
Soviet-Chinese rivalry in, 176
urbanism, 33
Watch Tower Movement in, 66
White settlers, 51

The African Political Dictionary

1. Land and People

Central Africa That area embracing the former French Equatorial Africa (Chad, Central African Republic, Gabon, and Congo), Cameroon, Equatorial Guinea, São Tomé and Príncipe, and Zaire (formerly the Belgian Congo). *See also* EAST AFRICA, p. 3 INDIAN OCEAN AREA, p. 7; NORTH AFRICA, p. 8; SOUTHERN AFRICA, p. 15; WEST AFRICA, p. 17.

Significance Central Africa extends from the heart of the Sahara Desert to the enormous Zaire (formerly Congo) River Basin. The southern part of this large area embraces the great rain forests (p. 13). The vast country of Zaire has rich mineral deposits as well as petroleum sources that exist along much of the Atlantic coast. French is the major *lingua franca* of Central Africa since France dominated the four states of the former French Equatorial Africa and Belgium dominated Zaire (formerly the Belgian Congo). Spanish is the *lingua franca* of Equatorial Guinea (because of Spain's colonial domination). In São Tomé and Príncipe, Portuguese (because of Portugal's rule) is the *lingua franca*.

East Africa An area of Africa containing Ethiopia, Djibouti, Somalia, Kenya, Uganda, Rwanda, Burundi, and Tanzania (formerly Tanganyika and Zanzibar). Some scholars exclude Ethiopia, Djibouti, and Somalia from East Africa, preferring to place them in a separate category called the "Horn." *See also* CENTRAL AFRICA, p. 3; HORN, p. 8; INDIAN OCEAN AREA, p. 7; NORTH AFRICA, p. 8; SOUTHERN AFRICA, p. 15; WEST AFRICA, p. 17.

Significance Ethiopia is a direct descendant of Aksum (Axum), an early state formed in the fourth century B.C. In the fourth century A.D.

the Coptic form of Christianity was introduced, which is still extant. Islam, which is present in Ethiopia, dominates in Djibouti and Somalia, and is important in the rest of East Africa (p. 196). Islam and Arab influences, especially along the coast, have integrated much of East Africa into a far-flung commercial network for at least 1,000 years. European involvement in the area began only in the nineteenth century during the scramble for Africa (p. 48). In the early part of the twentieth century, European settlers were attracted to the highlands of Kenya, complicating colonial relations (p. 51).

Geographical Factors: Climate   Average weather conditions as revealed in temperature, wind velocity, and precipitation. Most of Africa is situated in the tropic zone between the Tropic of Cancer and the Tropic of Capricorn. Africa has almost half of the tropical lands in the world, and consequently sustained heat covers much of the continent. Seasons vary mainly from hot and wet to hot and dry in most of West and Central Africa. Great temperature variations, however, occur in desert and semidesert areas between day and night. The Mediterranean coast and highland areas are predominantly temperate, and southern Africa is often quite cool. *See also* LOCATION, p. 4; SIZE, p. 5; TOPOGRAPHY, p. 5.

Significance   Because of the hot climate, Africans have little need for heated shelters or heavy clothing. In fact, in many parts of the continent, cooking, eating, and socializing are done outside in traditional settings. Furthermore, two and sometimes three harvests per year are possible in some places, and certain crops, such as bananas, papaya, coconuts, and citrus fruits, grow with little human effort. On the negative side, heat, especially when combined with high humidity, is uncomfortable for all people. Furthermore, tropical soils are low in organic and mineral content and tend to be easily eroded. Such soils therefore require great care and hard work by farmers. Finally, the uneven spread of rains divides the agricultural year into periods of intense activity and periods of inactivity, and occasionally hunger and deprivation.

Geographical Factors: Location   Africa sits astride the equator between the Atlantic and Indian Oceans. It extends as far north of the equator as it does south, although two-thirds of its land mass is situated in the north. While the Mediterranean Sea constitutes the northern boundary of the continent as a whole, the Sahara Desert can be said to constitute the northern boundary of sub-Saharan or Black Africa. *See also* CLIMATE, p. 4; SIZE, p. 5; TOPOGRAPHY, p. 5.

Significance Africa's location has resulted in different contact patterns with the rest of the world. North Africa has been integrated into the Mediterranean world since the beginning of the First Millennium B.C., and closely linked to the Middle East after the spread of Islam beginning in the seventh century. East Africa has been connected with the Indian Ocean-Arab-Asian world for at least 2,000 years and especially since the rise of Islam. European and New World areas have been in contact with western, Central, and Southern Africa since the fifteenth century. Even so, to Europeans during the Age of Exploration, sub-Saharan Africa was considered a barrier along the sealanes to south and east Asia.

Geographical Factors: Size Physical extent. Africa is a continent of 11,682,000 square miles (30,432,500 square kilometers). It is almost 5,000 miles (8,045 kilometers) from Tunis, Tunisia, to the Cape of Good Hope, Republic of South Africa. It is about 4,400 miles (7,079 kilometers) from Dakar, Senegal, to the eastern tip of Somalia.

Significance Africa is the second largest continent (after Asia). It is larger than all of North America and India plus Great Britain, France, West Germany, Norway, Sweden, Spain, Italy, Switzerland, Holland, and Belgium. It makes up fully 20 percent or one-fifth of the landmass of the earth.

Geographical Factors: Topography The configuration of the earth's surface. Africa's surface is massive, more or less flat rock with few folds or deep undulations. However, highlands over 3,000 feet (914 meters) in height and 600 to 800 miles (965–1,287 kilometers) wide, stretch from Ethiopia to the Republic of South Africa. From these highlands rise the spectacular Mount Kilimanjaro (19,340 feet; 5,895 meters); and its nearby neighbor Mount Kenya (17,040 feet; 5,194 meters), as well as the Great Rift Valley (p. 7) and the Great Lakes, a string of lakes running from Ethiopia to Malawi. Most of the continent is under 3,000 feet (914 meters) and can be characterized as a vast plateau with small mountains here and there. The volcanic peak of Mt. Cameroon (13,353 feet; 4,070 meters), much of the eastern area from Ethiopia to the Drakensberg Mountains in South Africa, and the Atlas Mountains in Morocco and Algeria are exceptions to this pattern.

Great inland basins catch water and help to form some of the world's great rivers. The Nile flows north from Lake Victoria and other sources to empty into the Mediterranean. The Niger rises in Guinea and flows over 2,500 miles (4,023 kilometers), first northeastward into Mali, then southeastward into Nigeria, and finally south to the Atlantic. The Zaire (Congo) begins in southeast Zaire and flows over 3,000 miles (4,827 kilometers), first north, then west, and ultimately southwest to empty into the Atlantic. The Zambezi begins in Botswana, flows between Zambia and Zimbabwe (formerly Southern Rhodesia) and through Mozambique to the Indian Ocean.

Africa also has the largest desert in the world, the Sahara, which extends from the Atlantic to the Red Sea. Its western portion appeared in the last 10,000 years and thus is of relatively recent origin. Rock paintings attest to the facts that the Sahara was once much more densely populated than now and contained forests, rivers, and tropical game. Other large, and very dry deserts are the Kalahari in Namibia (formerly South West Africa) and Botswana (formerly Bechuanaland) and the Namib, running along the coast of Namibia.

A rain forest runs along the west coast of Africa from Guinea to Nigeria with an important gap in Benin (formerly Dahomey). It spreads inland from Cameroon to Angola and eventually extends to the eastern portion of Zaire (formerly the Belgian Congo). Between the rain forest and the Sahara Desert is the Sudan or savannah, grasslands that extend across the width of the continent from Senegal to Ethiopia and at its eastern end curve southward around the rain forest into southern Africa (p. 16). The coasts are remarkably smooth with no great indentations and few natural ports. Rapids are found on many rivers just before they reach the coast and prevent easy access from the sea. *See also* CLIMATE, p. 4; LOCATION, p. 4; SIZE, p. 5.

Significance The great deserts are sparsely populated. Most Africans live in the grasslands, the highlands, and the rain forests. The great rivers provide a means of transportation and communication, as well as a source of food. The rivers are sluggish and tend to ebb and flow with rainy and dry seasons. The smooth coastline made the continent as difficult to depart from as to enter, and partly explains why there was little ocean exploration from Africa. The Sahara has served as a bridge to much trade and cultural interchange, but today appears to be something of a barrier in political relations. Technologically the desert is becoming more and more of a bridge between North Africa and the sub-Saharan region. But as one scholar has noted, "What technology has opened, politics has often closed" (Zartman, 1963, p. 21). National boundaries divide the Sahara into many parts, each manifesting a national interest that looks away from the desert rather than toward it. Many border disputes involve ill-defined boundary lines in the desert. And North African perceptions of the world differ from those of sub-Saharan Africans (p. 16).

Great Rift Valley   A fault in the earth's surface that runs the length of the Red Sea, through Ethiopia, Kenya, and Uganda, southward from Rwanda to Mozambique, thence into the Indian Ocean. Part of the rift is a deep escarpment centered mainly in Kenya and Ethiopia, while other portions of the rift appear in the Great Lakes, all on the eastern side of the continent.

Significance   The Rift Valley in Kenya and Ethiopia has been especially generous in preserving the remains of the earliest known protohumans. Through the indefatigable efforts of the late Dr. Louis B. Leakey and, more recently, Richard Leakey and Donald Johanson, the paleoanthropological record not only places the origin of man in eastern Africa but pushes that origin back to well over 3 million years ago.

Horn, The   A protrusion off the east coast of Africa that juts into the Indian Ocean, where it is joined by the Gulf of Aden. On a map, the region resembles a V or a horn lying on its side. It embraces Somalia, Djibouti, and eastern Ethiopia.

Significance   The Horn is especially important as a strategic outpost overlooking the Gulf of Aden, the passageway connecting the Red Sea to the Indian Ocean.

Indian Ocean Area   Island countries in the Indian Ocean attached to the continent of Africa through membership in the Organization of African Unity (OAU). These include the Comoro Islands, Madagascar (formerly the Malagasy Republic), Mauritius, and Seychelles. Réunion is also located in the Indian Ocean but is a department (district) of France, not an independent state. Mayotte likewise is a part of France, although it is one of the four islands of the Comoros. *See also* EAST AFRICA, p. 3; CENTRAL AFRICA, p. 3; NORTH AFRICA, p. 8; SOUTHERN AFRICA, p. 15; WEST AFRICA, p. 17.

Significance   There was never any question that the large island of Madagascar and the small Comoro Islands, located between Madagascar and the mainland, would be associated with Africa. Mauritius and Seychelles were further from the continent, and had stronger Indian and southeast Asian influences, so it was not clear that their governments would identify with Africa. As these areas became independent, however, they sought membership in the OAU and were readily admitted. The Indian Ocean Area has become important to Africa because of the continued presence of a colonial power (France) there. Further east and closer to India is the British possession of the Chagos Archipelago, where Diego Garcia Island is located and on which the United States has a military base. African states have agreed that the Chagos belongs to Mauritius. They are motivated by (1) the belief that Mauritius and the Chagos Archipelago were once governed together; (2) the goal of eliminating all vestiges of colonialism from anywhere near Africa; and (3) the desire to make the Indian Ocean a "Zone of Peace" (p. 175).

Maghreb Northwestern Africa, particularly Morocco, Algeria, and Tunisia. The Maghreb became the granary of the Roman Empire, providing grains as well as olives and grapes to the Mediterranean world. In the seventh century, the Maghreb (from the Arabic word for "west") became the western outpost of Islam in Africa. Arabs established Islam in the region along with their language.

Significance The people of the Maghreb have had a long common history, which contained a dream of ultimate unity. In fact, the area was united briefly in the eleventh century. It has been divided into three parts, however, longer than it was ever unified. Even as French colonies, all three areas were ruled as separate entities. Nevertheless, there is a pan-Maghrebic perspective in the area that supports some efforts at cooperation. On the other hand, nationalism precludes close cooperation, and indeed today Morocco and Algeria are in a state of hostility over the Algeria-supported Polisario movement (p. 160), which is seeking independence from Morocco.

North Africa An area embracing the five states that border the Mediterranean (Morocco, Algeria, Tunisia, Libya, and Egypt), Western Sahara, and usually the Sudan Republic, although the southern half of Sudan contains cultures more akin to sub-Saharan Africa than to North Africa. *See also* CENTRAL AFRICA, p. 3; EAST AFRICA, p. 3; INDIAN OCEAN AREA, p. 7; SOUTHERN AFRICA, p. 15; WEST AFRICA, p. 17.

Significance The identifying characteristics of this area are the Arabic language, overwhelming acceptance of Islam, and historical ties with the Middle East. As the southern shore of the Mediterranean, however, North Africa has played a vital role in western affairs for over 2,000 years. The Roman Empire included a strip of North Africa along the entire length of the Mediterranean shore from Morocco to Egypt.

Population: Demographic Transition The theory that human population expanded very slowly throughout history until the Industrial Revolution intervened, first in Europe and then in the rest of the world, to produce unprecedented growth. The pattern in Europe after 1650 reflected a situation of (1) high birthrate/high deathrate, being replaced by (2) high birthrate/low deathrate, and finally (3) low birthrate/low deathrate. The transition, therefore, was one of very slow growth followed by more than a century of very high growth, followed by the present pattern of low growth, although not yet as low as that before the Industrial Revolution. But the pattern is clear: a decline in deathrate accompanied the process of industrializing, and a decline in birthrate occurred after industrialization had been achieved. Assuming the same forces to be operating in Africa, that continent is now in the second phase of high growth rate, which may last as long as a century. This is what is meant by "population explosion." *See also* POPULATION: DENSITY, p. 9; GNP/PC, p. 10; GROWTH RATE, p. 10; SIZE, p. 11.

Significance The demographic transition theory places heavy emphasis on rapid industrialization as a way of balancing population growth. Nonetheless, a population that is doubling in only 20 to 25 years interferes greatly with rapid industrialization. Wealth that could be invested in general economic growth is siphoned into the health and education of a sizable nonproductive population (i.e., those under 15 years of age).

Population: Density The number or compactness of people per measured area. The number of people per square kilometer of arable land in Africa is about 50, which is about half of what it is for the world in general (98) and about the same as for North America. However, four mainland countries (Benin, Liberia, Burundi, and Rwanda) have over 2.5 times the population density of the world, and eight (Gambia, Nigeria, Sierra Leone, Togo, Djibouti, Malawi, Uganda, and Zimbabwe) considerably exceed the world average. Among the island states, Cape Verde, Comoros, Mauritius, Réunion, Seychelles, and São Tomé and Príncipe have densities ranging from 230 persons per square kilometer to over 1,300. *See also* DEMOGRAPHIC TRANSITION, p. 9; GNP/PC, p. 10; GROWTH RATE, p. 10; SIZE, p. 11.

Significance African states in general are not densely populated, at least as measured against economically advanced Europe, where population density per square kilometer of arable land exceeds 200. The greater the density, however, the greater the pressures on arable land. In the developing states of Africa, population density is simply another problem with which these states must cope.

Population: Gross National Product/Per Capita (GNP/PC)

The total worth of goods and services for one year divided by the population size. The Population Reference Bureau estimates the GNP in Africa in 1980 to be $383 billion. On a per capita basis this provides an average income of $770 per year for every man, woman, and child. On a comparative basis this makes Africa the poorest area of the world: for Asia the GNP/PC is about $920; for Latin America, about $1910; for the Soviet Union, about $4,550; for Europe, about $7,990; and for North America, about $11,240. In Africa, however, there is a great disparity between countries (see Table B-1, p. 200). Thus, while one-third of the countries have a GNP/PC of $560 or more, the other two-thirds have less; Chad with a mere $120 has the lowest. *See also* DEMOGRAPHIC TRANSITION, p. 9; DENSITY, p. 9; GROWTH RATE, p. 10; SIZE, p. 11.

Significance GNP/PC is an average and therefore only a crude measure of the per capita wealth of a country. It gives no indication of the economic worth of any particular individual. Wealth is not evenly distributed in any country; therefore, if there is a low average income but a number of very wealthy people, the poorest are indeed destitute. Since GNP is calculated on the basis of goods and services in the public arena, personal goods and services (such as growing and eating one's own food or spinning, weaving, and sewing one's own clothes) are not counted in measuring the wealth of a country. Since this applies to all countries and continents, comparisons are still fairly useful. By all such measures, Africans are generally among the poorest people on earth.

Population: Growth Rate

The difference between births and deaths per year per thousand persons in the population. African birth-rates are about 46 per thousand, while the deathrate is about 17 per thousand. Thus, the population is growing at the rate of 29 per thousand per year or 2.9 percent. Africa's growth rate is now the highest of any continent. The growth rate, however, varies from state to state, with many countries growing at 2 percent or less. Gabon's increase, for example, is estimated at only 1.2 percent. What makes the rate so high in general for Africa is the rate of the most populous countries (see Table B-2, p. 200). These 13 states contain over 71 percent of all African peoples, and their average growth rate is 3 percent. Kenya's growth rate of 3.9 percent is the highest in the world. These high rates are not due to an increase in the number of births but rather to lowered death rates resulting from the impact of modern medicine, health care, and improved diets, which allow more people to survive longer. Thus, in periods when births remain the same but deaths per year decline, the total population can increase rapidly. Africa's extreme position is shown comparatively by reference to the growth rate of other areas: Europe, 0.4 percent; North America, 0.7 percent; Soviet Union, 0.8 percent; World, 1.7 percent; Asia, 1.8 percent; and Latin America, 2.3 percent. *See also* DEMOGRAPHIC TRANSITION, p. 9; DENSITY, p. 9; GNP/PC, p. 10; SIZE, p. 11.

Significance   A population growing at 1.0 percent per year will double in 70 years; at 2.0 percent in 35 years; at 3.0 percent in 23 years. Thus Kenya with a population of 17,900,000 and growing at 3.9 percent per year will double its population to 35,800,000 in only 18 years. At 3.2 percent growth rate, Nigeria's 82,300,000 people will double to 164,600,000 in 22 years. Another way of depicting this population increase is to point out that Nigeria has over 2.5 million new babies each year. This number is in excess of what it takes to replace the number who die. As a result, the population boom each year requires thousands of new clinics, thousands of tons of additional food, thousands of new classrooms and teachers, and very soon will necessitate the creation of millions of new jobs. Because of this rapid growth rate, 45 percent of all Africans are under the age of 15 (compared with a world average of 35 percent and only 24 percent for developed areas). This is the highest percentage of nonproducing youth in the world and is one more major burden that African states must bear that is greater than that borne in the rest of the world.

Population: Size   The number of people inhabiting a country or area. The total population for Africa in 1982 was estimated by the Population Reference Bureau at 498 million. Sub-Saharan Africa has about 381 million inhabitants. West Africa is the largest region with 150 million people, which is almost 40 percent of sub-Saharan Africa, and 30 percent of the continent. The West African country of Nigeria has over 80 million people, making its population the largest on the continent, and the tenth largest in the world. See Table B-3 for the estimated population of each state in each region in descending order. *See also* POPULATION: DEMOGRAPHIC TRANSITION, p. 9; DENSITY, p. 9; GNP/PC, p. 10; GROWTH RATE, p. 10.

Significance The average population size per country in the world is 26 million. Only five states in Africa (Nigeria, Egypt, Ethiopia, Zaire, and South Africa) exceed the world average. Consequently, Africa is a region of small states. In fact, only eight (Morocco, Algeria, Sudan, Tanzania, Kenya, Uganda, Mozambique, and Ghana) have populations of between 10 and 22 million. There are 26 states with populations of less than 5 million and 12 of less than 1 million. Many large cities in the world are larger than two dozen African states. If, as is argued by economists, a population size of about 15 million is necessary for economic viability, then most African states are doomed to permanent underdevelopment. On the other hand, since Africa's ministates are all members of the United Nations, which functions on the principle of one vote for each state, the African continent can dominate UN voting more fully than any other although it contains only about 11 percent of world population.

Race A gene pool; a group of people who share a number of physical characteristics because they are part of the same gene pool. *See also* RACISM, p. 13.

Significance There are four distinct gene pools in mainland Africa reflecting varied physical characteristics and usually referred to as Negroid, Pygmoid (or Negrillo), Khoisan (or Bushmanoid), and Caucasoid. A strong Mongoloid gene pool exists on the island of Madagascar. Except for North Africa, where Caucasoids predominate, the Negroid type prevails. The Pygmoid type is limited mainly to areas west and north of Lake Victoria and numbers only a few ten-thousands. Even fewer in number are the Khoisan peoples, who are restricted primarily to the Kalahari Desert region. Among the predominant Negroid peoples are a number of subraces with physical characteristics that distinguish them from other types, such as the Fulani of West Africa and Nilotic peoples of East Africa. While it is possible to classify people scientifically according to physical characteristics shared by the gene pool, race is not significant in the study of cultures. One race or subrace is not mentally or intellectually superior or inferior to another. Great cultural inventions, such as the Agricultural, Urban, and Industrial Revolutions, cannot be explained by reference to the gene pool of the inventors. Consequently, race is merely a descriptive term showing variation within the single species of mankind, *Homo sapiens*.

Racism The belief that some races are inferior or superior to others; the act of attributing to an individual the assumed stereotypes of his race or gene pool. In Africa, racism was practiced primarily by Europeans who came to dominate and in some cases to settle the area. They frequently stereotyped all dark-skinned people as lazy, stupid, uneducable, and childlike. Even individuals who clearly did not fit the stereotype were treated as if they did. While present in varying degrees throughout Africa, racism was especially widespread in eastern, Central, and Southern Africa, where European minorities came to dominate African majorities and Asian settlers. Today, racism still prevails in its most virulent form, *apartheid*, in the Republic of South Africa. *See also* APARTHEID, p. 35; BLACKS, p. 39; COLOREDS, p. 41; RACE, p. 12; SETTLERS: WHITES, p. 51.

Significance In the study of culture it is known that in any large population or gene pool the distribution of abilities will be spread out randomly in basically the same way as in any other large population or gene pool. Racism, nevertheless, ignores that fact and stereotypes all members of the gene pool with the good or bad qualities attributed to the race. It thus became possible in Africa for a minority of Whites, who also gained control of the machinery of government, to allege their racial superiority over all non-Whites. If one race controls all power in the society, it can reserve the desirable goods for itself and deny them to all others.

Rain Forest A tropical area with an annual rainfall of at least 100 inches (254 centimeters) and marked by lofty trees, especially evergreens, forming a continuous covering. In sub-Saharan Africa the rain forest constitutes a narrow belt along the entire Guinea Coast (except for a gap in Benin) from Guinea to Nigeria, which then moves eastward in a wide swath to cover all of the western coast from Cameroon to the mouth of the Zaire (Congo) and thence to the eastern side of Zaire (formerly the Belgian Congo).

Significance The great variation between the rain forest and the desert, both prominent characteristics of Africa, is a result of the contrast between high and low rainfall. High precipitation depends on wind direction: the heaviest rains come when the winds blow in from the Atlantic. Rainy seasons are intermixed with dry seasons, but it is the rainy season on which so much of life depends, especially farming and water storage (such as replenishing wells). Many people live in the rain forests, where they are sustained by a wide variety of yams, vegetables, fruits, and seeds. Cocoa is an important cash crop grown in the rain forest. Clearing of the forests, however, is damaging to the ecological balance. Because the soil is low in organic and mineral content, exhaustion and erosion soon make the land difficult if not impossible to farm unless fallow periods are permitted. The strenuous lives of people who inhabit the forests have given rise to complex social institutions based on the principle of mutual dependence.

Sahara Desert The large desert dominating the geography of northern Africa. West to east, it extends from the Atlantic Ocean to the Red Sea. South to north, it stretches roughly from the 15th parallel to a line approximately 25–100 miles (40–161 kilometers) from the Mediterranean Sea, thus having an average width of 1,500 miles (2,414 kilometers). About 10,000 years ago the western portion was a fertile plain, so we must recognize that a large part of the Sahara is of relatively recent origin. Rather than being simply a pile of sand, the Sahara is dotted with numerous oases, in which permanent habitation occurs and which have long served as terminals for the many caravan routes that crisscross the area. These caravans for centuries transported goods and people to North Africa and Europe and brought goods, people, and ideas to Black Africa.

Significance The Sahara was once thought of as a vast barrier between the north and the savannah area. Now it seems more accurate to regard it as a land bridge. From the north, across that bridge, came Islam (in the last 1,000 years), a continuous supply of salt, and probably ironworking technology (as early as 400 B.C.). From the south, a variety of items including gold and, to a lesser extent, slaves have been dispatched northward. In fact, trade has flowed both ways for many centuries. Nevertheless, the Sahara has also served as a boundary line between the peoples and states of North Africa and the peoples and states to the south. North Africa, because of the prevalence of the Arabic language, a more homogeneous history, and a long period of direct links with the Middle East, is generally identified with the Middle East in a way which Africa south of the Sahara is not. It is possible that the gradual spread southward of Islam may eventually reduce the distinctions between these regions.

Sahel A narrow strip of land between the Sudanic Belt (p. 16) and the Sahara Desert (p. 14) stretching from Mauritania to Ethiopia. *Sahel* comes from Arabic, meaning "edge, border, or coast," and in this case refers to the edge of the desert. The strip ranges from about 120 to 180 miles (193–290 kilometers) in width, has intermittent rainfall, and contains low scrub and grasses. Pastoral peoples attempt to exploit the grasses for their herds, and in some areas with a little more than average rainfall, marginal farming occurs.

Significance The Sahel has always supported a thinly scattered population of nomadic peoples. In the last generation or two, however, the number of pastoral and agricultural people attempting to exploit this area increased substantially, probably due to general population growth. They overgrazed and overfarmed these marginal lands and consequently had no reserve areas when one of the worst droughts of the century struck the Sahel. Starting in Mauritania in 1969, the drought spread eastward to Ethiopia by 1972, and lasted overall approximately five years. Hundreds of thousands of people and animals perished. (In fact, it is estimated that 100,000 Ethiopians died because of drought or subsequent disease between 1972 and 1975.) In 1975, the Organization for Economic Cooperation and Development (OECD), composed of Western industrialized nations and Japan, joined with the affected African countries to form the Sahel Club in order to explore ways to salvage the Sahel area. Plans are now under way to dig wells for irrigation, start a reforestation program, and initiate soil conservation. By 1981, only a fraction of the money needed had been raised, and political instability in many of the affected states retarded any serious moves to solve the crisis. With conditions little changed, the possibility exists that the crises of 1969–74 will soon be repeated.

Southern Africa That area embracing Angola, Zambia (formerly Northern Rhodesia), Malawi (formerly Nyasaland), Zimbabwe (formerly Southern Rhodesia), Mozambique, Namibia (formerly South West Africa), Botswana (formerly Bechuanaland), Swaziland, Lesotho (formerly Basutoland), and the Republic of South Africa. Some scholars also include the Indian Ocean Area, although their ties are with Africa as a whole (through membership in African international groupings) rather than with the southern mainland areas. *See also* CENTRAL AFRICA, p. 3; EAST AFRICA, p. 3; INDIAN OCEAN AREA, p. 7; NORTH AFRICA, p. 8; WEST AFRICA, p. 17.

Significance At one time Great Britain dominated Southern Africa except for Angola and Mozambique (controlled by Portugal) and Namibia (controlled by the Republic of South Africa). Two common characteristics of much of the area have been the prominent role played by White settlers in delaying independence movements and the predominance of racial inequality. To this day, South Africa's delay in granting independence to Namibia, as well as its extreme racist policies, have brought South Africa into conflict with the rest of the world and leave it almost friendless among nations. Nevertheless, South Africa controls the sealanes between the Atlantic and Indian Oceans and is thus of commercial and strategic importance. The entire area of southern Africa, furthermore, is the source of abundant mineral wealth, especially chromium, copper, diamonds, gold, and uranium, and is consequently of great importance in the world's economy.

Sub-Saharan Africa That part of Africa south of North Africa; the 42 countries of West, Central, East, and Southern Africa.

Significance The primary distinctions between sub-Saharan Africa and North Africa include not only the differences in peoples and cultures, but also the long association and identification of North Africa with Europe and the Middle East. Islam spread across North Africa in the eighth century, followed by the spread of Arabic. In the fourteenth century much of North Africa was incorporated into the Ottoman Empire. While Islam spread slowly south of the desert from Senegal to the Horn and along the east coast to mid-Mozambique, most of the area south of the Sahara has developed with little knowledge of the rest of the world. In turn, much of sub-Saharan Africa was little known by the rest of the world before the sixteenth century. Its isolation, while not absolute, has served to differentiate most of sub-Saharan Africa from North Africa.

Sudanic Belt A strip of land between the Sahara Desert and the rain forest extending about 3,000 miles (4,827 kilometers) from Senegal to Ethiopia. The word *Sudan* comes from the Arabic phrase, *Bilād al-Sudān*, meaning "the country of the black people," but now is closely associated with the word *savannah*, meaning "rolling grasslands dotted with scattered trees." The Sudanic belt is sometimes called the "belt of vegetation," and has moderate rainfall demarcated by wet and dry seasons.

Significance The Sudanic Belt is an area of high population concentration. It is a major cattle-herding area, although horses, sheep, goats, and camels are also found there. In addition, it is an area of grains, cotton, and peanuts. These features help to explain why the Sudanic Belt was the home of some of the great territorial empires of West Africa, notably ancient Ghana, ancient Mali, and Songhai. After the eleventh century, Sudanic Belt cities became the main centers from which the teachings of Islam spread into the forest areas. It is today the area where Islamic and traditional African law blend.

Land and People 17

Tropical Africa That portion of Africa located between the Tropic of Cancer and the Tropic of Capricorn. *See also* other geographical areas.

Significance Some people use the term *tropical Africa* to refer to the populations and cultures of Black Africans as distinguished from the populations and cultures of both the extreme north and the extreme south of the continent. While the term has some validity in reference to the north, it misrepresents the extreme south by leaving the impression that, historically, people of Black African ancestry did not inhabit that area and are relative newcomers.

West Africa That area of Africa west of Lake Chad, embracing the following countries: Mali, Upper Volta, and Niger in the landlocked portion, and the coastal states of Mauritania, Senegal, Gambia, Guinea-Bissau, Guinea, Sierra Leone, Liberia, Ivory Coast, Ghana (formerly the Gold Coast), Togo, Benin Republic (formerly Dahomey), and Nigeria. *See also* CENTRAL AFRICA, p. 3; EAST AFRICA, p. 3; INDIAN OCEAN AREA, p. 7; NORTH AFRICA, p. 8; SUDANIC BELT, p. 16; SOUTHERN AFRICA, p. 15.

Significance West Africa embraces the largest number of states of any area of Africa, contains one-third of all its people, and is the area of the largest number of distinct ethnic groups. It also provided the greatest number of slaves to the Atlantic slave trade (p. 000). Perhaps more importantly, West Africa was the area of large precolonial states and empires. In the Sudanic Belt were Ghana (700–1200), Mali (1200–1500), Songhai (1350–1600), Kanem-Bornu (800–1900), and the Hausa city-states (1300–1800); and in the forest zone were Benin (1500–1800), Oyo (1600–1850), Ashanti (Asante) (1650–1900), and Dahomey (1700–1900). Towns and cities originated independently in West Africa, and many of them served as the southern terminals of the extensive trans-Saharan caravan routes.

2. Culture and Tradition

Acephalous Society   A headless or stateless society, i.e., one which makes public decisions or resolves conflict through varying and differing individuals and groups, depending on the question at issue. It also means the absence of a fixed executive, judicial, or legislative role above the level of a family. If conflict occurs between two groups, such as two villages that do not recognize any authority superior to them, then they must resolve the conflict by negotiation, compromise, or warfare. In the precolonial period, there were a few dozen acephalous societies in Africa, located in all major regions. While hunting and gathering societies are always acephalous, stateless agricultural communities have also existed in Africa. Agricultural societies can become quite large, embracing a few million people, and still operate an acephalous political system, as the Igbo (Ibo) of eastern Nigeria demonstrated before 1900. Other large acephalous societies in traditional Africa were the Tiv of central Nigeria and the Nuer of southern Sudan. *See also* STATE, p. 31.

Significance   Acephalous societies, made up of groups that share the same cultural patterns and language, lack a unifying, formal political structure. Each village, clan, and/or family regarded itself as an independent entity bound only by agreements made with other similar groups (very much like the system of international relations today). These societies have faced considerable change by being incorporated into one of the present states of Africa. Those Africans who already lived in states had to make fewer adjustments than those who had lived in acephalous societies.

Europeans, on encountering such societies, regarded them as anarchic, i.e., devoid of government in the sense of orderly decision making. This assessment was incorrect. Acephalous societies are orderly.

They do make decisions and resolve conflict, but they do it without a centralized governmental institution of fixed rulers. They operate among their various segments (such as families, clans, villages, and regions) not unlike the contemporary world of independent states, which operates without a world ruler or a world lawmaker or a compulsory world court. Segments of acephalous societies regarded themselves as members of a particular culture just as independent states today regard themselves as part of the world of states. Often segments will band together to fight off an attack from an outside culture, just as world states today might band together to try to ward off an extraterrestrial attack. The weakness of acephalous societies is apparent: Unless they unite before the threat, they are often unable to ward off an outside menace. Yet, unification is the one thing such communities reject in order to maintain their valued independence.

Age Groups Groups in traditional societies embracing all males (and in some societies all females) of a common age in some social function. Two types exist. An *age set* is a group formed of persons born within a designated time (perhaps in the last year or the last four years) who remain identified for the rest of their lives with that age set. An *age grade* consists of one or more age sets that perform a specific function or occupy a particular status. An age set is formed early in a person's life, usually at puberty. While great variations occur in the formation and function of age groups, a common sequence in East Africa is as follows: (1) initiates, youths who have recently been initiated into an age set; (2) warriors, young men responsible for the defense of the society; (3) one or more grades of mature men who take part in government; and (4) elders, old men who advise and adjudicate. While age groups function in many acephalous societies (p. 19), they were particularly widespread in eastern and southeastern Africa.

Significance Age groups are devices by which some societies without the usual state hierarchy (p. 31) can nevertheless defend themselves and settle disputes among their members. Those who govern do so only when their age set is in the right grade, and after their period of rule, they move to the next grade. An age set cuts across kinship, clan, or status lines and is thus free of class connotations since it includes all individuals of the proper age. Age groups allow the society to recognize and utilize various stages of human development from growing childhood, to vigorous youth, to mature adults, to sage elders.

Agriculture The control of plant and animal reproduction so as to maintain and enhance the quantity and quality of each. The Agricultural Revolution occurred at various times and places (beginning about 10,000 years ago). In Africa, it is probable that agriculture was independently invented in parts of West Africa and Ethiopia. Agriculture, including herding, has been the principal form of production and livelihood in Africa. Conducted without machine technology and applied science, most agriculture has been of a subsistence nature. In the last few decades, cash crops (such as cocoa, coffee, cotton, sisal, tobacco, and rubber) have become important in many parts of the continent. Even so, most Africans today still survive by some form of subsistence agriculture. *See also* HERDING, p. 25; HUNTING AND GATHERING, p. 26; IRON USE, p. 26; STATE, p. 31.

Significance Agriculture was man's first great technological revolution after tool using and fire. It is a far more reliable way of human survival than hunting and gathering. Africans have engaged in this form of human survival for many centuries. Agriculture made settled living possible, which in turn led, in Africa as elsewhere, to urbanization. The Agricultural Revolution produced food surpluses which (1) increased population; (2) produced competition for land, leading to systems of organized warfare; (3) greatly enhanced specialization of labor by freeing some people from food production to engage in other full-time activities such as politics, religion, military defense, craftsmanship, art, or intellectual pursuits; and (4) made the creation of the state possible. While in Africa, as elsewhere, the adoption of agriculture has not always led to state formation, state formation has always rested on an agricultural base.

Atlantic Slave Trade The system by which slaves captured in Africa were bought, transported across the Atlantic Ocean, and sold in the Americas. The trade began in 1441 when two Portuguese captains took 12 African slaves to Lisbon. It spread to the Americas in 1502 when Africans began to replace Carib Indians in Hispaniola. Masters of European slaving vessels would sail to slaving stations along the coasts of Africa where they would exchange such items as salt, cloth, guns, hardware, and rum for slaves who had been captured inland by other Africans. As many as 40 slave forts once existed along the Guinea Coast of West Africa, the source of most New World slaves. (Some captives did come from Central and East Africa as well.) Portugal dominated the slave trade in the sixteenth century, Holland in the seventeenth, and Great Britain in the eighteenth. In 1807, Britain declared the trade illegal for its own citizens and ships and thereafter seized slaving vessels and freed their captives. Later, other countries joined in the ban against the slave trade, and the commerce decreased to a trickle by the middle of the nineteenth century. *See also* RETURNED SLAVES, p. 29; SLAVERY, p. 31.

Significance The Atlantic slave trade was especially noteworthy, although it was not the only slave route for Africans. Captives were also transported across the Sahara and the Indian Ocean, primarily to Muslim lands. The horror of the Atlantic trade, however, was odious: captured and marched in chains to the slave forts; incarcerated (often for months) in filthy slave barracks; packed like logs in the foul holds of the slave ships; and finally, chained and offered for sale to some master in the New World who regarded them as pieces of chattel. The impact on Africa was the loss of probably four to five million inhabitants in West Africa alone. The trade also resulted in the creation of African slave-trading states (such as Dahomey), the increased importation of firearms, intensified warfare for slaves, and the breakup of many traditional societies. Probably only the advanced social complexity of most African societies explains their ability to survive as well as they did the three and one-half centuries of the Atlantic Slave Trade. One benefit from this period, however, was the European introduction into Africa of a great number of New World crops, which Africans, in turn, adapted as staples: maize (corn), manioc, papayas, sweet potatoes, peanuts, tomatoes, and tobacco. It should be noted that the slave trade and slavery also affected those who profited from the system; it was probably the primary factor in the establishment of ingrained ideas of racial superiority that still plague Western civilization.

Bantu-Speaking Peoples The predominant language family of an area roughly from Nigeria to Kenya and southward to the Republic of South Africa. Bantu languages seem to have linguistic relationships to some languages of West Africa and not to the older Khoisan languages (the "click" language of the San hunters of southern Africa and the now-extinct Khoi-Khoi herders) of the area. All the Bantu languages are closely related, indicating their relatively recent separation from the language center. Scholars are not in agreement, however, about either the location of the center or the process by which the languages spread and took on their present forms. The most common explanation accepted by most (but not all) scholars is that the earliest Bantu languages (called proto-Bantu) were located in what is today southeastern Nigeria and western Cameroon. From there, beginning before the Christian era, Bantu speakers migrated eastward and southward, possibly motivated by population pressures associated with the spread of agriculture and iron metallurgy. Gradually, they populated the vast area described, displacing the Khoisan speakers, except in southwest Africa. (See Vansina, 1980.) *See also* BLACKS, p. 39, LANGUAGES, p. 27.

Significance   Bantu is a linguistic term, although it has been incorrectly used in the Republic of South Africa to refer to Black Africans in general. The close relationships among the various Bantu languages and their ubiquity south of the equator indicate a recent period of vast population migration and thus provide information on precolonial African history, even in the absence of written records.

Culture   The nonbiological aspects of human beings. Biology determines that humans must eat, work, defecate, sleep, copulate, speak, feel, hear, see, menstruate, and bear children; but culture sets the boundaries on when, where, how, and why humans do these things. Culture is the way a people uses the earth's resources for survival, organizes to carry on its activities, and explains life. Thus culture includes the technological base of human survival that has been learned; the social institutions in which people function, which is learned; and the ideas, beliefs, and values people hold, also learned. Culture, therefore, is learned behavior. A particular culture is one that has its own combination of technological, sociological, and ideological characteristics. It is estimated that in 1900 there were as many as 800 to 1,000 distinct cultures and mutually exclusive languages in Africa. Each particular culture constituted an ethnic group and defended itself against other cultures that might threaten it. Because individuals learn their own culture rather than another, this process becomes the way by which people are divided into "we" and "they." The blending of two or more cultures into a single one takes many generations of often violent struggle. *See also* ETHNICITY, p. 24; NATIONALISM, p. 76.

Significance   Culture is the lens through which people see other cultures. To the extent that the perceived culture differs from one's own, it is usually regarded as strange or improper and thus to be condemned. On the other hand, one culture will occasionally find something good and useful in another and will borrow it. Sometimes a culture will impose its characteristics on another. By these means, cultural traits diffuse. Generally, it seems, cultures borrow technical processes from each other rather willingly (although some cultures will refuse even technology that is alien); they are more cautious about borrowing social institutions (political structures, economic systems, family organizations); and they strongly resist borrowing the ideological aspects of another culture (e.g., a religion, a philosophy of individualism, a work ethos, the value of time). African cultures have been especially entangled with matters of cultural diffusion. In almost every colonially defined territory, the dominant power ruled numerous ethnic groups with a variety of cultures. Over these different cultures, the foreign power superimposed its technologies, social institutions, and values. After independence, each new state has been gripped by the need to blend its indigenous cultures, and at the same time to incorporate what it wants of the alien forms. The ultimate objective of the amalgamation of cultures is to produce a new national culture. For these reasons, African societies are often said to be enmeshed in a grand "rub of cultures."

Ethnicity   The state or quality of affiliation identified by race, culture, and/or language. Ethnicity in Africa is reflected in the strong sense of belonging that possesses most people. The group to which a person belongs is often identified as narrowly as the family, clan, or village. Ethnicity is partly a function of communication: One communicates most easily with people who share one's own values, language, and experiences. It is also a function of separation: People who see themselves as different from others identify with each other rather than with the outside groups. (This identification may be the source of the we-they dichotomy in all social relations.) Nationalism attempts to prompt people to raise their level of identification from the ethnic group to the nation. This process is undertaken by introducing such things as common education, mass communications, political participation, uniform laws, consistent and fair public administration, and national holidays. *See also* CULTURE, p. 23; NATIONALISM, p. 76; TRIBALISM, p. 32; TRIBE, p. 33.

Significance   The term *ethnicity* has replaced *tribalism* in many scholarly analyses. *Tribalism* had come to have an element of changelessness about it, has often been used in a pejorative sense, and is difficult to distinguish from nationalism. The term *ethnicity* is free from these restrictions while still allowing people to be identified by characteristics that set them apart from others. Ethnicity in Africa refers to the collection of people with whom the individual identifies himself. He may think of himself almost exclusively as a member of a family, a clan, a village, a region, a religion, a language group, or a race. As barriers between these various identification groups diminish (and benefits are perceived from the new arrangement), he may come to think of himself as a national citizen; this is the hope of African political leaders.

Family   A household of people related by marriage and offspring. A family consists of a father and mother and their children, but may also include a father and several mothers and their offspring and the offsprings' spouses and children. Polygyny was common in 98 percent of African societies, with monogamy restricted primarily to Berber society in North Africa and Christian society in Ethiopia. Because of the cost of plural marriages, most men in traditional Africa had one wife but were not legally restricted to one. Today monogamy is widely practiced among Christians, although not all Christians are monogamous. As elsewhere, most people in Africa marry. Since marriage ties two families together as much as it unites two individuals, most marriages are arranged by families. A gift from the groom's family called "bridewealth," is usually given to the bride's family. Should the bride prove unfaithful or barren, the bridewealth is returned to the groom's family; should the groom prove unworthy by maltreating the bride, the groom's family forfeits the bridewealth, even if the bride leaves her spouse. In polygynous relationships, the husband, in part to minimize jealousy, rotates his attentions to the different wives on a strict basis and usually provides each wife with her own house. An extended family may include a man, his wife or wives, his unmarried children, his married sons, and possibly the wives of his grandsons.

Significance   Marriage throughout Africa traditionally was far more than an individual affair. It tied extended families together so that the welfare of each was a common concern. Polygyny meant not only that every woman had a male provider, but she also had someone to share in the duties of maintaining a home and caring for the children. Since the various wives cared for all the offspring, children always had a "loving parent" to go to when the biological parent was angry, ill, or absent. Extended families remain complex units that even today allow for cooperation in economic and social matters on a grander scale than small families can provide. In fact, Africans grow up surrounded by many important and influencial people, not all of whom are blood relations. This developmental process is believed to engender an "otherness" awareness that is stronger among members of extended families than those in small nuclear families.

Herding   A form of survival based on the raising of livestock. All herding in Africa is confined to the savannah or grasslands. Most herding is of cattle, which are kept throughout the sub-Saharan savannah, as well as the area from eastern Africa to the Cape. In the Sahara itself, camels are herded. Goats are ubiquitous throughout herding areas (as well as elsewhere), and sheep are frequently kept also. Most herders practice transhumance, that is, the movement of livestock into desert areas during the brief period each year when grazing is possible, and then moving them to better pastures for the rest of the year.

Herding families have milk as their major diet, and sometimes blood, and occasionally meat. The small animals provide an essential food supplement to that supplied by the large animals. The proud herder, however, is likely to identify himself exclusively in terms of his large animals. All herding societies except the Maasai have established a kind of symbiotic relationship with agricultural peoples whereby they acquire vegetables in exchange for animals or animal products. The best known modern herders are the Maasai of Kenya and Tanzania (formerly Tanganyika and Zanzibar), the Somalis of the Horn, and the pastoral Fulani of West Africa. *See also* AGRICULTURE, p. 20; HUNTING AND GATHERING, p. 26; IRON USE, p. 26.

Significance Although Africans are overwhelmingly agriculturalists, only 4 or 5 percent are herders. In an age when modernization is the key objective of state leaders, herders can present many problems related to their reluctance to live in settlements. These vary from the difficulty of providing education and other amenities for a mobile population to the herders' resistence to being integrated into the larger, more industrialized nation-state.

Hunting and Gathering The process of survival by foraging plants and animals in their natural state. This way of living was common to all people until it was replaced by agriculture and herding. In Africa today it is restricted to fewer than 0.25 percent, primarily to the Mbuti (Pygmies) in Zaire and the San in southern Africa. Hunters and gatherers live in small bands of 20 to 50 people. Women tend to gather near the campsite and men to hunt farther away. *See also* AGRICULTURE, p. 20; HERDING, p. 25; IRON USE, p. 26.

Significance Hunting and gathering is a doomed way of life and has all but disappeared in the world. The great challenge to the states that contain such bands is how to integrate them into their modernization programs.

Iron Use The utilization of iron in the making of tools and weapons. Ironworking was probably invented in the Middle East in the fourteenth century B.C. and diffused westward to Greece and thence into Africa by way of Carthage, and southward into Kush (in present-day Sudan) and Aksum (Axum, in present-day Ethiopia). By 200 B.C., iron use had diffused throughout West Africa, and by the first century A.D., it had reached as far south as Zimbabwe (formerly Southern Rhodesia). The making of iron-tipped hoes and iron-shod axes permitted the spread of agriculture into the African forests. In addition, superior weapons of iron made conquest possible. The introduction of iron and the spread of agriculture probably explain the great migrations of Bantu-speaking peoples (p. 22) during the last two millenia. *See also* AGRICULTURE, p. 20; HERDING, p. 25; HUNTING AND GATHERING, p. 26; URBANISM, p. 33.

Significance The Iron Age was a vast technological improvement over the Neolithic (New Stone) Age in the same way that agriculture had been a vast improvement over hunting and gathering. In Africa ironworking helped to produce increased food supplies (through agricultural improvements), rapid population growth, large-scale migrations, the trend toward urbanization, and the impetus to conquest. These developments, in turn, resulted in new forms of political organization needed for governing large territories and nonrelated peoples.

Languages The articulated, meaningful sounds by which specific groups communicate feelings and concepts. There are in Africa approximately 800 to 1,000 distinct, mutually exclusive languages, perhaps one-quarter of all the languages in the world. Joseph H. Greenberg, the widely respected linguist, has divided African languages into 4 major families and subdivided these into 22 branches. By far the largest family is the Niger-Congo, which extends from Senegal to Kenya and south to the Cape, with a small pocket in Sudan. This family has 5 major branches in West Africa, the widespread Bantu branch in Central, Eastern, and Southern Africa, and the small Kordofanian branch in Sudan. The second family is Nilo-Saharan, stretching mainly from northern Chad southeasterly to Kenya, but embracing some people on the Niger River in West Africa. The third family is Afro–Asiatic, dominating North Africa but extending southward into West Africa and southeasterly into the Horn. Finally, there is the Khoisan family, located mainly in southwest Africa. Other important languages include the *lingua francas* of Afrikaans, English, French, Portuguese, Spanish, Swahili (in East and Central Africa), and Hausa (in the savannah area of West Africa), and several creole languages (mixtures of African and European languages) spoken in various places. In the Indian Ocean Area, Malayo-Polynesian languages are spoken on Madagascar, and Hindi and other Asian languages are spoken on Mauritius. *See also* BANTU-SPEAKING PEOPLES, p. 22.

Significance The many languages spoken in Africa create profound problems for political integration. Each group desires its language to be the national language. By default, therefore, most states in sub-Saharan Africa are forced to use the European language of their former colonial ruler as the national language, which means mainly

English or French, and, to a lesser extent, Spanish and Portuguese. An exception is Swahili, which is being deliberately cultivated as a national language in Tanzania and Kenya.

Oral Tradition   Inherited patterns of thought or action revealed through word of mouth. Oral tradition is contrasted with written tradition, which has long existed in Islamic regions as well as among the Coptic Christians of Ethiopia and the Swahili groups of East Africa. Oral tradition, however, is present in many parts of Africa, including areas of written tradition. Throughout Africa one finds praise-poems that are either sung or recited and deal with ethnic groups, animals, geographical features, and such contemporary topics as bicycles and automobiles. Prose narratives are also used throughout Africa. Nonliterate societies, in particular, have relied on historical stories that provide official accounts of the histories of states, ethnic groups, clans, families, migrations, wars, and famines. Fictional narratives are also common and include animal trickster stories and supernatural tales as well as various riddles and proverbs. The *griot* of West Africa is a professional oral-historian who sometimes sings his story accompanied by a musical instrument.

Significance   The recitation of stories, praise songs, riddles, and proverbs is a familiar way to create rich shared cultural attitudes, beliefs, values, and the sense of time, place, and history. In the past, the oral historian also provided support for the reputation of individuals and groups by recounting the great events of their ancestors. Rulers especially benefitted from praise poems. Often, however, official versions of oral histories differed from the common or folk versions of the same tale, thus creating a problem for modern historians who try to determine which of these various versions, if any, is the most correct. Nevertheless, through oral traditions Africans have a sense of history and continuity as well as an appreciation and respect for ancestors.

Religion   An ideological system based on a belief in extraterrestrial beings or forces not subject to empirical investigation. Traditionally, Africans have been as religious as other people. In general, indigenous African religions postulate: (1) a high god who created the earth and mankind but remains aloof; (2) a pantheon of gods and spirits or ancestors who intervene between man and the high god; and (3) a direct relationship between their ethnic group and their religion. Africans do not perceive their religions as exportable and do not proselytize. They believe in prayers, sacrifice, and rituals, in the sacredness of life, and in good and evil.

Christianity has been in Africa almost from its beginnings, in its Coptic form in Egypt and Ethiopia. In fact, Ethiopia, despite its religious diversity, is still regarded as a Christian country. Islam, founded in the seventh century, spread quickly to North Africa, where it predominates. By the eleventh century it had penetrated sub-Saharan Africa, where it continues to spread southward. Islam now predominates in West Africa, except along the coast, and in much of East Africa, especially along the littoral to mid-Mozambique. In contrast, Christian missionaries began to operate in sub-Saharan Africa at about the time that the Atlantic Slave Trade commenced (p. 21). Their activities spurted ahead in the nineteenth century and spread inland from all shores. Thus sub-Saharan Africans tend to be Muslim, Christian or "traditional," or amalgams of Islam or Christianity with the "traditional." Christianity is divided between the Catholic and Protestant factions. In turn, Protestants are divided among the numerous missionary denominations. *See also* CHRISTIAN MISSIONS, p. 48.

Significance Unlike the Muslims, Christian missionaries built, financed, and staffed schools that became the source of the education of most African elites until recently. However, in spite of great religious diversity and missionary zeal, there is remarkably little open hostility among religions.

Returned Slaves Africans who had been enslaved but later were freed and returned to Africa. After 1807, British and other European ships patrolled the Atlantic Ocean hunting down slave ships and freeing their captives. Many freed slaves were settled in Sierra Leone by the British government, where they formed a Creole class. Likewise, after 1820, freed slaves in the United States were settled in what they called Liberia (from the word liberty) and became the ruling class until the late 1970s. *See also* ATLANTIC SLAVE TRADE, p. 21; SLAVERY, p. 31.

Significance While some freed slaves were able to return to their place of origin, most were not. The majority remained in the New World or in Europe. A few, however, returned to Africa, especially to Sierra Leone and Liberia where, because of their different customs and languages, they constituted a small but privileged and Westernized class.

Rites of Passage Formal, routinized, group-directed behavior associated with major status changes in life. The most significant change is from childhood to adulthood, but other transformations involve marriage, the birth of children, installation in high office, and death. When formal procedures or rites accompany the passage from one status to another, and involve a great portion of the population, it is called a "rite of passage." Such rites, although common throughout Africa, vary greatly. Many African communities held grand ceremonies for initiating children at puberty into adulthood. In some societies the main feature of the rite was the circumcision of boys, as among the Tiriki of Kenya and the Kpelle of Liberia, and in some, clitoridectomy was performed on girls, as among the Kpelle. Other aspects of the rites often included months or even years of seclusion during which youths were taught to bear suffering and pain, how to deal with the opposite sex, the history of their people, basic rules of conduct, and religious values. In addition, boys were instructed in methods of hunting and warfare, while girls learned correct procedures for maintaining a household. Other societies (such as the Yoruba, Igbo, Tiv, and Hausa of Nigeria) maintained the educational aspects described above but conducted circumcision at another time, often with little ritual. Some communities (such as the Hausa and Yoruba) conducted clitoridectomy operations independent of the rites associated with puberty. The Somalis both circumcise boys and permit them to pass into adulthood without ritual, although they are initiated into adulthood when they are assigned the care of herds of camels. The essential rite of passage for the Hausa of northern Nigeria occurs not at puberty but at marriage. *See also* AGE GROUPS, p. 20; FAMILY, p. 24; SECRET SOCIETIES, p. 30.

Significance   Rites of passage, where they existed, have undergone much change as a result of colonialism and formal education. Circumcision and clitoridectomy, if maintained, tend to be performed now on infants. Formal schooling interferes with the long periods of seclusion formerly associated with puberty rites. Marriage and death rites, on the other hand, are often maintained as in the past or combined with new practices (such as Christian ones).

Secret Societies   Groups formed in certain societies to regulate various kinds of behavior in conformity with supernatural forces. In organization and ritual, secret societies in Africa resemble fraternal orders of Western societies. In their supernatural role, they resemble the medieval church in Europe, which prescribed conduct for members of society and alone could remit certain sins. The primary purposes of secret societies were to initiate young people into the adult world, to regulate sexual conduct, to supervise political and economic affairs, and to provide various social services (ranging from medical treatment to entertainment). Once one has been initiated into the society, he or she is bound by oath not to reveal the secrets of the society and to conform to its code of conduct. The *Poro* of the Guinea-Liberia-Sierra Leone area is probably the best known of such societies, but they exist throughout much of West Africa and in the Zaire area.

Significance Secret societies are valuable in cultures that do not have formal state structures, age groups, or kinship groups for enforcing social values and conduct. In Sierra Leone, the *Poro* (men's society) and *Sande* (women's society) once exercised important political functions, similar to lawmaking.

Slavery The state of a person who is the chattel, or property, of another. Although a person may sell himself into slavery as an indentured servant, most slavery in history has resulted from capture in warfare or slaving raids. Occasionally, for economic or social reasons, parents will sell their children into slavery. Slavery has been quite common historically throughout Africa. However, in most forms of indigenous African slavery, slaves had rights as well as duties. Often, they aspired to and achieved high standing in a family or society, and, in turn, were able to pass their status on to their children. *See also* ATLANTIC SLAVE TRADE, p. 21; RETURNED SLAVES, p. 29.

Significance Slavery has long been an aspect of life in indigenous Africa. Even before the commencement of the Atlantic slave trade, the trans-Saharan slave trade and slaving along the East African coast were centuries old. (Neither, however, compared to the Atlantic slave trade in the number of captives taken.) Slavery has been known in all parts of the world, but no people have suffered the ravages of this nefarious institution as have Africans.

State A society with formal, centralized, fixed political roles, always involving a recognized head or executive, and usually a bureaucracy. Before the age of colonialism, many African societies were run as states. Some of these states were small, numbering only a few thousand people, under the rule of a king (but often called a chief in Africa). Other states were large kingdoms involving millions of people and having many intermediate kings (or chiefs) serving as mediators between their people and the supreme king (sometimes called emperor). Many rulers had to consult councils of elders or representatives of clans, although some held absolute authority. Many of the great states of Africa, at their height, rivaled their contemporaries in Europe in size, population, scholarship, and opulence of their courts: for example, Ghana (700–1200 A.D.), Mali (1200–1500 A.D.), Songhai (1350–1600 A.D.), or the Hausa city-states (1300–1800 A.D.), all in West Africa. Other states of considerable size and population and lasting 200 or more years were: Ashanti (Asante), Dahomey, Oyo, Benin, and Kanem–Bornu in West Africa; Buganda and Bunyoro in East Africa; and Kongo, Luba, Lunda, Lozi, Mutapa, and Changamire (Rozvi) in Central and Southern Africa. These states had well-developed urban centers and efficient agriculture. They were formed not only for defense but as complex trading systems, external as well as internal. *See also* ACEPHALOUS SOCIETY, p. 19; TRIBE, p. 33.

Significance By the time of European conquest, a variety of African states had been established across the continent. The existence of such organized states made European conquest easier than it would have been with acephalous societies. European nations were able to capture African states because of superior technology, not superior state structures. African states, when defeated by European ones, had formal officials to grant the surrender and formal structures through which victors could rule their new possessions. By way of contrast, the most difficult societies to conquer and rule were the acephalous ones.

Tribalism The concept that some act or belief is based on defense of a so-called "tribal" interest in contrast to a larger interest. People in Africa are accused by other Africans of being "tribalistic" when they defend a practice, language, ritual, tradition, social organization, or region against an alleged incursion by a similar group ("tribe" against "tribe") or against a proposed action by the larger state ("tribe" against the state or nation). For example, "tribalism" is charged when a group opposes the location of a highway through what it regards as sacred territory, or insists that political boundaries exclude or include some particular people, or seeks a special political privilege for itself, or demands independence from the state of which it is a part. *See also* TRIBE, p. 33.

Significance Most scholars reject the term "tribalism" on the grounds that it simply refers to ethnic or regional conflicts found in all parts of the globe. By labeling such antagonisms in Africa as "tribalism," one inaccurately suggests that Africa is different from the rest of the world. Ethnic and regional conflicts are intense in many states in Africa. Wherever they occur, people opposed to the action or belief of any particular group are apt to charge their enemies with "tribalism." Thus the term is widely used in Africa as a pejorative expression.

Tribe   A vague term referring to a group of people who regard themselves as bound together by kinship traceable to a common ancestor (real or imagined). The vagueness of the term makes precise definition difficult, and for this reason most scholars avoid it. Where used, however, *tribe* refers to a group of people that inhabits a particular area, speaks a common language, practices common rituals, and shares common social institutions and values. Many scholars believe that there may be as many as 800 to 1,000 such groups in Africa. Such figures may cause one to infer incorrectly that African "tribes" are all small societies. While many such groups are small, some contain millions of people (for example, the Hausa, Yoruba, and Igbo of Nigeria), and many number in the hundreds of thousands. *See also* ETHNICITY, p. 24; STATE, p. 31; TRIBALISM, p. 32.

Significance   The fact of size alone makes the term *tribe* suspect. It might be better to think of eight or ten million people as a "nation" rather than a tribe, although *nation* itself implies a unity of identification that some large so-called tribes have never had. But the word *tribe* has other defects. It has been used at times to refer also to subgroups inside a larger group, to village states, to language groups, and in a pejorative sense to groups that are disliked. For these reasons, many social scientists avoid the term *tribe* and refer instead to "ethnic group" or "people." Nevertheless, the term *tribe* is commonly used by Africans and still appears in a few scholarly books, although its contemporary use is declining.

Urbanism   The state of aggregating people into compact areas for trade, governmental institutions, specialization of labor, manufacturing, and finance. West Africa especially was the locus of many urban centers long before it came into contact with Europeans. Among the more important urban centers were: Timbuctu (in what is now Mali), Kumasi (in what is now Ghana), Oyo, Ile-Ife, Benin, Kano, Katsina, and Zaria (in what is now Nigeria). Urban centers also existed in other parts of Africa: Mogadishu (in Somalia), Mombasa (in Kenya), Zanzibar City (in what is now Tanzania), Luanda (in Angola), Zimbabwe (in what is now Zimbabwe), and Aksum (Axum, in Ethiopia).

Significance   In cultural evolution, urbanization is the second major revolution of human societies after the Agricultural Revolution. The existence of sophisticated precolonial urban centers throughout Africa attests to the fact that Africans had advanced, complex cultures before the arrival of Europeans.

3. Colonial Perspectives

Afrikaner   A South African White of Dutch-German-French descent. Afrikaners constitute about 58 percent of the total White population (the remainder being mainly of English descent), but only about 9 percent of the total population of the country. In South Africa only Whites have full political rights. Since Afrikaners politically dominate the other Whites, they consequently dominate the country. They are an extremely homogeneous group, speaking their own language (Afrikaans), practicing their own religion (Dutch Reformed), supporting their own political party (National Party), and implementing the Afrikaner policy of *apartheid* by which they protect their privileged position by subjugating the Black, Colored, and Asian peoples in the country. *See also* APARTHEID, p. 35; BLACKS, p. 39; BOERS, p. 39; BOER WAR, p. 40; BROEDERBOND, p. 41; COLOREDS, p. 42; GREAT TREK, p. 46; SETTLERS: ASIAN, p. 50; SETTLERS: WHITE, p. 51.

Significance   The Afrikaner National Party, representing White minority rule, speaks as the official voice of the Republic of South Africa. The Afrikaners are so united in their fear of losing their racial and cultural identity (as well as their privileges) that to date they have refused to make any significant concessions to majority rule. Afrikaners have for over 30 years formed a tight-knit, intolerant, and intransigent ruling class that has controlled all aspects of public life in the country. Buttressed by a siege mentality, they dominate not only the formal lawmaking and administrative powers of government, but also the police, the army, the judiciary, the education system, and many of the religious institutions.

Apartheid   An Afrikaans word (pronounced uh-part-ate) meaning apartness or separateness. It describes the policy of the National Party (in charge of the government of the Republic of South Africa since 1948) that segregates the races according to its own definitions. By numerous laws, the non-White majorities are denied all political rights such as voting or serving in public office, are required to carry identity passes when traveling in "White" areas, and are severely restricted in their jobs, housing, land ownership, and education. *Apartheid* is the most extreme form of government-sanctioned segregation of people on alleged racial factors in the contemporary world. *See also* AFRIKANER, p. 35; BLACKS, p. 39; COLOREDS, p. 42; BOERS, p. 39; BOER WAR, p. 40; BROEDERBOND, p. 40; GREAT TREK, p. 41; RACE, p. 12; RACISM, p. 13.

Significance Apartheid is a policy directed by a White minority against a vast majority of non-Whites, and specifically against Black Africans. This policy is the cause for antagonistic relations between Black African states and the Republic of South Africa, and the near-unanimous efforts of Black states to persuade the United Nations to impose economic sanctions on that White redoubt. The intransigence of the White government and the rise of anti-*apartheid* guerrilla movements have caused many people to fear that South Africa may erupt in a racial civil war. Such a conflict would soon embroil other African states and then perhaps the great powers of the world.

Assimilado Policy The Portuguese policy for assimilating Africans who achieved a certain level of Europeanization. The Portuguese maintained no official color-bar, tolerated mixed marriages, and allowed Africans who became literate in Portuguese and earned a specific income to become *assimilados*. According to theory, assimilados were permitted to enjoy all the rights of Portuguese citizenship. The assimilado policy of Portugal contrasted significantly with the openly racist policies of other colonial powers. However, the rights of Portuguese citizens were never very great under that country's dictatorships, and the assimilado policy can therefore be overemphasized. Nevertheless, the policy, if not the practice, was quite different from that followed elsewhere. *See also* ASSIMILATION, p. 37; ASSOCIATION, p. 37.

Significance As envisioned by the Portuguese, the assimilado policy required the extirpation of African cultures, and their replacement by Portuguese values, traditions, institutions, and language. Such a policy depended overwhelmingly on education, but Portugal made little effort to educate its colonial subjects. Thus by 1950, after over 300 years of colonial rule, there were only 30,000 assimilados in Angola and a mere 4,500 in Mozambique. Therefore, assimilation was more a hope than a promise. Even so, it is generally conceded that the Portuguese colonies in southern Africa were never as overtly racist as settler societies established in other parts of the continent.

Assimilation   French colonial policy that defined the French objective as one of integrating Africans into French culture. The assimilation policy required Africans to be so inculcated with the French language, French history, and French values that they were to be regarded as Black Frenchmen. *See also* ASSIMILADO POLICY, p. 36; ASSOCIATION, p. 37.

Significance   Although assimilation was for a time a goal, and some Africans were actually assimilated, it soon became clear that the investment in education and time made assimilation an unrealistic goal for most Africans under French rule. Assimilation thus gave way to association. Nevertheless, when Africans attained the status of Frenchmen—in facility with the French language, manners, customs, dress, and values—the French granted them full political rights including running for election and serving in the French National Assembly and French cabinet (as, for example, did Felix Houphouet-Boigny, now President of the Ivory Coast).

Association   French colonial policy that dismissed assimilation as unrealistic, but, nonetheless, offered a related plan called association. According to this policy, Africans should be made into Frenchmen as soon as reasonably possible, and all African territories under French rule should be governed as part of indivisible France. Until Africans were Frenchmen, they would remain associated with France. *See also* ASSIMILATION, p. 37.

Significance   By defining their policy as "association" rather than "assimilation," the French were freed from full-scale and very costly efforts to transform millions of Africans into Frenchmen in a short time. Furthermore, association had a superior-inferior aura about it, whereas assimilation implied equality. It took little foresight for the French to realize that if all Africans under their rule were assimilated then Black Frenchmen would outnumber White Frenchmen.

Belgian Empire   A territory (now Zaire) known as the Congo Free State that was removed from King Leopold II's personal rule by the

Belgian Parliament in 1908 and thereafter called the Belgian Congo. After World War I, Belgium acquired as mandates of the League of Nations the former German colony of Ruanda-Urundi (now Rwanda and Burundi). *See also* BRITISH EMPIRE, pp. 40–41; FRENCH EMPIRE, p. 45; GERMAN EMPIRE, p. 46; ITALIAN EMPIRE, p. 48; PORTUGUESE EMPIRE, p. 49; SPANISH EMPIRE, p. 52; TABLE B-5, p. 204.

Significance King Leopold's methods of exploiting the Congo Free State (including forced labor and the leasing of vast tracts of land to private companies) were so ruthless that the population was reduced by a large fraction in 20 years. The notoriety of Leopold's personal rule so embarrassed the Belgian government that it seized the property and made it into a colony, which survived as such until 1960.

Berlin Conference of 1884–85 An international conference of great powers convened by the German Chancellor Otto von Bismarck to seek agreement on the principles for partitioning Africa. Representatives came from Great Britain, France, Germany, Spain, Portugal, and Belgium, with an observer from the United States. The conference agreed: (1) to utilize the principle that title to colonial territory rested on "effective occupation and management;" (2) to recognize the claims of Britain and France to areas of West Africa inland from their coastal possessions; and (3) to acknowledge the Congo Free State as a private estate "belonging" to King Leopold II of Belgium. *See also* BELGIAN EMPIRE, p. 37; BRITISH EMPIRE, p. 40; COLONIALISM/IMPERIALISM, p. 41; FRENCH EMPIRE, p. 45; GERMAN EMPIRE, p. 46; ITALIAN EMPIRE, p. 48; PORTUGUESE EMPIRE, p. 49; SCRAMBLE FOR AFRICA, p. 49; SPANISH EMPIRE, p. 52.

Significance The Berlin Conference, by producing agreement among the great powers, defused the growing tensions in Europe. The participants recognized certain parts of Africa as subject to particular European countries or (as in the case of the Congo area) under the control of one man. The principle of effective control and management meant that a European country could only claim title to areas it actually controlled. This condition was inserted to counter Portugal's claim over all of East and southcentral Africa. (Its claim was contradicted by the fact that its soldiers and officials operated only in Angola and Mozambique.) The major impact of the "effective control" principle was that it provided a basis for resolving other conflicts which grew out of the scramble (p. 49). For example, the British and German confrontations over Zanzibar, Tanganyika, Kenya, and Uganda were finally settled in 1890, partly on the basis of the "effective control" principle.

Blacks (Black Africans)   An imprecise term referring to the dark skin color and physiological stereotype of persons born in sub-Saharan Africa whose ancestors were also of sub-Saharan origin. It is also sometimes used to include the so-called Colored people and even the people of Asian descent in South Africa. *See also* BANTU-SPEAKING PEOPLES, p. 22; RACISM, p. 13.

Significance   More and more people born in sub-Saharan Africa whose ancestors were of sub-Saharan origin call themselves Blacks or Black Africans to distinguish themselves from: (1) people whose ancestry was not African (such as Europeans and Asians) but who were themselves born in Africa; and (2) North Africans (who tend to be perceived by sub-Saharan Africans as racially linked with Europe and culturally linked with Arabia). In South Africa the term becomes especially imprecise when applied to the Colored people whose ancestry may be more non-African than African. To apply it also to Asians is to make the term strictly a political one referring generally to mistreated people. In 1978, however, the Government of the Republic of South Africa agreed to use the term "Blacks" in place of "Bantu" in referring to inhabitants of exclusively African ancestry, and changed the name of the Bantu Affairs Department to the Department of Plural Relations and Development.

Boers   A Dutch word for the farmers of Dutch-German-French origin who settled in South Africa after 1652. They lived inland from the administrative center of Cape Town and became the core of what would later be known as Afrikaners. *See also* AFRIKANER, p. 35; APARTHEID, p. 35; BOER WAR, p. 40; BROEDERBOND, p. 41; GREAT TREK, p. 46; SETTLERS: WHITE, p. 51.

Significance   The Dutch settlers from the Netherlands were often poor farmers, artisans, and laborers who practiced a rigid form of Calvinism and who, augmented by Germans, became employees of the Dutch East Indian Company in the Cape area. Some of them became farmers in their new land. In 1685, Louis XIV of France withdrew his protection of Protestant Calvinists (Huguenots) who, to escape persecution, emigrated to South Africa and mixed with the Dutch-German population. All became known as Boers and acquired a sense of being

South African rather than Dutch, German, or French. Their particular belief was that only those selected by God for salvation could be saved; the "elect" were those who adhered to the traditional Calvinist precepts. From the beginning, the concept of the "elect" excluded the local San (Bushmen) and Khoi-Khoi (Hottentots) from salvation. This view was later extended to all non-Whites and was, in part, the basis for the contemporary policy of *apartheid.*

Boer War (South African War, 1899–1902) The war between Great Britain on one hand and the Boer republics of Transvaal and Orange Free State on the other. The Afrikaner states sought independence from British interference in their internal affairs. After the discovery of gold in the Transvaal (1886), Great Britain attempted to gain control over the region by charging that Afrikaner leaders were obstructing British mining interests. British imperial policy and economic interests as well as Afrikaner intransigence led to war. Britain eventually won after a lengthy and bitter struggle. See also AFRIKANER, p. 35; APARTHEID, p. 35; BOERS, p. 39; BROEDERBOND, p. 41; GREAT TREK, p. 46; SETTLERS: WHITE, p. 51.

Significance The Boer War determined the composition of what became, in 1910, the Union of South Africa, a federation of the two defeated Boer states, English-speaking Natal, Cape Colony, and several African polities. The new state contained an overwhelming African majority, but indigenous opinion was not sought at its creation, nor was consideration given to indigenous rights. The Union was a self-governing territory within the British Commonwealth, with political power shared by shifting coalitions of English-speakers and moderate Afrikaners who favored cooperation between the two White groups and with Great Britain. In contrast, however, less moderate Afrikaners (after 1902) began the systematic development of an exclusive cultural nationalism based on the Afrikaans language, membership in the Dutch Reformed Church, hostility toward Britain, and a commitment to the creation of a racially stratified society dominated by Afrikaners only. This movement came to fruition in the 1948 general election victory of the National Party under the leadership of Dr. D. F. Malan. Since then, the principles of *apartheid* have been applied by successive National Party governments. The long-standing Afrikaner dislike of Great Britain reached its logical conclusion in 1961 when the Union of South Africa cut its last formal connections with that country and with the Commonwealth and became the Republic of South Africa.

British Empire Those areas of the world, including much of Africa, that by 1914 had come under the colonial domination or influence of Great Britain. In North Africa this included Egypt and Sudan; in West Africa, Nigeria, Ghana, Sierra Leone, and Gambia; in East Africa, Kenya, Uganda, Zanzibar, and part of Somaliland; in southern Africa, Zambia (formerly Northern Rhodesia), Zimbabwe (formerly Southern Rhodesia), Malawi (formerly Nyasaland), Botswana (formerly Bechuanaland), Lesotho (formerly Basutoland), Swaziland, and the Republic of South Africa; and in the Indian Ocean, Mauritius and Seychelles. After World War I, the British also acquired, as mandates of the League of Nations, one former German colony (Tanganyika) and portions of two others (Togo and Cameroon). *See also* BELGIAN EMPIRE, p. 37; FRENCH EMPIRE, p. 45; GERMAN EMPIRE, p. 46; ITALIAN EMPIRE, p. 48; PORTUGUESE EMPIRE, p. 49; SPANISH EMPIRE, p. 52; TABLE B-5, p. 204.

Significance Great Britain at one time ruled half of the people of Africa and was therefore the most influential of the imperial powers there. English is today the most widespread *lingua franca* on the continent. After World War I, the Empire became the "British Commonwealth," and after World War II, simply the "Commonwealth."

Broederbond An Afrikaans word meaning "brotherhood" that refers to a closed and secret organization in the Republic of South Africa to which most prominent Afrikaners belong. Formed in 1918, the *Broederbond* is composed of "true believers," who vow to maintain the religion of the Dutch Reformed Church, *apartheid,* permanent subjugation of all non-White people, and the permanent control of government in their own hands. It was once believed to control the government by monitoring all policies and legislation for doctrinal purity and by condemning all deviations. Its power was probably always exaggerated, but today it is clearly subordinate to the National Party. *See also* APARTHEID, p. 35; BOERS, p. 39; BOER WAR, p. 40; GREAT TREK, p. 46; RACISM, p. 13; SETTLERS: WHITE, p. 51.

Significance Afrikaners control the formal government through the National Party, but have relied on the secret *Broederbond* to infiltrate the churches, schools, clubs, and public offices in order to build and maintain unswerving, uncompromising support for rigid racial separation and Afrikaner domination of South African society. The *Broederbond* also has helped to select "right-thinking" Afrikaner candidates for office, coalesce Africaner opinion behind all policies that support *apartheid,* and marshal *en masse* Afrikaner opposition to equality for non-Whites.

Colonialism/Imperialism The rule of one people over another. Originally, colonialism referred to the hiving off of some members from a larger group in order to migrate to a new location while remaining under the rule of the parent group. From this concept came the terms *colony* and *mother country* (as in the American colonies before 1776). However, as peoples of different races and cultures came under European rule, their lands too came to be called colonies, even though they were not of European descent. Gradually colonialism and imperialism (the imposition of imperium or absolute rule over alien lands and peoples) came to be used almost interchangeably.

Colonialism/imperialism takes many forms: direct rule by occupying forces and administrators, rule on behalf of international organizations (League of Nations mandates, United Nations trusts), protectorates where the dominant power controls only foreign policy, domination through local surrogates loyal to the imperial ideology and wishes (as in the Soviet satellites in Eastern Europe). Thus, in part, the results of colonialism/imperialism are political subjugation and economic exploitation. *See also* BERLIN CONFERENCE, p. 38; DIRECT RULE, p. 43; INDIRECT RULE, p. 47; SCRAMBLE FOR AFRICA, p. 49.

Significance Africa came to know colonialism/imperialism well, especially after 1885, when the entire continent except for Ethiopia and Liberia came under the domination of European powers. The age of colonialism/imperialism for Africa will basically end with the independence of Namibia (p. 182).

Coloreds (Coloureds) People in the Republic of South Africa who are officially identified as being of mixed racial ancestry, partly White. Their origins, dating to 1657, involved White men and slave women from tropical Africa, Madagascar, and Java as well as local San and Khoi-Khoi women. Today, Coloreds comprise about 2.6 million people, or about 9 percent of the population. Most of them speak Afrikaans, the remainder, English. Almost all are Christians except for about 6 percent who are Muslim and known as Cape Malays. (Islam arrived with the slaves imported from Java.) In the past they identified mainly with the Whites, but recently the Coloreds have begun to associate themselves with the Blacks. They live mainly in the western part of Cape Province in their own internally defined class system. Under the *apartheid* system, they are denied political and social rights, but Coloreds do have more privileges and higher material standards than Blacks. *See also* APARTHEID, p. 35; BLACKS, p. 39; RACE, p. 12; RACISM, p. 13; SETTLERS: ASIAN, p. 50.

Significance In spite of the fact that Whites established the social patterns that produced the Colored population, twentieth-century laws attempt to stop any further mixing of races. A 1927 law prohibits sexual intercourse between Whites and Blacks (Black Africans) and a 1950 law prohibits sexual relations between a White and any non-White (including Colored and Indian). The Coloreds constitute a strange problem for the *apartheid* policy since they are partly or even mainly white themselves and have no ancestral "homelands" to which to return. Because many Coloreds still identify with Whites, they present another problem for those who attempt to organize all "non-Whites" in the struggle against *apartheid*.

Direct Rule   A system of colonial rule that applied colonial policies to its subjects with little regard for local tradition or interests, usually associated with French and Belgian practice. While the French might appoint a traditional ruler to administer an area, he was merely the agent of the French; his duties were always spelled out to him and he could be (and often was) removed if he violated those duties. In addition, the area and people the appointee administered were not necessarily the ones traditionally under his rule. Thus, when the colonial officer spoke to the local chief (whether traditional ruler or merely appointed), the instructions were always regarded as orders by both parties. The objective was to determine local behavior in the colony as directly as possible. *See also* COLONIALISM/IMPERIALISM, p. 41; INDIRECT RULE, p. 47.

Significance   Direct rule usually fits the stereotype of colonial rule. While it was less sensitive to tradition than indirect rule, nevertheless, few colonial powers tried to ignore local traditions completely. Often the semblance of observing tradition was necessary to get anything done. The population of a colony was usually more receptive to innovation if it seemed to support tradition in some way. Conversely, direct rule could probably destroy undesirable behavior (as viewed by the colonizer) faster than indirect.

European Exploration of Africa   The era when individual Europeans, motivated largely by curiosity, began to penetrate the interior of Africa. Except for some Portuguese explorations of the interior beginning in the mid-sixteenth century, most European governments whose citizens and firms were trading along the coasts continued to display little interest in the interior until the nineteenth century. By 1800, the picture was changing. Explorers began to search for answers to questions that had puzzled scientists, such as the origins of the Nile and the Congo Rivers and the course of the Niger as well as the nature of the peoples and cultures of the interior. In 1795, Mungo Park began to explore the middle and upper Niger, followed by the Frenchman, René Caillié. But it was not until 1830 that H. Clapperton and R. Lander put a canoe in the Niger River and drifted all the way to the Atlantic through the huge delta in Nigeria (which Europeans had thought until then to be a number of independent rivers). In the 1850s, Dr. H. Barth crossed the Sahara and explored Hausaland and the Niger River. Similarly, in the 1850s and 1860s, R. Burton, J. Speke, and J. Grant explored the Great Lakes area in search of the origin of the Nile. During the same period, Dr. David Livingstone explored the area between the Lualaba and the Zambezi Rivers. In the 1870s, H. M. Stanley showed that the Congo and the Lualaba were the same river. Such explorations by 1900 provided Europeans with much accurate scientific and geographical information about the vast interior of Africa.

Significance With the demise of the slave trade, Europeans and Africans began to show a greater interest in other items of trade. The era of explorations supplied Europeans with greater knowledge about the cultures of the interior, trade opportunities, routes of land porterage, and navigable rivers. It also expedited the colonial era, although that was not a primary purpose of exploration.

French Community The title of the relationship between France and its African colonies as a result of the *loi-cadre* (framework law), in effect from 1958 to 1960. The proposal for the French Community had resulted largely from negotiations between President de Gaulle of France and Felix Houphouet-Boigny, leader of the Ivory Coast. Each territory was permitted to hold an election in 1958 on the question of whether to accept or reject the loi-cadre. A "yes" vote was an agreement to join the Community, and thus maintain close ties with France. A "no" vote was to reject the Community and become totally independent, with the severance of all ties with France, including the loss of all aid. Only the people of Guinea, under the leadership of Sekou Touré, voted "no," resulting in immediate and precipitate independence. The remaining territories voted "yes," thus entering into the new arrangement. The vote meant that the territories, in contrast to their status in the French Union, lost their representation in the French Assembly (parliament). In exchange, each individual territory (for example, Ivory Coast, Chad) emerged as an autonomous, but not independent, state. Each state then set up its own government with an executive and legislature, and sent representatives to an Executive Council presided over by the President of France.

In actuality, however, the Community turned out to be merely a transitional device leading to full independence barely two years after its formation. In 1960, in response to insistent demands, President de Gaulle granted independence to 14 French territories, excluding only Algeria, Comoros, and Djibouti. The irony was that while in 1958 France broke all relations with Guinea because of its "no" vote, independence was granted in 1960 to the other states with de Gaulle's blessing and continued close ties and assistance. *See also* ASSIMILATION, p. 37; ASSOCIATION, p. 37; FRENCH EMPIRE, p. 45; FRENCH UNION, p. 45.

Significance The loi-cadre was the device for breaking up the large areas of French West and Equatorial Africa into the separate territories that very shortly became independent states, as they now exist. Under the Community, Africans could still be associated with France but not assimilated. They were to remain African (not Black Frenchmen) and be ruled by Africans (not Frenchmen), under the general supervision of France. Nevertheless, autonomy was not the same as independence (for example, states of the Community were not able to join the United Nations). Furthermore, the gaining of independence by other states was an irresistible lure to the African leaders in the Community, prompting their insistent demands for total independence.

French Empire The areas of Africa that by 1914 had come under the colonial domination of France. These regions included the North African territories of Morocco, Algeria, and Tunisia; French West Africa (now Senegal, Mauritania, Mali, Upper Volta, Guinea, Ivory Coast, Niger, and Benin); the central African area, later known as French Equatorial Africa (now Chad, Central African Republic, Gabon, Congo); Djibouti (on the Red Sea); and in the Indian Ocean, the large island of Madagascar and the small islands of Comoro and Réunion. After World War I, France also acquired parts of Cameroon and Togo as League of Nations mandates. *See also* ASSIMILATION, p. 37; ASSOCIATION, p. 37; DIRECT RULE, p. 43; FRENCH COMMUNITY, p. 44; FRENCH UNION, p. 45; TABLE B-5, 204.

Significance While France had the largest land empire in Africa, it ruled only about 40 percent as many people as Britain. Its method was by direct rule, and its policies were based on assimilation and/or association.

French Union The formal title of the French government and territories (including European France and its possessions) during the

Fourth Republic from 1946 to 1958. The African possessions became part of Overseas France. Africans under the Union structure were permitted to participate in their own governance by electing (usually indirectly through communal bodies) representatives to territorial assemblies and to the French National Assembly in Paris. Even so, French governors continued to be posted to the African territories, indicating the French commitment to remain the dominant partner in the Union. *See also* ASSIMILATION, p. 37; ASSOCIATION, p. 37; FRENCH COMMUNITY, p. 45; FRENCH EMPIRE, p. 45.

Significance The French objective for the African colonies was to integrate Black Frenchmen (those who had acquired French language and culture) into the political culture of France. No other colonial power had made it possible for Black Africans to sit side-by-side in its democratically elected legislature with citizens from the metropole (ruling country). Some Africans (e.g., Felix Houphouet-Boigny of Ivory Coast) even became ministers in the French government. This feature of French rule partially explains the remarkably friendly relations still maintained between France and many of its former colonies.

German Empire The areas of Africa that before 1914 had come under the colonial domination of Germany. These regions included what are now known as Tanzania (exclusive of Zanzibar), Burundi, Rwanda, Cameroon, Togo, and Namibia. These colonies were all lost to Germany as a result of World War I and assigned as mandates to Britain, France, and Belgium. *See also* BELGIAN EMPIRE, p. 37; BRITISH EMPIRE, p. 40; FRENCH EMPIRE, p. 46; ITALIAN EMPIRE, p. 48; PORTUGUESE EMPIRE, p. 49; SPANISH EMPIRE, p. 52.

Significance Germany, unified only in 1871, almost immediately began to acquire colonies. However, after winning some valuable areas, Germany lost them all following World War I. Despite this, German influence remained strong in these former colonies for many years, especially in South West Africa (now Namibia), where the German language and culture persist to this day.

Great Trek The mass movement and resettlement of Boers (1835–37), with their possessions and animals, from their areas in the Cape Colony northeastward across the Orange and Vaal Rivers, and, to a limited extent, into Natal. The Colony of South Africa (established by the Dutch) had come under British rule in 1814. The British began to impose their language and culture as well as laws regarding landholding and slavery. They further antagonized the Afrikaner population by espousing rights for Africans. In a desperate effort to escape liberalism (which they regarded as heresy), thousands of Boers began the Great Trek with the intention of establishing their own independent governments beyond British control. *See also* AFRIKANER, p. 35; APARTHEID, p. 35; BOERS, p. 39; BOER WAR, p. 40; BROEDERBOND, p. 41; SETTLERS: WHITE, p. 51.

Significance The Great Trek has had a vast psychological impact on Afrikaners. It and the Boer War are two pillars of Afrikaner nationalism. It represents not only frontier self-reliance but also the effort of Boers to escape any identification with the British. In addition, it represents their attempt to escape "ungodly equality" with the Africans, and thus symbolizes everything held sacred by today's Afrikaners. The British, however, did not recognize the right of its citizens to escape British laws simply by moving to other territory. Consequently, the areas to which the Boers fled were constant foci of conflict between Britain and the Boers until their status was finally resolved by the Boer War.

Indirect Rule A system of colonial rule utilizing traditional authorities. The policy was designed to disturb local polities as little as possible while at the same time effecting colonial rule. The British employed this method of rule first in Northern Nigeria, which served as a model for its other colonies where traditional rulers existed. The colonial officer acted primarily as an advisor to the traditional ruler except in extreme cases, when he exerted his actual authority. *See also* COLONIALISM/IMPERIALISM, p. 41; DIRECT RULE, p. 43.

Significance Indirect rule was regarded by many during the era of colonialism as the most humane way to administer a colony. It extended colonial relationships while masking the power involved. Traditional rulers could be seen by their subjects to be performing their time-honored functions even when, on instructions from the colonial officer, they ordered their subjects to do nontraditional things. The system also permitted rulers to utilize traditional practices for doing new things, like consulting with confidants, elders, or nobles before building a new road or school. In some cases, such as the emirates of Northern Nigeria, it entrenched traditional rulers in office who had theretofore been subject to removal by traditional means. Furthermore, indirect rule affected African societies by causing people to realize that their traditional institutions and rulers were increasingly meaningless, bereft of everything except long-accustomed prestige.

Italian Empire   The areas of Africa that before 1914 had come under the colonial domination of Italy. These included Libya, Eritrea (now part of Ethiopia), and a portion of Somalia. *See also* BELGIAN EMPIRE, p. 37; BRITISH EMPIRE, p. 40; FRENCH EMPIRE, p. 45; GERMAN EMPIRE, p. 46; PORTUGUESE EMPIRE, p. 49; SPANISH EMPIRE, p. 52; TABLE B-5, p. 204.

Significance   Italy, only unified in 1871, entered the competition for colonies late. Beside the areas mentioned above, it tried also to add Ethiopia to its empire in 1896 by sending an army to conquer that ancient land. To the great surprise of the Italians, the Ethiopian army proved to be superior and routed the invaders at Adowa, thus preserving Ethiopian freedom until 1936, when Italy recovered its lost "honor" through military conquest. Ethiopia was then added to the Italian Empire, which came to an end during the North African campaigns of World War II.

Missions (Christian)   Church-sponsored agencies represented by individuals sent to Africa to convert local peoples to a particular version of Christianity. The Portuguese were the earliest (in the fifteenth century) to be concerned with propagating Catholicism along the coast near Cape Verde and in Benin, the Congo, Angola, and Mozambique, but these efforts had little lasting impact. Until the nineteenth century, Europeans were primarily interested in trade, mainly in slaves. However, in the latter part of the eighteenth century, there swept through the Protestant churches of northern Europe an unprecedented zeal for converting to Christianity the heathen of the world. By the early nineteenth century, numerous Protestant missionary societies began to operate in southern Africa and then in West and East Africa. A revived Catholic missionary effort developed also in the nineteenth century, primarily from France. By the 1870s missionary activities took on a momentum that has continued to the present, and is important in the fields of medicine and education. *See also* RELIGION, p. 28.

Significance   Christian missionaries realized very early that the most effective way to make and keep converts was through education. Thus, long before colonial governments became interested in the education of Africans, missionaries, especially Protestants, were building schools and teaching children to read the Bible, especially in English. Education also served to propagate various aspects of European culture. One unforeseen impact was that the missionary schools became the incubating grounds for young nationalists determined to destroy colonialism.

Portuguese Empire   The areas of Africa that before 1914 had come under the colonial domination of Portugal. These included Cape Verde Islands off the coast of West Africa, Guinea-Bissau in West Africa, São Tomé and Príncipe in the Bight of Benin, and the large territories of Angola and Mozambique in Southern Africa. *See also* BELGIAN EMPIRE, p. 37; BRITISH EMPIRE, p. 40; FRENCH EMPIRE, p. 45; GERMAN EMPIRE, p. 46; ITALIAN EMPIRE, p. 48; SPANISH EMPIRE, p. 52; TABLE B-5, p. 204.

Significance   By the sixteenth century, Portugal had made contacts and established enclaves along the west coast as far as Angola and in eastern Africa along the Mozambique littoral. Lisbon was interested mainly in slaving, other trade, and missionary work. Little concern was shown for developing the colonies, even after the slave trade was abolished in the nineteenth century. After the scramble for Africa began, Portugal attempted to connect its two giant possessions, Angola and Mozambique, but was thwarted by the more powerful British.

Scramble for Africa   The competition among European powers to gain control over African territories and/or to keep their rivals from gaining such control. The scramble extended from about 1880 to 1914. Before the scramble began, Africa had already faced the intrusion of various European governments, many of which occupied coastal enclaves from Senegal to Tanzania. In the interior explorers and missionaries had previously made contact with many African cultures. In contrast to the earlier period, the scramble was rapid and explosive. European powers acted from mistrust of each other. Each feared that a rival would acquire so large a part of the continent or so much of its wealth that the balance of power would be upset. Traders also began to pressure their governments to acquire African territory so as to have governmental protection for their markets. After King Leopold II of Belgium assumed private control of an area over three times the size of Texas (what is now Zaire), the rivalry intensified and led to the Berlin Conference of 1884–85 (p. 38). At the conference, principles of competition were agreed upon, and the scramble thereafter mainly involved questions of effective territorial occupation. Except for Ethiopia and Liberia, all of Africa came under European domination by 1914. *See also* BELGIAN EMPIRE, p. 37; BERLIN CONFERENCE, p. 38; BRITISH EMPIRE, p. 40; COLONIALISM/IMPERIALISM, p. 41; CONGO FREE STATE, p. 31; EUROPEAN EXPLORATION OF AFRICA, p. 43; FRENCH EMPIRE, p. 45; GERMAN EMPIRE, p. 46; ITALIAN EMPIRE, p. 48; MISSIONS: CHRISTIAN, p. 48; PORTUGUESE EMPIRE, p. 49; SPANISH EMPIRE, p. 52.

Significance In part, the scramble for Africa may have postponed World War I until 1914. In Africa, it brought under foreign rule many disparate peoples and stimulated them to begin the process of building independent nation-states. The boundaries established by the imperial powers are essentially those of today's independent states, and the peoples competing there are those thrown together as a result of the scramble. Many ethnic groups lost portions of their populations to competing colonies as boundary lines were drawn through their midst; others have been forced to embrace traditional enemies in their nation-building efforts.

Separate Development An Afrikaner term for a policy of separating all ethnic groups and allowing them to develop independently of others. *Apartheid* is but one example of separate development as conceived by the National Party of South Africa. As early as 1913, three years after the formation of the Union of South Africa, the Natives Land Act was passed to enforce territorial separation between Whites and other groups. Since then, all non-Whites have been "separated" from political roles in their own country. Such separation is never the result of socially agreed-upon policies, but rather conditions imposed by Whites on non-Whites. Whites thus determine what is development not only for Whites but also for non-Whites, who are not even consulted in the matter. *See also* AFRIKANER, p. 35; APARTHEID, p. 35; BROEDERBOND, p. 41; HOMELANDS IN SOUTH AFRICA, p. 149.

Significance Afrikaners have been the main defenders of the idea of separate development. In fact, the Afrikaner founders of the National Party at one time advocated separate development for both White groups, Afrikaners and English-speakers, under the domination of Afrikaners. The present Afrikaner leaders, however, seek to rule South Africa with the support of English-speaking Whites. The so-called homelands policy is but one further example of efforts by a ruling elite to dispose of an ethnic problem by driving the target group into a different (imposed) polity.

Settlers: Asian People of Asian (mainly Indian) origin imported by the British in the nineteenth and early twentieth centuries as contract laborers to work in East and Southern Africa. In East Africa, the largest Asian population today is found in Kenya, although it constitutes only a small fraction of the total population. Most Asians in Uganda were expelled by Idi Amin in 1972. Those who remain in Kenya, Uganda, and Tanzania have for the most part opted for local citizenship and have thus cast their lot with the African states.

In South Africa, Asians were imported into Natal between 1860 and 1911 to work on the sugar estates. Today, they number about 700,000 and thus make up about 2.5 percent of the total population. In South Africa, Asians have a high degree of cultural homogeneity, even though their ancestors came from a variety of linguistic, religious, and caste distinctions in India. Although most speak an Indian language, the vast majority also speak English. Eighty-five percent of the Indians live in Natal (with most of the rest in the southern Transvaal), where they are mainly small traders and clerks. Under the *apartheid* system they are defined by law, segregated into their own communities, and denied political and social rights. See also APARTHEID, p. 35; SETTLERS: WHITE, p. 51.

Significance The Asians basically constitute unassimilated and perhaps unassimilable groups. They have consciously maintained their own communities, married among themselves, and generally shunned close contacts with the indigenous populations. They have thus often been as much a target of Black antagonism as White settlers.

Settlers: Levantines People from Lebanon and Syria who settled in parts of West Africa in the late nineteenth century. Living in the extremely poor Levant, they were attracted to West Africa by the growing commerce between that area and Europe. Rather quickly, due to their business skills and willingness to live in West Africa, they became the middlemen in trade between Africans and Europeans. Today, though tiny in numbers, they own a great number of small retail businesses. See also SETTLERS: ASIANS, p. 50; SETTLERS: WHITE, p. 51.

Significance For many West Africans, the Levantines represent another case of foreigners exploiting them. However, there has been very little overt violence directed at these settlers, many of whom go out of their way to cooperate with the local governments.

Settlers: White (Europeans) An imprecise term referring usually to people of European ancestry who have migrated to, or been born in, Africa. (The term "White" is invalid when used as a synonym for Caucasoid, since North Africans and most of the settler Asians are also Caucasoid, but are not referred to as White in Africa.) Whites have settled mainly in East and Southern Africa, and more specifically in Kenya, the Republic of South Africa, Zimbabwe, and Namibia. They constitute a minority wherever they have settled: 0.2 percent in Kenya, 4 percent in Zimbabwe, 16.5 percent in the Republic of South Africa, and 20 percent in Namibia. See also RACE, p. 12; RACISM, p. 13.

Significance People of European descent have settled only a few places in sub-Saharan Africa. However, where Whites settled and expropriated land, they dominated the politics of the area by racist policies. It was the presence of White settlers that delayed the independence of Kenya and more recently, Zimbabwe. (Even today, Europeans continue to deny independence to Namibia.) White settlers completely dominate the politics and government of the Republic of South Africa. Consequently, they face the wrath of increasing guerrilla activity by the disenfranchised majority.

Spanish Empire The areas of Africa that had by 1914 come under the colonial domination of Spain. These areas included Equatorial Guinea, Western Sahara, and the extreme northern and southern parts of Morocco. See also BELGIAN EMPIRE, p. 37; BRITISH EMPIRE, p. 40; FRENCH EMPIRE, p. 45; GERMAN EMPIRE, p. 46; ITALIAN EMPIRE, p. 48; PORTUGUESE EMPIRE, p. 49; TABLE B-5, p. 204.

Significance Spain's African empire was the smallest of the imperialist possessions and embraced the fewest people.

Warrant Chiefs Persons appointed by colonial authorities as "chiefs" in acephalous societies through whom the dominant power expected to rule. Acephalous societies created a problem for Great Britain when the latter became committed to indirect rule: There were no traditional rulers to serve as intermediaries between the ruling officials and the people. As a result, the British appointed so-called warrant chiefs for such people. The warrant chiefs held their authority by a warrant, that is, a commission or document granting them certain powers. See also ABA WOMEN'S RIOTS, p. 53; ACEPHALOUS SOCIETY, p. 19.

Significance Warrant chiefs probably did more harm than good. When they attempted to settle a local dispute or collect taxes, they aroused the resentment of the local population. Their power was regarded by the people as illegitimate since it had little or no relationship to the society's traditional methods for ruling or making decisions.

4. African Resistance to Colonialism

Aba Women's Riots   A riot by market women in the Aba district of Eastern Nigeria in 1929 in protest of British rule. The British had decided, in this chiefless society, to create "chiefs" through whom they could rule. These warrant chiefs, as they were known, were extremely unpopular because they were artificial creations. In 1926, the British imposed a personal tax, called a "poll tax," of 2.5 percent of annual earnings on all males. In 1929, a warrant chief near Aba, contrary to the tax law, began to count not only men but also women, children, and animals for tax purposes. As a result, organized groups of women sacked stores, burnt down native courts, and attacked warrant chiefs and Europeans. By December, the ferocity of the riots led the police to fire on a group of women, killing as many as 50 and injuring an equal number, and thus finally quelling the rebellion. The riots were spontaneous and carried out solely by women. The women were all illiterate and committed to a return to traditions that for them included the expulsion of the British from the region. The riots of these market women are partly explained by the fact that they were all members of an age grade that united them in terms of values, common experiences, and long associations. *See also* AGE GROUPS, p. 20; WARRANT CHIEFS, p. 52.

Significance   The Aba women's riots illustrate resistance by Africans to colonial rule—in this case about 30 years after the British had penetrated the area. The insult of being ruled by foreigners was heightened by the British attempt to impose their rule through the installation of African intermediate rulers (who had no traditional authority) as well as by the imposition of an alien tax.

African Independent Churches Church ministers and congregations in Africa that have seceded from the parent body or formed their own churches in opposition to racism, colonialism, and foreign denunciation of African customs. In 1884, Nehemiah Tile, a South African Wesleyan Methodist minister of Tembu origins, broke away from the parent body to form the Tembu National Church, which he opened to persons of all races. In the 1890s, other ministers broke from the Wesleyan Methodist Church and founded the Ethiopian Church based on the motto "Africa for the Africans." While a segment of the Ethiopian Church remains, most of its congregations affiliated with the pioneer Black church in the United States, the African Methodist Episcopalian Church (AME). It is now one of the largest non-White churches in South Africa. In 1891, the United Native African Church in Nigeria seceded from the Anglican Church. Other groups followed suit not only in Nigeria but throughout West Africa; their common aim was the independent governance of their churches. The independent churches, though frequently fundamentalist in tone, tended to be tolerent of polygyny, encouraged colorful vestments, and accompanied the vigorous singing of hymns with drums and calabashes. Some of these churches have taken on Zionist overtones, tending to stress the Old Testament over the New. Others, such as the Watch Tower Movement, have put their own emphasis on the received doctrine. Some Africans, however, have simply formed their own Christian congregations, such as the Order of the Seraphim and Cherubim in Nigeria. *See also* WATCH TOWER MOVEMENT, p. 66.

Significance Independent African churches were born of many causes. Christianity itself came to Africa in many forms, often accompanied by fierce doctrinal conflicts. Africans simply continued this process. Despite the often widespread appeal of Christianity, Africans soon had to abandon certain elements that accompanied its introduction: racism, association with imperialism, and missionary intolerance of revered African customs. These defects were overcome by the assumption of African control of African churches. It is important to note that this form of resistance to foreign domination began to express itself even before political domination had been completed.

Ashanti (Asante) Resistance Resistance to British colonial rule by the Ashanti of the Gold Coast (now Ghana). In 1888, Kwaku Dua III, also known as Prempeh I, became the Asantehene, King of the Ashanti. He set about rebuilding the kingdom, which had been weakened by British incursions on the coast. Within three years he had restored a measure of unity among the Ashanti and was confident of restoring the

Ashanti Empire. Thus, when the British offered in 1891 to make his kingdom a British protectorate, Prempeh rejected the proposal on the grounds that his kingdom "must remain independent as of old" and must at the same time remain "friendly with all white men" (Boahen, 1966, p. 128). As Prempeh continued to rebuild his empire, the British attempted to gain control of the area north of Ashantiland. Finally in 1896, the British invaded Kumasi, the capital, arrested the king and five of his regents, and established a protectorate. The British broke up the Ashanti confederacy by making separate treaties with each of its members while leaving Kumasi without a ruler. In 1900, the British Governor insulted all Ashanti by demanding to sit on the golden stool, a sacred symbol of the Ashanti kingdom and spirit. Not even the true Asantehene could actually sit on the stool without defiling it. A rebellion broke out that took a year to suppress. In 1901, the British formally annexed Ashanti as a colony. It was not until 1924 that Prempeh was permitted to return from exile, as a private citizen. *See also* FULANI RESISTANCE, p. 57; SANUSIYYA RESISTANCE, p. 63.

Significance The Ashanti Empire had risen in the late seventeenth century and expanded considerably in the eighteenth century. In the following century, it faced conflict with the coastal state of Fante, an ally of the British. In 1873–74, the British and Fante armies invaded Ashantiland and defeated the country. The British imposed a peace treaty by which the Ashanti renounced all claims to the coastal states and agreed to allow trade between the coast and Kumasi. As conflict continued (and British aspirations to control the northern part of the Gold Coast remained thwarted by the Ashanti), it was only a matter of time before Britain used its superior weaponry to subdue the Ashanti. Ashanti resistance is another example that dispels the European myth that Africans welcomed colonial domination.

Central African Federation The ill-fated amalgamation into a federation of the three British colonies of Northern Rhodesia (Zambia), Southern Rhodesia (Zimbabwe), and Nyasaland (Malawi) in 1953. Despite the new governmental arrangement, the Federation was to remain under British control and was expected, by British policy and intention, to produce a "partnership" of races. At that time there were about 300,000 Whites (mostly in Southern Rhodesia) and 9,000,000 Blacks. White settlers held control of the self-governing colony of Southern Rhodesia, and British administrators ruled the other two. Most Africans opposed the Federation from the beginning because they would not be granted an equal voice in running the government. Some Blacks also feared that Southern Rhodesian Whites would simply expand their control over all three colonies and thus create an *apartheid* state north of the Limpopo River. Movements toward self-rule under Blacks continued in Northern Rhodesia and Nyasaland and, in large part, killed the Federation. In 1964, both gained their independence.

Significance Southern Rhodesian Whites had no intention of establishing a multiracial "partnership." Following the collapse of the Federation, they remained adamant in maintaining their minority rule for another 17 years before guerrilla warfare, British pressure, a United Nations' boycott, and world public opinion finally forced them to yield to a government established by majority vote. In 1980, "Rhodesia" became independent as Zimbabwe under Black rulers who promised to develop a multiracial society. Thus, from the beginning, African resistance to a colonially dictated policy that ignored Black interests prevented any possibility of success for the federation of the three territories.

Chilembwe, John An early African martyr of resistance to European colonialism. Chilembwe was born in Nyasaland (Malawi) and was taken to America in 1897 by the missionary, Joseph Booth. He studied at a Baptist college in Virginia and returned home to set up his own mission. At first he seemed to be concerned only with his religious calling, but over time he came more and more to resent the insolence and brutality of White settlers. Only with World War I was Chilembwe provoked to act. Fighting between British and German forces had actually occurred in northern Nyasaland, and he became angered that a European war could endanger African lives. Chilembwe wrote a letter to a newspaper protesting the conscription of Africans and suggested that in their place, rich, White bankers, farmers, and shopkeepers should go to war and be shot. When his letter was suppressed, he decided that an armed rebellion, much like that of John Brown in the United States, must be undertaken to dramatize the helpless position of Blacks. In the ensuing revolt, a European estate manager was killed and his head displayed in Chilembwe's church. Chilembwe eluded the police for two weeks before he was shot (in 1915) trying to escape to Mozambique. His death made him a martyr to the cause of resisting foreign rule. *See also* KIMBANGUISM, p. 57–58; KITAWALA MOVEMENT, p. 58; WATCH TOWER MOVEMENT, p. 66; VARIETIES OF AFRICAN RESISTANCE, p. 63.

Significance John Chilembwe dramatizes the intensity of feelings and violence of actions that can result from mistreatment because of one's race. While many people learn to tolerate perpetual subservience, some people eventually lash out in desperation. Chilembwe was one of the latter. He also illustrates the fact that resistance was often highly individualistic as well as collective in style.

Fulani Resistance Resistance by Fulani emirates to British colonialism. After Britain had subdued southern Nigeria, and the British flag had been hoisted over Lokoja at the confluence of the Niger and Benue Rivers in 1900, Sir Frederick Lugard, the administrator, decided to invade the north. The north was under the authority of Muslim emirs (rulers) who controlled trade routes and engaged in slave raiding. Some, as in Kano, were securely ensconced behind huge walls. In May 1902, the Sultan of Sokoto learned of Lugard's intentions and sent the following blunt message:

> From us to you. I do not consent that any one from you shall ever dwell with us. I will never agree with you. I will have nothing ever to do with you. Between us and you there are no dealings except as between Mussulmans and Unbelievers, War, as God Almighty has enjoined on us. There is no power or strength save in God on high. This with salutations. (Crowder, 1962, p. 199.)

Lugard had one overwhelming advantage: He had maxim guns, and the emirs did not. By February 1903, he had captured Kano and installed his own emir to replace the one who had fled. The following month, Lugard marched on Sokoto, which he captured quickly because the sultan had escaped before the British arrived. The sultan, however, joined the king of Keffi, but the British routed the two rulers, pursued them across country, and killed both at the battle of Burmi. By 1906, Lugard was in firm control of the Fulani north. *See also* ASHANTI (ASANTE) RESISTANCE, p. 54; SANUSIYYA RESISTANCE, p. 63.

Significance Fulani resistance to British rule was the normal reaction of any state and its rulers to invasion and conquest. The Fulani reaction dispels the European myth that Africans welcomed colonial domination. Superior weapons, not superior social institutions, forced most Africans to yield to foreign rule.

Kimbanguism A variant of Christianity that arose in the Belgian Congo (Zaire) as a protest against foreign rule. The movement was named after Simon Kimbangu (1899–1951), a Baptist minister. He began to preach in 1921 and soon won a reputation as a healer. He did not, however, challenge either orthodox Christian doctrine or European rule. On the other hand, he spoke with such authority that he became a hero to the indigenous population, "a black David to be set against the white Goliath" (Hallett, 1974, p. 465). The Belgian authorities grew anxious after some of his followers left their jobs and refused to pay taxes. Eventually, the Belgians arrested him and sentenced him to prison, where he died in 1951. The arrest and imprisonment made Kimbangu a martyr, and from his prison cell he found himself deified by his followers. They regarded him as a "Savior of the Black Peoples" and likened him to Moses, Jesus, Muhammed, and Buddha. Kimbanguists were openly anti-European, but they nonetheless eschewed violence. Their resentment, however, stimulated the growth of more vigorous movements, such as the Kitawala. *See also* AFRICAN INDEPENDENT CHURCHES, p. 54; JOHN CHILEMBWE, p. 56; KITAWALA MOVEMENT, p. 58; WATCH TOWER MOVEMENT, p. 66.

Significance Kimbanguism seems to have grown as much out of the psychological need of people for a Black role model as from religious conviction. Belgian rule in the Congo (Zaire) did not permit indigenes any political participation until the 1950s, much later than either British or French colonial powers, who permitted limited political activity as early as the 1920s. Kimbanguism, while offering religious hope for the future, at the same time stimulated anti-European sentiment in the area of the lower Congo (Zaire) River.

Kitawala Movement A religious movement in the Belgian Congo (now Zaire) that strongly resisted White dominance. The Kitawala Movement was an offshoot of the Watch Tower Society (*kitawala* means "tower") that blended with Kimbanguist prophecy. It also developed some unique religious ideas. God, it was claimed, had three sons, an Asiatic Jew, a European, and a Negro. The first two mistreated and mocked the third, making him feel inferior. In a forthcoming apocalypse (God-induced catastrophe), Negroes would be the only survivors and, with newly acquired white skins, would establish a theocratic government. *See also* KIMBANGUISM, p. 57; WATCH TOWER MOVEMENT, p. 66.

Significance The Kitawala Movement undoubtedly had purely religious impulses, but it is difficult to ignore the political-protest aspects of the doctrine. European rule in the Congo (Zaire) involved, as elsewhere, the destruction of much of traditional society. With overt political activity prohibited, it was an adaptive maneuver to convert political protest to religious expression. The Kitawala Movement provided a more satisfactory explanation of human existence for many subjected people than they could get from colonial rulers.

Maji Maji Rebellion   A rebellion against German colonial policies in Tanganyika (now Tanzania) in 1905–07. The Germans had faced chronic violent resistance from the mid-1890s, related to hut taxes, forced labor, German settlers, and a particularly harsh system of direct rule. Local rulers, institutions, and traditions were ignored or swept away. Experimental farming schemes that threatened traditional livelihood were imposed on the population. German administrators and their appointed subordinates (often local Arabs) were deeply resented. Seething unrest came to permeate the area. Religious leaders in the south began to distribute a potion of millet and maize mixed in water, called maji, that was alleged to make warriors immune to the effects of bullets. This act created hope among the oppressed, united a number of diverse groups, and instilled a fanatical will to resistance among the people. The resultant Maji Maji Rebellion soon spread far beyond its point of origin. The Germans needed two years to crush the rebellion, and they finally resorted to scorched-earth tactics in which they destroyed houses and crops. It is believed that more than 70,000 Africans died in the rebellion, many of whom succumbed to disease and starvation. *See also* DIRECT RULE, p. 43.

Significance   The Maji Maji Rebellion demonstrated that African masses were as likely as organized states to resist foreign domination. In this case, harsh administrators forced people to undertake activities that could be regarded as life-threatening. The custom-shattering behavior of an alien culture (such as Germany) has frequently led Africans to violent resistance. The Maji Maji Rebellion is but one example of African opposition to foreign rule.

Mau Mau   The name given by White settlers in Kenya to a guerrilla organization of poor Kikuyu in the early 1950s that was secretive, anticolonial, anti-Christian, and violent. To win support from other Kikuyu, the Mau Mau leaders forced them to take a loyalty oath based on a distorted traditional Kikuyu ritual. Mau Mau's major objectives were to regain Kikuyu land occupied by White settlers and obtain freedom from foreign domination. The movement was directed primarily at fellow Kikuyu, who were frightened into joining the crusade. In fact, less than a hundred Whites were killed; most of the victims (numbering in the thousands) were Kikuyu. With the help of traditional Kikuyu (who explained the true use of the oath) and of Kikuyu Christians (who were not afraid of the oath), the British army finally suppressed the movement. *See also* SETTLERS: WHITE, p. 51.

Significance   Many authorities believe that the Mau Mau movement was a true nationalistic movement in that its aim was to drive out White settlers and turn government over to Africans. However, it was so closely tied to one ethnic group, the Kikuyu, that some scholars question this assertion and point out that the oath Mau Mau required was a Kikuyu oath (unrelated to the traditions of other ethnic groups) and the land displaced by White settlers was restricted largely to Kikuyu areas. Nevertheless, Mau Mau did involve Africans in organized resistance to White settler colonialism, an important feature in East and southern Africa. It forced the White settlers and the British administration to admit the legitimacy of African aspirations. Indigenes were first brought into the government in 1954, and by 1963 Kenya was independent.

Muhammad Ali An Albanian reformer who was appointed by the Ottoman Sultan to govern Egypt after Napoleon had been forced to withdraw in 1801. Muhammad Ali set out to found his own dynasty of foreign princes by ousting the Mamluks, an ex-slave caste of Turks and Asians that had ruled Egypt for five centuries. Muhammad Ali recognized that Western military and technological superiority had made Egypt vulnerable, so he set out to develop Egypt economically and militarily, hoping to stave off further foreign incursions. Borrowing from the West, he built a strong army, set up protective tariffs, and created a stable currency and marketing system. He conquered Sudan and extended Egypt's influence as far south as the lakes region. By the 1820s, he was more powerful than his overlord, the Ottoman Sultan. In 1831, he took over Palestine and Syria from direct Ottoman control. Only Britain and other European states, determined to sustain the faltering Ottomans, kept him from taking over the entire Empire in 1839. Even though most of Muhammad Ali's industrialization efforts and educational reforms did not survive, and Egypt eventually fell to the British (later in the century), he must be credited with initiating a modernization program in the Egyptian state.

Significance Muhammad Ali was not an Egyptian but he, like Egyptians, was a citizen of the Ottoman Empire. He opposed European incursions, however, not so much as an Ottoman but rather as a non-European who did not want to be under foreign rule. Nonetheless, he recognized the importance of Western science and technology and sensed that only economic development could stave off European dominance. Had his successors been as wise, his policies might have succeeded; even so, he left a legacy of modernization that influenced the course of Egyptian history. His resistance to European dominance provides another example of African opposition to foreign rule.

Ndebele-Shona Rebellion of 1896–1897 A rebellion against foreign rule by two African societies in what is now Zimbabwe. The British South Africa Company under Cecil Rhodes established control over Mashonaland (land of the Shona) in 1890 and provided 3,000 acres of land to each of 200 White "pioneers." In nearby Matabeleland, the Ndebele feared the possibility that Rhodes' action would interfere with their raids of Shona cattle and eventually encroach upon their land. In 1893, the Ndebele raiders attacked the southern Shona area, seizing cattle and killing a number of Shona villagers. Pressed by the White settlers, Rhodes' forces attacked and destroyed the Ndebele kingdom. In 1896, however, the two former enemies rebelled against the harsh realities of White rule: confiscation of cattle, forced labor, loss of land, excessive taxation, brutal mistreatment (by both settlers and African police), and constant humiliation. As resentment mounted, former Ndebele warriors secretly collected a cache of guns. The bloody eruption began in March 1896 and was not ended until September 1897, when the last Shona were flushed out of hillside caves by the official forces. On both sides, the losses were staggering. In fact, victory had cost the settlers 10 percent of their population. *See also* ABA WOMEN'S RIOTS, p. 53; ASHANTI (ASANTE) RESISTANCE, p. 54; FULANI RESISTANCE, p. 57; SANUSIYYA RESISTANCE, p. 63; VARIETIES OF AFRICAN RESISTANCE, p. 63.

Significance The Ndebele-Shona Rebellion provides an example in which two groups hostile to each other simultaneously attacked their common foe to try to escape foreign domination. As elsewhere on the continent, their effort proved futile because the Europeans had more advanced weapons as well as a long-range strategy.

Proto-Nationalism Resistance to foreign domination that seeks autonomy rather than sovereignty. Proto-nationalism is generally ascribed to African resistance from the initial imposition of European rule in the last decades of the nineteenth century to World War II. Some resistance movements, such as the Ashanti Wars or the wars of Samori Touré, were nationalistic in that the leaders sought to achieve or maintain sovereign states. Following the firm establishment of European rule, resistance was often proto-nationalistic because the protestors sought not independence from foreign rule but involvement in the governing process. Examples of this process include the African National Congress in South Africa in 1912, the National Congress of British West Africa formed in 1920, and the Aborigines' Rights Protection Society formed in the Gold Coast (now Ghana) in 1897 (p. 65). *See* *also* AFRICAN NATIONAL CONGRESS, p. 121; NATIONALISM, p. 76; VARIETIES OF AFRICAN RESISTANCE, p. 63.

Significance Proto-nationalism is a term that recognizes that early forms of resistance to colonialism stemmed from many motivations. Some resistance movements were simply spontaneous revolts against alien rule or institutions. Some were reactionary efforts to revive traditional ways and institutions. And some movements were motivated by attempts of Africans to acquire a role in their own governance, but not become the sole, independent government. This is what distinguishes proto-nationalism from nationalism.

Samori Touré A military genius and founder of a state stretching across the area now known as upper Guinea and northern Ivory Coast and into northern Ghana. Samori was a soldier-trader, the son of a local Malinka (Mande) woman (from what is now upper Guinea) and a *juula* (Muslim trader) father. Beginning about 1870, he set out to build a Mande empire. He gathered together several hundred blacksmiths to build breach-loaded guns and cartridges, each laboriously handmade. One small African state or area after another fell to his forces. Unfortunately, his state-building coincided after 1879 with French designs on the same area. Since they were occupied with other struggles, the French decided at first not to engage Samori in direct combat but to wear him down by attacks on his periphery. Samori turned to guerrilla warfare. While one part of his army would resist the French at some point, another part would be expanding his area of control. In addition, Samori engaged in diplomacy; he attempted to establish alliances with other African states and even with the British. Finally, in 1891, the French decided to concentrate on Samori's defeat and soon discovered the excellence of his military skills. It took seven more years of French superior weaponry to capture Samori in 1898 and send him into exile. *See also* ASHANTI (ASANTE) RESISTANCE, p. 54; FULANI RESISTANCE, p. 57; SANUSIYYA RESISTANCE, p. 63; VARIETIES OF AFRICAN RESISTANCE, p. 63.

Significance Samori Touré illustrates that state formation was still occurring in Africa even as Europeans attempted to justify their incursions by suggesting that Africans were incapable of governing themselves. Had the French not intervened, there might well be a large, indigenously created state in West Africa embracing all or parts of some of the present states. West Africans had, in fact, been creating great states for over 1,000 years and did not require European help. The great irony here was that as Africans began to recover and regroup after the end of the Atlantic slave trade, Europeans again intervened to suppress the freedom, not merely of unfortunate captives, but of all Africans.

Sanusiyya Resistance Resistance to Italian colonialism by the Sanusiyya Brotherhood in Libya. Italy invaded Libya in 1911 to establish for itself a colony in Africa, as other European powers had done. The Sanusiyya Brotherhood had been founded in Libya in 1835 to promote Muslim purity. By good administration the Sanusiyya established over 100 local branches or lodges in Libya and more in the Sahara Desert, devoted to piety, learning, and commerce. They soon formed a powerful, homogeneous organization of people with closely shared values. When Italy invaded, the Sanusiyya began a long battle of resistance against the Italians that lasted until 1932. Although the Italians had superior weapons, the Sanusiyya fought with stubborn, fanatical resistance. By the time of their defeat, it is estimated that the Sanusiyya population had been reduced in 20 years by one-half to two-thirds. *See also* ASHANTI (ASANTE) RESISTANCE, p. 54; FULANI RESISTANCE, p. 57; VARIETIES OF AFRICAN RESISTANCE, p. 63.

Significance Sanusiyya resistance is but another example of how many people react to alien rule. Most people finally yield to superior force when it is apparent that they will lose; the Sanusiyya represent those people who seem psychologically unable, even in the face of almost certain death, to yield to the force of others. They provide another rebuttal to the myth that Africans welcomed European rule.

Varieties of African Resistance The various methods and social forms used by Africans to respond to the early stages of European penetration. Contrary to many European claims, resistance to colonialism was intense, varied, and widespread. Although European dominance was welcomed in a few places and tolerated in others, violence was required in most places to secure and maintain foreign control. Numerous dramatic examples of responses to colonialism appear under other headings in this chapter. A brief overview of the methods and social institutions is given here. For example, the French decided in the 1880s to press eastward from their Senegal territory to the headwaters of the Niger River and thence to Lake Chad. They were forced to fight one ethnic group after another before finally reaching Timbuctu in 1894. They fought local groups in that area for another dozen years and contended with Samori Touré (p. 62). In 1896–97, they conquered the area now known as Upper Volta, and by 1900 they were marching toward Lake Chad.

To help the Royal Niger Company (which had a British charter to administer much of what is now southern Nigeria), the British sent troops to the Niger Delta area in 1887. Their purpose was to capture and deport (to the West Indies) King Ja Ja, whose control of the palm oil trade obstructed the commerce of the Royal Company. In Uganda in the 1890s, with the help of local African Christians, the British had to drive the *kabaka* (king) into exile before they could rule the area. Also in the late 1890s, they had to deploy Indian troops to disperse Africans who obstructed the building of the railroad from Mombasa, Kenya, to Lake Victoria. When a British expedition to Benin City (Nigeria) was ambushed in 1897, the British quickly retaliated by destroying the city and surrounding towns and villages.

In 1906, the British declared martial law when the Zulus under Bambata in South Africa refused, among other things, to pay a toll tax. The Zulus responded with violence, using a military technique invented around 1820 by their great ancestor Shaka. The technique involved close-order fighting using short-handled stabbing spears from behind body-length shields. They were no match, however, for modern weaponry, and the British killed Bambata and 500 of his men. In 1881, the Turko-Egyptian authorities in Sudan faced a revolt by a religious group led by Muhammad Ahmad al-Mahdi. With British support and leadership, a force was sent to quell the revolt of the Mahdists (as they were called), but it suffered a humiliating defeat. The British for a time maintained a "cold war" posture toward the Mahdists. Finally, in 1896, they decided to take vigorous action to rid themselves of the Madhi's successor. So well and stubbornly did the Mahdists fight that it took the British 30 months to bring the war to a successful end in September 1898.

King Leopold of Belgium set up the Congo area (now Zaire) as a private personal estate, where indigenes were expected to work for him: growing rubber, collecting ivory, building roads, and so forth. Africans refused to "volunteer" for such work, and, as a result, murder and torture were introduced. In spite of such brutality, African resistance continued, which led the foreign intruders to engage in more torture. The carnage became the subject of a major scandal so heated that, in 1908, Leopold was forced to turn the area over to his government as the Belgian Congo.

In 1898, in Sierra Leone, a local chief named Bai Bureh led a rebellion against a house tax levied by the British. In response to British force, Bai Bureh resorted to guerrilla tactics. The rebellion spread to other parts of the area before the British were able finally to quell it, capture Bai Bureh, and exile him.

Another form of African resistance materialized among such organizations as the Aborigines' Rights Protection Society, formed in the Gold Coast (now Ghana) in 1897 to protest British attempts at land seizure. It brought to prominence J. R. Casely-Hayford, the Society's attorney, who became the most articulate advocate of African consciousness by the turn of the century. He later, in 1920, became one of the founders of the National Congress of British West Africa, which organizers formed, not to claim independence, but to demand a voice for Africans in their own governance. Although rejected at first by the British, it is believed that the group's demands were helpful in persuading the British to permit local citizens to serve on official councils of government.

Yet another aspect of resistance to foreign domination appeared in the form of African labor unions in urban industrial areas. Clements Kadalie of Nyasaland (Malawi), a migrant worker in South Africa, founded the Industrial and Commercial Workers' Union (ICU) in 1918 and promptly called a series of strikes to protest unequal racist treatment. Internal dissension and implacable White opposition finally destroyed his union, but his ideas survived and appeared elsewhere. In Northern Rhodesia (Zambia) in 1935 and again in 1940, Africans engaged in violent strikes to protest the brutalities of White workers against Black and the wage disparities based on race. (In one copper mine the average White earned 27 times as much as the average Black.)

Resistance thus appeared in a variety of forms, including reliance on traditional chiefs and religious leaders, spontaneous outbursts, and individual reactions. Some reactors resorted to violence, while others attempted to channel protest into acceptable means. Some resistance was led by state organizations, others by village and local groups. All parts of the continent were involved. *See also* the other headings in this chapter and NATIONALISM, p. 76.

Significance The varieties of African resistance attest to the fact that Africans in general did not welcome foreign rule. While some rulers collaborated with European powers in order to gain allies against more powerful neighbors (as the Fante of Ghana did for security against the Ashanti), most Africans resented foreign rule. Superior European weapons (especially machineguns and rapid-loading rifles) could not be matched by Africans, and they yielded one by one to European control. After that, individuals and groups emerged to show their resistance, taking the forms described above and elsewhere in this chapter. These early resistance movements were not nationalistic in the sense of seeking nationhood for the colonially defined territory, but they presaged the nationalistic movements.

Watch Tower Movement A millenarian religious movement (better known in the United States, where it originated, as Jehovah's Witnesses) that formed its own unique resistance to foreign dominations. The Watch Tower Movement was introduced in Nyasaland (Malawi) from South Africa in 1908, and in various forms it became prominent in what is now eastern Zaire, Zambia, and Zimbabwe. Eliot Kamwana, the first prophet of the movement in Nyasaland, prophesied the end of British rule. He would point to the offices of local British administrators and prophesy openly to the people that they would soon cease to see the foreign officials. Instead, he stated, "we shall make our own ships, make our own powder, make or import our own guns" (Hallett, 1974, p. 529). Kamwana's boldness and impertinence soon led to his arrest and deportation. Even in his absence his movement spread and contributed to Kimbanguism and especially the Kitawala Movement in Zaire. *See also* KIMBANGUISM, p. 57; KITAWALA MOVEMENT, p. 58.

Significance The Watch Tower Society, since its origins in the United States in 1879, has emphasized church governance over secular governance. It was therefore a logical step for African adherents to resist foreign rule, although in resisting alien domination the movement did not differ from many other resistance groups.

5. Political Culture and Ideology

African Personality   The concept that Africans have a particular personality that distinguishes them from other people. Among Africans, it is an assertive concept that alleges that Africans have a homogenous culture that has produced a rationalist, communalistic, sensitive, intuitive personality type. It developed, at least partially, in response to European stereotypes of Africans as having a lazy, immature, childlike, and violent personality. Kwame Nkrumah of Ghana, who tried unsuccessfully to instill the concept in English-speaking Africa, attempted to eliminate its racist elements by stating that it merely referred to an African philosophy or spirit related to the common degrading experience of colonialism. He offered "African personality" as a substitute for the concept of Negritude that had appeared in French-speaking areas. *See also* NEGRITUDE, p. 77.

Significance   The concept of African personality that appeared in the 1960s has had no lasting impact in English-speaking Africa. As a racial stereotype, whether positive or negative, it has no relevance in empirical studies—Africans vary in their personality developments as widely as peoples of other continents. Even as a philosophical concept, it is clear that colonialism did not produce a homogeneous view or perception of the world in Africa. There seems to be no more of a distinct African personality than there is an Asian, European, or North American personality.

African Socialism   A belief that traditional societies in Africa had characteristics that today make them more compatible with a certain form of socialism than with capitalism. Among these characteristics were communal land ownership, the extended family, and elaborate concepts of kinship. Accompanying such concepts was the practice of sharing; it was inconceivable in most African societies that anyone should go hungry while others had food. In addition, African values generally emphasized cooperation rather than competition and were concerned with the group rather than the individual; these concepts are regarded today as being closer to socialism than to capitalism. It is an African socialism, however, not a Marxist or Soviet form. African socialists (e.g., Leopold Senghor of Senegal) tend to reject the Soviet system's call for class struggle, atheism, and a dictatorship of the proletariat. In Tanzania (under Julius Nyerere), they insist (contrary to Marx but in accord with Mao) that socialism can be built on a peasant base. *See also* MARXISM, p. 74; SOCIAL CLASSES, p. 81; SOCIALISM, p. 82.

Significance African socialism, widely proclaimed throughout Africa, is an egregiously imprecise term. The late J. B. Danquah of Ghana claimed to be a "socialist liberal." Dr. Michael Okpara, former premier of Nigeria's Eastern Region, in 1960 said, "Socialism means fellowship, freedom and opportunity for all." As recently as 1981, a legislator in Kenya said: "I will never be a [communist] comrade ... I am a capitalist. I believe in African socialism." In fact, President Kenneth Kaunda of Zambia even seems to identify socialism and humanism. There is little evidence that African socialism has produced a clearly defined and distinct form of government or economic system. To date, it appears to be largely an emotional term sufficiently vacuous to be generally accepted by many Africans.

Arusha Declaration A formal document issued in the town of Arusha in 1967 by President Julius Nyerere of Tanzania (formerly Tanganyika and Zanzibar) committing the country to socialism based on peasant farming, democracy under "one party," and self-reliance. A socialist state, the Arusha Declaration proclaims, "is one in which all people are workers and in which neither capitalism nor feudalism exists." It states also that Tanzania has erred in attempting to develop by the use of money and industrialization, neither of which it has in adequate supply. What it does have are peasant farmers and a few workers, and it must build socialism on its agricultural potential. "One-party" democracy is to be assured by permitting only peasants and workers to have political rights in the single "party" and by denying political rights to anyone who is "associated with the practices of Capitalism or Feudalism," owns shares in any company, holds a directorship in any private enterprise, has two or more salaries, or owns houses for rent. Self-reliance refers to the avoidance of most foreign aid and investments, a commitment to hard work, and the application of intelligence to productive activity. In summation, the Arusha Declaration avers that: "Industries will come and money will come but their foundation is the people and their hard work, especially in agriculture. This is the meaning of self-reliance."

Significance   The Arusha Declaration became the blueprint by which Tanzania has attempted to develop. Agricultural collectives and village cooperatives were established throughout rural areas, businesses were nationalized, and parastatals (government corporations) were created. Peasants were exhorted and coerced to produce more. Thus far, however, the experiment seems to have been largely a failure. In his ten-year review, President Julius Nyerere could only note successes in some changed attitudes, in the decrease in income differentials between the rich and poor, and in improvements in health, education, and transport. But in the areas of production, he excoriated the state industries for operating "well below capacity" and for "not producing sufficient surplus to finance new investment." He also noted that "agricultural results have been very disappointing." Nyerere attributed agricultural failure to the fact that local political leaders refused to learn "good husbandry" and join peasants in production; they preferred rather to "shout at peasants and exhort them to produce more." As a result, agricultural collectivization was dropped, and some private enterprise was given official encouragement. Nevertheless, Prime Minister Edward Sokoine asserted in 1977 that "Tanzania will not sacrifice socialist goals for productivity."

Communism   The ideology, or belief system, that advocates that all people in a society share equally the wealth of the society. The concept of communism has been a part of the history of Western civilization since at least the time of Plato in the fourth century B.C. One of the first attempts to practice communism occurred in the early Christian community at Antioch and is described in the Acts of the Apostles, Chapters 4 and 5. The notions of noncompetition, equalitarianism, and collective ownership appear in the philosophies of many people and were concerned less with amassing material goods than with finding some way of distributing them equally. In the last century and a half communism has come to be linked with (although it is not identical to) socialism. Under the influence of Karl Marx and his followers, communism today is associated with many beliefs that were not originally related to the term. Today, communists are those who usually belong to organizations calling themselves communist and who identify with Marxism-Leninism and the Soviet Union. Part of their philosophy includes: the violent overthrow of capitalist governments, subjugation of those who differ with the ruling elite, denial of certain civil rights, condemnation of individualism, near-absolute control of people's lives, centralized planning and government ownership of all means of production, the state as the employer of all people, strong nationalism, fanatical devotion to ideology, and a dictatorship by a small, self-appointed elite through a mobilization machine called a "communist party." *See also* AFRICAN SOCIALISM, p. 67; MARXISM, p. 74; SOCIAL CLASSES, p. 81; SOCIALISM, p. 82.

Significance No state in Africa today is controlled by a ruling elite that calls itself a communist party, although Ethiopia's rulers are reportedly attempting to form themselves into such a political machine. Known communist organizations exist in the Republic of South Africa (banned), Egypt (banned), Sudan, Madagascar, Senegal, Tunisia, and Algeria. (Various states, however, are ruled by people who call themselves Marxists but eschew the term *communist*.)

Constitutionalism Regularized restraints upon government. To be regularized means that the restraints are predictable because they are spelled out either by formal law or by tradition and practice. Such restraints today are usually specified in a document known as a constitution that sets forth the organs (legislative, executive, judicial, administrative), powers, and procedures of government, and more importantly describes the restraints on government (such as prohibiting ex post facto—retroactive—laws, listing of civil rights, balancing of powers, and requiring strict methods for amending the constitution). Since constitutionalism is a system whereby governments are restrained (and conversely individual liberty is enhanced), some governments without formal constitutions may nevertheless be constitutionalized (e.g., Great Britain), and some governments with formal constitutions may nevertheless be nonconstitutionalized (e.g., the Soviet Union, where there are no effective formal restraints on government). If governors, regardless of written rules, may do as they wish (coerce, restrain, and even kill citizens) and generally behave as if their only restraints were their own beliefs, then the system is not constitutionalized. In traditional Africa, many polities practiced constitutionalism, even in the absence of a formal document called a constitution. Governors and governments were often restrained in many ways. Many rulers were selected by councils whose members held positions according to tradition and whose choices of rulers were traditionally defined. Most rulers were required to consult elders, councillors, priests, or other prestigious persons on various matters. Many harsh or unfair rulers could be deposed by long-established procedures. In addition, rulers often had unavoidable obligations regarding sacrifices, feasts, and celebrations that constrained them. There were, therefore, many means to keep rulers from abusing their powers. Such means embodied regularized restraints on government and consequently reflected constitutionalism. For example, many of the Yoruba states in what is now western Nigeria had a form of checks and balances on the use of political power, as when a king had to accept the decisions of a council of chiefs whose members in turn represented the interests of their people. In Africa today, however, constitutionalism hardly exists. Since most of the states operate under the control of either a single "party" or a military clique, they cannot be regarded as constitutionalized. The exceptions today appear to be Egypt, Gambia, Mauritius, Nigeria, Senegal, Zimbabwe, Botswana, and possibly Morocco. *See also* AGE GROUP, p. 20; DEMOCRACY, p. 71.

Significance Constitutionalism, as regularized restraints on government, has been a part of Western political philosophy since at least the time of Plato and Aristotle. Likewise, African political behavior, if not formal political theory, often reflected the same concern: how to keep governments from abusing political power. Whereas Western constitutionalism was usually effected by formal documents spelling out restraints on governments, African constitutionalism (like the British form) was many generations in the making and was effected through custom and experience as well as the expectations of the politically active portion of the population. In Africa as in the West, however, many societies never achieved constitutional restraints and merely reflected the arbitrary use of power. Constitutionalism is always difficult to establish, primarily because many rulers prefer unfettered decision-making power and subjects are unable or unwilling to attempt to impose restraints. This difficulty is especially apparent in Africa today where (1) strong central governments are generally preferred, (2) there are intense pressures to develop economically as rapidly as possible, (3) collective and social responsibilities are regarded as more valuable than individual concerns, (4) much divisiveness among ethnic groups exists, (5) rulers control a monopoly of force in the society, and (6) there are few effective organized groups (such as political parties, labor unions, chambers of commerce, farmers' cooperatives, consumers' groups) to challenge the powers of government. Under these circumstances, in Africa today the term "constitutionalism" is rarely used in theoretical treatises on government, and there is little commitment to its implications except in a few countries.

Democracy A political system and form of government in which individuals are free to hold and propagate ideas and to compete with others for the prevalence of those ideas. The concept of democracy holds that all people who are permitted to participate in political affairs are to be regarded as equal in that participation. Thus, democracy may involve a consensus process, as in African acephalous societies, where all adult males of a clan or village participated in making decisions in which all participants eventually agreed; it may be the "town-meeting" type, in which interested people may participate in making decisions; or it may involve a procedure in which the view or preference of a majority of participants prevails. The latter system entails the open and competitive election systems found in numerous Western countries and in about 16 percent of the African countries. Most countries of the world, including those in Africa, are not democracies, and many do not regard democracy as an ideal. On the other hand, since the term has now become popular, regimes that do not satisfy the definition often call themselves democratic. This is especially true of rulers who claim (even without open, competitive elections) to rule in the interest of the masses, or workers, or peasants. Such regimes cannot be regarded as democratic because they lack the freely expressed preference of the politically active citizenry. Such regimes need not be harsh or cruel, and the masses may not feel deprived of their rights; nevertheless democracy is not a feeling but a process. At least one ruler, President Houphouet-Boigny of Ivory Coast, acknowledged in the 1960s that his government was not democratic and asserted that the population was not yet qualified for democracy. *See also* COMPETITIVE PARTY SYSTEM, p. 85; LEGITIMACY, p. 74; MILITARY RULE, p. 133; "ONE-PARTY" SYSTEM, p. 97.

Significance Democracy of the consensus and "town-meeting" types is possible only in small communities and does not exist in large states. No African state today attempts either form. Majoritarian democracy is not widespread on the continent; most regimes are either "one-party" or military dictatorships, both of which are nondemocratic by definition. On the other hand, majoritarian democracy is being attempted today in Botswana, Egypt, Gambia, Mauritius, Morocco, Nigeria, Senegal, and Zimbabwe (formerly Southern Rhodesia). Furthermore, five "one-party" states (Algeria, Ivory Coast, Kenya, Tanzania, and Zambia) have introduced a democratic element: voters choose between two candidates in Kenya, Tanzania, and Zambia; among three in Algeria; and among three or more in Ivory Coast, all candidates having first been approved by the "party" officials. Democracy in public affairs is a difficult system to install and maintain anywhere, and especially in Africa. First, mass participation in public affairs was not widespread in many parts of traditional Africa. Second, the nondemocratic character of colonialism did little to encourage mass participation. Third, there is little popular demand for democracy in many of the countries (people use traditional methods of defending their interests, usually by group action through families, clans, villages, and ethnic groups). Fourth, democracy tends to encourage and emphasize differences rather than conformity among people, which counters the traditional African respect for consensus and social (rather than individual) good. Fifth, because many people in Africa hold strong views about politics, they often become intolerant of opposing views and may even attempt to suppress any opinion contrary to their own (in contrast to democracy). Sixth, democracy requires candidates and followers who are psychologically able and willing to lose elections, a condition that has been quite rare in the few truly competitive elections in Africa. Seventh, certain alleged prerequisites of democracy are absent in Africa: mass education, long experience with elections, the downgrading of ethnic identification and the upgrading of citizen identification, and the concept of nation in place of group or region. All eyes, therefore, will be focused on the few democracies to see if they are able to operate such a system even in the absence of the alleged prerequisites. At this time, even though it is a frequently stated ideal, democracy has not become widespread in Africa and may never be adopted in some countries.

Ideology A set of beliefs, values, attitudes, and preferences about how society ought to be organized and for what purposes. The function of ideology is to create organizational solidarity among like-minded people and thereby enhance enthusiastic commitment. All people have ideologies, although for many the principles are so ill-formed and conflicting that the ideology is not apparent. Many ideologies are deliberately couched in general terms (such as democracy, freedom, equality, constitutionalism, reformism, dignity, rights, competition, science, knowledge, progress, free thought, rule of law) that allow their holders considerable pragmatic flexibility and make it easy for people stressing different terms to accommodate one another. Other people, however, espouse a rigid set of beliefs and become fanatically devoted to them to the point of refusing any compromise with opponents. The latter group tends to be referred to as *ideologues,* represented in today's politics by communists, fascists, some socialists, some religious groups, and all terrorists. Ideologies are frequently used by governments to oppress those who have different beliefs. See also CONSTITUTIONALISM, p. 70; MARXISM, p. 74; TERRORISM, p. 83.

Significance Africa, considering the diversity and intensity of its challenges, has been remarkably free of ideologues. Those most closely fitting the term over the last 20 years include some socialist leaders (such as Sekou Touré of Guinea, Col. Muammar Qaddafy of Libya, and the late Kwame Nkrumah of Ghana), the avowed Marxists, and the defenders of *apartheid* in the Republic of South Africa. General ideologies guide most African elites, who seem to agree on the need for economic development but not on the means. The absence of clearly formulated ideologies is regarded by some scholars as a great weakness in the drive toward technological growth and development. The problem is how to build an ideology that will guide and inspire people without at the same time crushing those who hold other views. Ideologues, who claim to possess the one and only true belief, are willing to impose an ideology that prohibits any alternative belief. Nonideologues, even some dictators, seem more inclined to stress the value of nationalism and pay little or no attention to competing ideologies on economics, education, religion, etc. In the first generation of African independence there is little evidence that an imposed ideology has united people behind a certain belief more successfully than has a system of competing ideologies. Nor do systems run by ideologues show a more rapid development rate than those with competitive ideological systems, although differences may emerge over time.

Legitimacy The belief among the general population that the people in charge of government are entitled to rule. Legitimacy means that rulers are thought to have acquired power by proper procedures, such as an election, selection by an appropriate body, or inheritance (as in monarchies); and to maintain power by honest and fair rule in accordance with accepted principles. Rulers are regarded as illegitimate if they acquire their power by fraud or violence, or deny the masses a role in the selection process, or behave in what is regarded as an improper way. Legitimacy, therefore, is an attitude held by a high proportion of the people and is not the same as legality—a legitimate regime may enact a law that the people regard as illegitimate. *See also* COMMUNAL INSTABILITY, p. 124; COUP D'ETAT, p. 125; MASS INSTABILITY, p. 129; POLITICAL VIOLENCE, p. 134.

Significance Many African states lack legitimacy. These include military regimes and regimes that face organized resistance (see Table B-6, p. 208). Also included in this category are regimes in which a minority has gained a monopoly of force to coerce the majority, as in Burundi and the Republic of South Africa. Legitimacy, on the other hand, is most apparent where elections (even when noncompetitive) are held. Legitimacy is doubtful wherever the army is highly visible and frequently engaged in exercises to subdue "dissidents."

Marxism An ideology or belief system based on the theories of the German social philosopher, historian, and economist Karl Marx

(1818–83) and his collaborator Friedrich Engels (1820–95). Marxism vehemently criticized nineteenth-century capitalism and modified earlier concepts of communism/socialism. Marx claimed to have discovered the actual workings of history by which to explain the human condition at any time. Three concepts dominated his theory. First, he offered a materialist interpretation of history, which maintains that social relations are built primarily on economic and technological concerns. Therefore, economic production determines or substantially conditions the social structure and belief systems of a people. Second, social change comes about because of a struggle between social classes, and classes are determined by ownership (or nonownership) of the means of production. The class that owns the means of production dominates all other classes, primarily through control of the state. Third, the value of what is produced is determined solely by the amount of labor put into it. Any difference between the labor costs of any item and the price it sells for is "surplus value."

Marx utilized these three concepts to analyze nineteenth-century advanced industrial societies. The societies were all organized around the concept of private capitalism, which, he emphasized, was to date the most advanced way to create wealth. The capitalists (the bourgeoisie) owned all the means of production and consequently composed the dominant class. The landless workers (the proletariat) were the dominated class, and were paid only the labor cost of what they produced, which was a subsistence-level wage because of competition. Workers as a class were unable to buy what they produced, which generally led to overproduction (or as Marxists claimed, underconsumption). Successful capitalists began to devour the unsuccessful ones, exposing the contradictions in capitalism. In time this process will reduce the number of capitalists to a wealthy elite, and will increase the size of the proletariat, who will become poorer. At some unspecified moment, the workers will spontaneously rebel and overthrow the capitalists and will collectively acquire ownership of the means of production; that is, the society will become socialist. In a brief dictatorship, capitalists will be eliminated and therefore all classes will disappear. Since the state is nothing more than the means by which one class dominates another, after socialism is established, the state will wither away and all people will share equally whatever society produces. No state will exist to coerce any person. The guiding principle will be "From each according to his ability; to each according to his need." *See also* AFRICAN SOCIALISM, p. 67; COMMUNISM, p. 69; "ONE-PARTY" SYSTEM, p. 97; SOCIAL CLASSES, p. 81; SOCIALISM, p. 82; STATE, p. 31.

Significance In Africa, according to their leaders, the following states are Marxist: Angola, Benin, Congo, Ethiopia, Madagascar, Mozambique, and Somalia. (Zimbabwe, although headed by an avowed

Marxist, is not regarded as a Marxist state since it is organized as a competitive-party structure.) The Marxist states tend to seek close ties with the Soviet bloc and to reject ties with the United States, although Somalia is an exception on both counts. They are all governed by so-called one party systems, but this is also true of many non-Marxist states in Africa. Civil rights such as freedom of press, speech, and assembly are denied, but these are also denied in many non-Marxist states. The goals of Marxist states in Africa are couched in vague terms such as nationalism, national independence, anticolonialism, people's rule, anticapitalism, nationalization of the means of production, and economic betterment for all, but how a developed socialist society is to be established is unclear. What distinguishes an avowed Marxist regime from the other regimes in Africa seems to be a certain intense devotion to ideological slogans, an insistence on analyzing all social problems in terms of class conflict, a vanguard "party" not open to all citizens but restricted to true believers, and dictatorial rule. It should be noted that none of the conditions postulated by Marx as necessary for the advent of socialism is present in any of the so-called Marxist states, nor elsewhere in Africa with the exception of the Republic of South Africa. There is no advanced capitalism; industrialization is barely underway; workers (in the sense of landless wage-earners) constitute a tiny portion of the population; there is almost no mass awareness of being exploited by capitalists; and those who are getting richer are not so much capitalists as government officials, including some Marxist ones. To claim belief in Marxist principles in the absence of Marxist conditions is strange only if one ignores the fact that the Soviets, under the rubric of Leninism-Stalinism, discarded one principle of Marx, namely his belief in a temporary dictatorship to be followed by the withering-away of the state. Now, in the name of Marx, it is possible to espouse socialist and egalitarian ideals while building a permanent state of unlimited coercive power dominated by a self-appointed elite. Since the Soviet Union is the leading example of this type of Marxism, it can only be presumed that a Soviet-type society is the goal of avowed Marxist regimes in Africa, especially since Marxists have not claimed otherwise. However, considering the fluidity of politics in Africa, it may be decades before any clear-cut patterns of political rule emerge, including the nature of Marxist regimes. (See Albright, 1980, p. 222; Ottaway and Ottaway, 1981, p. 10.)

Nationalism   An emotional attachment to a defined group of people and a defined territory; the belief that a group of people together constitutes a nation and has, or ought to have, a territory of its own on which to build a state. Thus, when movements in Ghana or

Nigeria or Tanzania sought independence from British colonial rule, they were practicing a form of nationalism. Nationalism also stirred the people of Eastern Nigeria in 1967 when they sought independence (as Biafra) from Nigeria. Similarly, Eritreans in Ethiopia and Western Saharans in Morocco who seek to have their own state or Somalis in Ethiopia who seek to join other Somalis in Somalia are all practicing nationalism. Any effort by a group of people to form a state of its own is a form of nationalism. Within existing states, efforts to build greater loyalty or patriotic commitment to the present polity also are types of nationalist activity. Finally, efforts to merge present states into larger ones represent acts of nationalism, e.g., Pan-African nationalism. *See also* IDEOLOGY, p. 73.

Significance The period of most apparent nationalism in Africa was 1945–60, when Western-educated professional and skilled people formed political parties and demanded independence. During the colonial era, articulate spokesmen of the people stated that the colonial power should leave the area and turn the government and territory over to the indigenous people; nationalism was a claim by Africans in the colony to political power and control of their own destiny. People like Kwame Nkrumah of Ghana, Sekou Touré of Guinea, Nnamdi Azikiwe of Nigeria, Jomo Kenyatta of Kenya, and Julius Nyerere of Tanzania, leading spokesmen for such claims, became known as great nationalists. This form of nationalism, however, was largely negative in that it united people against the colonial ruler. Positive nationalism, the concept that people belong together as a nation because of reciprocal benefits, is far more difficult to build. Positive nationalism usually emerges slowly as various people come to share many things in common—such as language, religion, territory, markets, values, enemies, wars, history, and myths. It is the absence of ties that reveals the great problem of African states today. Positive nationalism rarely exists because most colonial-established boundaries embraced many different cultures as well as formerly antagonistic groups. Individuals are still more likely to give ultimate loyalty to their own ethnic group than to the central government that rules in the name of all people and all groups. This divided loyalty constitutes the most serious political difficulty for various African states.

Negritude Blackness (from the French); the concept that Black Africans by virtue of their race and enculturation see, feel, sense, and value differently from other peoples, and share among themselves an unconscious, physiological experience of blackness denied to other humans. Coined by the West Indian writer Aimé Césaire, it has come to be most fully identified with the poet and ex-President of Senegal, Léopold Senghor, who has argued that "Negritude is the whole complex of civilized values—cultural, economic, social and political—which characterize the black people." These values, he adds, are formed by intuition and above all "through primordial rhythms, synchronized with those of the Cosmos" ("What is Negritude?" *Negro Digest*, April 1962, p. 4). *See also* AFRICAN PERSONALITY, p. 67.

Significance Negritude is essentially a racist concept, attributing to Blacks basic insights that Whites and others do not have. It was developed during the colonial period as a statement of cultural nationalism. The concept of Negritude served to unite some Africans behind the anticolonial movements, but it never spread outside French-speaking Africa. Today it is receding in importance even in Francophone Africa.

Pan-Africanism A belief that existing states ought to merge into a single state. Pan-Africanists believe that there are sufficient common cultural characteristics among the hundreds of African societies to justify creating one huge African state to replace the existing ones. There is no agreement, however, on how this grand concept might be achieved. Kwame Nkrumah, a leading Pan-Africanist and former President of Ghana, argued that Africa had only three major philosophical systems—traditional, Islamic, and Euro-Christian—that could be accommodated by and integrated into a single state. Other leaders, such as Chief Obafemi Awolowo of Nigeria, argued that regions of Africa must first unite and only later take the next step of merging the regions. Still others regard Pan-Africanism as merely a long-range goal, taking perhaps centuries to accomplish. And some Pan-Africanists seem to envisage nothing more than a weak confederation of sovereign, independent states. *See also* CENTRAL AFRICAN FEDERATION, p. 55; EAST AFRICAN COMMUNITY, p. 146; NATIONALISM, p. 76; ORGANIZATION OF AFRICAN UNITY, p. 157.

Significance Pan-Africanism was a much-talked-about ideal of many African intellectuals and Western Blacks from 1900 until the mid-1960s (when most present-day African states became independent). Its exciting possibilities helped to arouse the enthusiasm of nationalists who envisioned independence for their country followed by the merger of all independent states into a single awesome world power. However, local, regional, ethnic, and national interests inside the new states and rivalries among the states quickly dashed any hopes for Pan-Africanism. The concept attracts little attention today and may be moribund. The problem can be illustrated by noting two recent conflicting "pan" ideals: the new "party" constitution of Tanzania (1977) that advocates "African unity" and the new Libyan constitution (1977) that pledges Libya's efforts "to achieving total Arab unity." Besides these different "pan" goals, other factors also work against Pan-Africanism. Africa has more independent states than any other continent, almost one-third of the world's total. Considering the difficulties of uniting even a few states, Africa's challenge in this direction seems impossibly formidable. Added to the problem of numbers is the fact that the present boundaries, drawn by colonial powers, do not embrace homogeneous peoples. Consequently, for most politicians, nationalism within present boundaries is regarded as more important than nationalism of some grander sort. Finally, it should be noted that the colonial process of mapmaking, while consolidating hundreds of cultures into the present 51 to 54, also produced a continent of small states: only five exceed the world average in population (p. 12). The result is a great number of similar states competing with each other to fulfill the same needs of their people. These are not fertile conditions for building Pan-Africanism.

Political Corruption   The practice by public officials or politicians of selling government privileges or rights for private gain; the giving or withholding of a government service or entitlement by a government official in exchange for dishonest personal gain. Political corruption involves such acts as the following: the politician who agrees to vote a certain way in exchange for some valuable gift; the minister who demands 10 percent of the total cost of a government contract from the recipient; the inspector who demands $100,000 from a road construction firm to certify the road as meeting contract specifications; the policemen who for a gift looks the other way; the clerk who refuses to issue a license until some gift has been received; the postal worker who "fails" to find a piece of mail until a gift suddenly appears.

Significance   Although the extent of political corruption in Africa is not known, everyone who does much business there, including both Africans and foreigners, believes it to be considerable and widespread. Corruption is often known as "dash," and even the lowest clerk in an office may expect a small dash to perform the work he is paid to do. At upper levels, corrupt government officials are often called "ten percenters," from the general norm that people doing business with the government should expect final costs of a contract to be 10 percent more than normal costs, with the extra winding up in the official's pockets. In fact, some officials will collect the bribe and distribute it in predetermined proportions to others who have a voice in the operation. If the businessman refuses to pay, he fails to "win" the contract. If he complains openly, he usually finds the practice is so widespread that nothing can be done about it. One explanation for so much corruption in Africa is that in earlier days it was traditional to give gifts to chiefs, priests, healers, etc., when one expected a service from them. Another explanation is that there is little sense of obligation to people outside one's own village, clan, or region, and therefore, one may get what one can from "strangers." Nonetheless, no government condones corruption, and some wage constant battles against the practice (Nigeria, for example, has banned both the giving and receiving of dash). There is, however, no evidence that corruption is declining. On the contrary, some people say privately that bribery is what gets things done; without it, official disinclination to work would soon bring all government to a halt. (See Eker, 1981, pp. 173–82; Ekpo, 1979.)

Political Culture The total environment of politics. Politics occurs in a technological setting, and its nature varies depending on whether the technology is one of hunting and gathering, subsistence agriculture, advanced agriculture and urbanization, or industrialization. Politics also occurs in a sociological setting of numerous structures or organizations such as families, clans, clubs, markets, religions, education, the military, guilds, and classes. Finally, politics also occurs in an ideological setting that rests on values, beliefs, and attitudes. Every individual exists in a technological, sociological, ideological setting that contributes, even in the least complex societies, to a complex political culture. Although similar societies behave basically alike, the political culture of each society has a certain uniqueness because individuals, groups, and interests contribute differently to the political culture. *See also* POLITICS, p. 81.

Significance In Africa, the political cultures of the different states are still forming. In fact, the twentieth century has witnessed massive alterations in all African cultures. First, colonialism carelessly mixed cultures that had never shared a political culture. Then independence permitted these cultures to compete with one another for the dominant role in shaping the emerging political culture. States are now trying to form their political culture around oil, agriculture, herding, trade, mining, mass education, new work habits, representative systems, central guidance, respect for individuals, respect for society, respect for ideology, or combinations of these features. There is no evidence that an African political culture is emerging, but many different political cultures in states may emerge in Africa in the next generation or two.

Politics The process by which authoritative decisions are made for a society; the process for authoritatively resolving conflict or making decisions for a society. The references to process emphasize that politics is a system for dealing with change and exists even in societies without formal political structures such as a state or a government of fixed roles by which to make decisions. Such acephalous societies, nevertheless, utilize politics to create variation or change. The term *authoritative* emphasizes the fact that the results of political decision making are binding upon all people in the political system. Whether a decision is rendered by an elder, priest, or warrior in an acephalous society or by a president, legislature, or court in a state society, it is the obligation of all members of the society to obey. How certain people acquire the right to render binding decisions (whether by tradition, inheritance, appointment, election, or violence) is also part of politics. Politics in any society is thus the process by which individuals (to the extent permitted by tradition, law, or force) defend their public interests against others. *See also* ACEPHALOUS SOCIETY, p. 19; STATE, p. 31.

Significance Almost all politics in Africa today is carried on within the framework of a state, even though some acephalous societies still exist. Politics is the primary social activity in African states because it is politics that determines the very nature of Africans' existence: who is to be included in the state, the powers of the state, who gets to wield power, how development shall occur, and how to deal with other African states and the outside world. The primacy of politics in Africa can hardly be doubted, since it is by the political process that the resolutions of conflicts and other decisions will determine the ultimate well-being of every African.

Social Classes The division of society into groups, each of which has a more or less inherited place in relation to its access to necessary and/or luxury material goods, political power, social security, and leisure. Social classes are usually described by such terms as landless and landed; commoners and nobles; poor and rich; lower, middle, and upper; proletariat and bourgeoisie; peasants, workers, and intelligentsia; oppressed and oppressors. Classes imply inequality, with lower classes, by definition, being those who gain the least of life's goods. Egalitarian societies are those that seek to eliminate class distinctions (the alleged goal of communists) or attempt to provide equal access to education and political participation, in effect, letting people choose their class (the alleged goal of democracies). *See also* AFRICAN SOCIALISM, p. 67; COMMUNISM, p. 69; MARXISM, p. 74; SOCIALISM, p. 82.

Significance Many Africans argue that traditional Africa did not have social classes and that consequently political movements based on class theories have no relevance in the African context. These people point to such examples as the stateless, egalitarian societies, such as the Igbo of Nigeria, Nuer of Sudan, Maasai of Kenya-Tanzania, and the Tallensi of Ghana. Opponents of this view, however, point to the long history of states in traditional Africa with aristocratic, common, and often slave classes. In addition, peasants, artisans, merchants, priests, and scholars frequently composed classes. Examples of the nineteenth century would include the Ashanti, Baganda, Ethiopian, Hausa-Fulani, and Yoruba kingdoms. Nevertheless, even where classes did not previously exist, they were imposed by the colonizers, who became a privileged ruling class and introduced the classes associated with capitalism. Finally, the political elites to whom independence was granted soon emerged as a highly privileged class, thus providing many African states today with a ruling class that lives opulently while the masses live poorly. Between the two there exists a small middle class.

Socialism An ideology or belief system that maintains that the entire society rather than private individuals should own the means of production, and that all individuals should share fairly (though not necessarily equally) in the wealth of the society. Socialism maintains that by owning the means of production, the society will be able to promote the collective good rather than individual good, and to promote cooperation and reduce (but not necessarily eliminate) competition. However, the precise meaning of socialism is far from agreed upon. Some socialists are antistatist and envisage a society guided by guilds rather than state governments. Others see socialism arising and being maintained only by the power of the state. Some socialists insist on authoritarian means to gain and maintain their ideal, while others defend democracy as the only process. Some even combine socialism with a qualified competitive market and see the state as a general control mechanism. Out of these various concepts arose the philosophy of Karl Marx, from which socialism received its greatest impetus. He maintained that he had discovered scientific socialism, a natural historical process by which advanced capitalist societies would spontaneously (probably violently) transform themselves into socialist ones. His followers later split into two major camps: one whose devotees called themselves socialists but stressed that socialism could come gradually, even democratically; and the other whose devotees called themselves communists and stressed the need for violent revolution to overthrow capitalism. While socialists do not necessarily regard themselves as communists, communists regard themselves as socialists. Consequently, states that emphasize socialism but not communism tend to downplay the use of violence. *See also* AFRICAN SOCIALISM, p. 67; COMMUNISM, p. 69; MARXISM, p. 74; "ONE-PARTY" SYSTEM, p. 97; SOCIAL CLASSES, p. 81.

Significance The following states in Africa are socialist in the sense that the leaders say the system is socialist or the dominant party claims to be socialist: Algeria, Cape Verde, Guinea, Guinea-Bissau, Libya, Mauritius, São Tomé and Príncipe, Senegal, Sudan, Tanzania, Tunisia, Seychelles, and Zambia. While these states may permit some private capitalism, their goal is to develop the society economically by government ownership of most means of production. All claim to operate so-called one-party systems except for Senegal and Mauritius, both of which are experimenting with competitive parties. Furthermore, even though many prominent politicians call themselves socialists, there seems to be little loyalty to the principles of socialism as described by Marx and Engels. In fact, socialism in Africa seems most generally to mean a commitment to the dominant role of government in initiating and guiding economic decisions. With few capitalists and with a sense of urgency to get on with economic development, Africans have tended to rely on governments to promote economic growth. Consequently, this policy is often viewed as a socialist solution. Furthermore, in an effort to avoid identification with foreign socialism and in a search for indigenous solutions, many Africans call themselves African socialists.

Terrorism The imprisonment, torture, or killing of innocent people for political ends. "Innocent" refers to behavior normally regarded as appropriate regardless of the victim's political views, such as riding in an airplane, working in an administrative position, serving as a policeman, or teaching. The terrorist's objectives are extraneous to the identity of the victim and focused on producing a change in policy in a government to whom the victim is important. Terrorists may be individuals, but they are most likely to be organizations or even governments. When a government is engaged in terrorism, it may be aimed primarily at producing change in other governments (as when Arab or Israeli governments practice terrorism). Sometimes, however, a government practices terrorism against its own people, and then the definition has to be modified: the imprisonment, torture, or killing of citizens to eliminate some nonviolent behavior, belief, or group deemed undesirable by the rulers. The objective is to eliminate the undesirable elements. The accidental, unintentional, or coincidental harming of innocent people that occurs in warfare is not regarded as terrorism. *See also* REFUGEES, p. 162.

Significance General terrorism has not been widespread in Africa, but governmental terrorism has reached alarming proportions in some states. The most drastic slaughter of citizens, numbering 100,000 or more in each case, was carried out by former President Idi Amin of Uganda, former Emperor Jean Bokassa of the Central African Republic, former President Francisco Nguema of Equatorial Guinea, and by the pogrom of the Tutsi against the Hutu in Burundi. Governmental terrorism has also been practiced by those regimes with large numbers of political prisoners (such as Guinea); by South African Whites against the Black majority; and by the numerous governments that have created the world's greatest refugee populations: Ethiopia, Zaire, Burundi, Rwanda, Guinea, Central African Republic, Equatorial Guinea, and Uganda. For example, Col. Mengistu, the Ethiopian ruler, has openly advocated that his followers spread "red terror" in the camp of reactionaries (Ottaway and Ottaway, 1980, p. 29).

6. Governmental Institutions and Processes

Competitive Party System A political system in which various interests in the society organize to compete with other similarly organized groups for the control of government. Political parties tend to be either ideological or nonideological. The former attract as followers those who essentially share an ideology, for example, Socialist, Christian Democratic, Labor, Vegetarian, Communist, Farmer, or Gold Standard parties. Ideological parties tend to appeal to a limited number of people in any society and, consequently, they tend to be small and numerous. Their chance of ruling usually depends on their willingness to coalesce with other parties once the election is over.

In contrast to ideological parties are nonideological parties that attempt to bring together as many interests as possible in order to appeal to the greatest number of voters. Where there is direct election of the country's chief executive, there is a tendency for nonideological parties to reduce in number to two parties, which are often coalitions of many interests loosely formed under such vague and imprecise terms as conservative, liberal, democratic, republican, national, progressive, and united. Thus, while ideological parties tend to identify themselves by reference to a basic belief, nonideological parties try to appeal to a broad spectrum of the population. Competitive party systems developed in Western democratic countries and have not fared well outside that cultural milieu. *See also* DEMOCRACY, p. 71; "NO-PARTY" SYSTEM, p. 97; "ONE-PARTY" SYSTEM, p. 97; POLITICAL PARTY, p. 99; TABLE B-5, p. 204.

Significance In Africa, competitive party systems exist in Botswana (formerly Bechuanaland), Egypt, Gambia, Mauritius, Morocco, Nigeria, Senegal, South Africa (for Whites only), and Zimbabwe (formerly Southern Rhodesia). Botswana currently has four political parties; Morocco, four; Nigeria, five; Senegal, at least six; and Zimbabwe, twelve. The power that the King of Morocco wields raises doubts as to the competitive nature of the parties there, and Prime Minister Mugabe of Zimbabwe has indicated that he would like to change from a competitive party to a "one-party" system in his state. Competitive party systems were quite common in the period 1957-65, when most African states gained their independence. After 1965, however, most African states turned to "one-party" or "no-party" systems, as a result of either the ideological preference of the ruling group or the advent of military rule.

Constitution The fundamental laws or rules by which a state is organized for governance and which spell out the powers of government, as well as the rights and duties of citizens. In most states today, a constitution is a specific written document, but a constitution can also consist of traditions as practiced by government accompanied by a series of legislative acts, as in Great Britain. The prime purpose of a constitution is to stipulate the powers of government by spelling out what government may do on the one hand (such as raise taxes, borrow money, or run national banks) and what government may not do on the other (such as prohibit speech, or favor one particular religion). However, constitutions are only as good as the political system. A dictatorship (whether military, "one-party," or "no-party") is usually unrestrained by the provisions of a constitution, and even in democracies rulers may try to avoid constitutional provisions. But constitutions (whether written or based on tradition) do provide the general principles by which a state is governed, whether unitary or federal, presidential or parliamentary, unicameral or bicameral. Normally, in order to provide continuity of ruling forms and behavior, constitutions are difficult to amend, but again the more dictatorial the government the easier it is to change the basic law. *See also* CONSTITUTIONALISM, p. 70; FEDERAL GOVERNMENT, p. 91; UNITARY GOVERNMENT, p. 102.

Significance In eight African states the constitution is currently suspended by military action (Burundi, Equatorial Guinea, Ethiopia, Ghana, Guinea-Bissau, Liberia, Mauritania, and Niger); in Djibouti its formation has been delayed; and in five states the picture is simply unclear at this time (Central African Republic, Chad, Lesotho, Swaziland, and Uganda). While many states have suspended their constitutions from time to time, currently 37 of them have some kind of formal document, ranging from detailed, complex efforts to spell out every governmental structure, power, and restraint, as in Nigeria, to a casual document which places no restraints on government, as in Libya. However, 28 of the 37 are also run by so-called "single parties," or mobilization machines, which mean in practice that rulers can do whatever they and their organization prefer. Constitutional restraints, in varying degrees, exist only in Botswana (formerly Bechuanaland), Egypt, Gambia, Mauritius, Morocco, Nigeria, Senegal, South Africa, and Zimbabwe (formerly Southern Rhodesia).

Decree   An order issued by an executive having the force of law. The power to issue decrees may be spelled out in the constitution or by tradition for certain situations, as when the executive issues a decree interpreting a legislative act; it may flow naturally from constitutionally recognized states of emergency; or it may simply be assumed by an executive with the power at hand to enforce his decrees, as in military regimes. Decrees may be recognized as valid by courts and thus treated as equal to statutes (which are legislative acts).

Significance   Rule by decree is normal in all emergency situations and thus characteristic of military regimes in Africa. It is common also in so-called one-party systems for heads of government to rule by decree, although they may from time to time send the decrees to a legislative body for automatic assent. Severe restrictions on decree law exist only in the nine states attempting to operate competitive, democratic systems (Botswana, Egypt, Gambia, Mauritius, Morocco, Nigeria, Senegal, South Africa—in relation to Whites only, and Zimbabwe).

Development Administration   The aspect of public administration that has been established to promote economic development. All states, whether developed or developing, have a system of public administration that traditionally is used to maintain law and order, promote justice, regulate utilities and communications, build roads, collect taxes, defend the country, and carry on diplomatic relations. The mark of the modern state, in fact, is that it has created a rational, efficient, representative bureaucracy to do these things. Developing countries inherited bureaucracies from the colonizing power to perform the usual tasks, always with too few qualified people with too little experience with too weakly instilled bureaucratic values. By the late 1960s it began to be believed that rapid economic development required people who deviated from the standard type of public administrator: rational, objective, oriented to law and order, devoted to hierarchy, committed to precedent, and preoccupied with why things *cannot* be done. On the contrary, development administration requires a person with a positive outlook, who is experimental, willing to be interdisciplinary in approach, not worried with hierarchy, and trained in economics and planning. This new kind of official, a development administrator, could then be assigned to new ministries such as national planning, social welfare, economic development, science and technology, and public works (to name some of Nigeria's ministries). In fact, some theorists even argued that "economic development can be met only by an oligarchic bureaucracy" that is itself in a constant struggle with political forces (Braibanti, 1961, p. 143). This has led other scholars to charge that development administration is merely a rationalization for autocratic rule, a device for making the bureaucracy a master rather than servant of society (Olugbemi, 1979, p. 97). Nevertheless, the concept of development administration serves to emphasize the constant struggle in Third World countries to try to find institutions that can speed up their drive to modernization and economic well being. *See also* MINISTRY, p. 94; PARASTATAL, p. 98; PLANNING, p. 99; PUBLIC ADMINISTRATION, p. 100.

Significance African countries have established the usual ministries to deal with foreign affairs, defense, justice, interior, finance, trade, posts, agriculture, education, health, and labor. But they have also demonstrated their concern for development administration by setting up ministries clearly devoted to development and planning, as Table B-4 (p. 204) demonstrates. Every independent African state except Djibouti and Swaziland has at least one ministry devoted to development or planning and some have three or four. Besides these ministries, 14 states have ministries devoted to scientific research, and 11 have ministries devoted to energy. Five states (Central African Republic, Gabon, Togo, Upper Volta, and Zimbabwe) have set up ministries devoted to women's affairs. It must be concluded, therefore, that African states are interested in development administration and willing to place some emphasis in that direction. However, there is little or no evidence to date that these specialized ministries have in any way expedited development in their areas. The individual different concerns of African states, however, range from general planning to quite specific development goals (see Table B-4).

Election The process by which some issue is referred to the general public for its reaction. The most common form of election involves the competition between two or more candidates for office in the executive, legislative, or judicial branch of government. However, in some societies (for example, the Soviet Union) such elections do not involve competing candidates; rather, the government allows only one candidate for a post, and the voting public is asked to approve or disapprove of the individual. Some elections are more accurately called referenda, in which voters are asked to approve some proposition, for example, a constitution, a tax rate, or a regulation on liquor sales. Elections have become very important and quite common in most developed countries in the last two centuries. Developing countries have greater difficulty in conducting elections, and they occur only sporadically, if at all, in many areas. However, the concept that the masses ought to participate in some way in the governing process prompts most governments everywhere to have elections from time to time or at least to promise to have them when conditions permit.

Significance All governments in Africa that are organized on some claim to democracy (Botswana, Egypt, Gambia, Mauritius, Morocco, Nigeria, Senegal, South Africa—for Whites only, and Zimbabwe) have regular elections. Most so-called one-party regimes also hold elections from time to time, but do not allow competitive candidates or parties. Exceptions are Algeria, Ivory Coast, Kenya, Tanzania (formerly Tanganyika and Zanzibar), Tunisia and Zambia (formerly Northern Rhodesia), where two or more officially approved candidates of the "single party" may be permitted to compete in elections. These elections are meaningful because they often result in the defeat and replacement of the incumbents. Military regimes usually do not hold elections until the ruling elite has decided to try to transform itself from a purely coercive ruling force to some kind of legitimate ruling force. Consequently, most Africans have had little experience with elections, and very few have participated in competitive elections. Africa's most populous country, Nigeria, did not have elections between January 1966 and the summer of 1979, a 13-year period dominated by military rule. In other countries (for example, Equatorial Guinea, Congo) elections have not been held for many years. Nevertheless, in many of the former French colonies of West Africa, noncompetitive elections occur rather frequently and are believed by the rulers to give an aura of legitimacy to the regimes. People are participating in government even when they vote in noncompetitive elections, so it is possible that such elections do provide some sense of legitimacy for regimes that hold them.

Executive The branch of government that executes laws, i.e., carries out the laws as given by a legislature or a monarch. The two main types of executives are the parliamentary and the presidential. In the former, the executive comes out of, and is responsible to, a legislature, as in Great Britain. The chief executive is usually called a prime minister or a premier, and the other top executives are usually called ministers. The prime minister is head of the majority party or the head of a coalition that can command a majority of votes in the legislature (usually called parliament). If the prime minister (and his fellow ministers, usually called the cabinet) fail to maintain the support of the majority in the parliament, he must resign or call for new parliamentary elections. In contrast to the parliamentary executive is the presidential executive, chosen independently of the legislature, as in the United States. The chief executive of this system is usually called a president and is often in direct conflict with the legislature. The prime minister and president in systems with effective legislatures are the single most powerful persons in the state because they propose policies and budgets to their legislatures, enforce the laws, and respond to and formulate policies on international events. A point of confusion, however, must be recognized in executive terminology: In parliamentary systems a largely ceremonial position known as head of state also exists and is usually called president if no ceremonial king or queen exists. It is thus a matter of empirical investigation whether the title of president refers to the powerful head of government and law enforcer, or to the head of state, a largely ceremonial role. *See also* LEGISLATURE, p. 93.

Significance In Africa there has been a decided move away from parliamentary to presidential executives. In the parliamentary system, the prime minister must always share some prestige and occasionally some power with the head of state (whether king or president). This has created conflict. The Constitution Drafting Committee of Nigeria, which drafted the 1979 Constitution, asserted that a division between head of state and head of government

> is meaningless in the light of African political experience and history. The tendency indeed of all people throughout the world is to elevate a single person to the position of ruler. In the context of Africa the division is not only meaningless, it is difficult to maintain in practice. No African Head of State has been known to be content with the position of mere figurehead. (Federal Republic of Nigeria, 1976, pp. xxix–xxxii.)

The accuracy of the Nigerian observation is easy to demonstrate. Only four states (Lesotho, Mauritius, South Africa—for Whites only, and Zimbabwe) have a true parliamentary system today in which there is both a head of government who wields political power, and a head of state who serves as the ceremonial symbol of the society. Morocco and Swaziland remain true monarchies since the king in each case wields ultimate authority and prime ministers serve only at the king's pleasure. All others have some form that merges the two offices, and the dominant person is usually called president. Even in truly presidential systems, however, the chief executive (the president) often designates one member of his council of ministers as prime minister, but the latter is not a truly independent executive but a servant of the true executive, the president (as in Algeria, Cameroon, Cape Verde, Central African Republic, Comoros, Congo, Djibouti, Egypt, Gabon, Guinea, Madagascar, Mauritania, Mozambique, Senegal, Sudan, Upper Volta, and Zambia).

Federal Government A geographical division of power in such a way that carefully defined regions of a country have some political authority independent of the central government. A federal structure means that every part of a country is under two governments, a regional one with powers that belong to it and a central one with its own authority. The distribution of power in federal systems varies from government to government, and a constitution is necessary to spell out what each government can and cannot do. Federal governments are created in recognition of the fact that the society is deeply divided on some issues, ranging from regional interests due to the sheer size of the country (as in Australia, Brazil, Canada, and the United States) to ethnic, linguistic, and religious divisions (as in India, Nigeria, and Switzerland). Federal structures permit local interests to resolve in their own way certain kinds of problems (such as the type of education, the support of religion, the source of taxation, and the exploitation of local resources). The proof that a system is federal is that the constitution cannot be changed without the approval of an extraordinary majority of the regions. The most common name of regions in federal governments is states, but they are also called provinces (Canada), laender (Germany), cantons (Switzerland), and regions (in Nigeria before 1967). Federal governments are difficult systems to operate because of constant jurisdictional disputes between the central government and the regions and among the competing regions. This helps to explain why federal systems are not popular, there being only about a dozen in the world. The United States was the first to make a federal system work, and has served as a model for other deeply divided societies that wanted also to have the benefits of a strong central government. Even so, the United States fought a civil war to determine finally the nature of its federal relations. *See also* UNITARY GOVERNMENT, p. 102.

Significance Almost every state in Africa is deeply divided by ethnic and linguistic differences, and many are divided by different regions due to sheer geographic size. The 600 or 700 ethnic groups on the continent would seem to attract federal solutions in order to give each group a sense of autonomy in at least some subjects. Nevertheless, only two federal systems (Comoros and Nigeria) and one quasi-federal system (Sudan) exist in Africa. (South Africa, because of some decentralization, is sometimes called federal, but the overriding power of the central government to act in all spheres without the consent of the provinces makes the system unitary.) Nigeria is a federation of 19 states with equal representation (five apiece) in the national Senate. The Constitution spells out 66 exclusive powers for the central government (foreign affairs, defense, banking, citizenship, police, nuclear energy, etc.) and a number of subjects on which both the central government and any state may act (taxation, electric power, agricultural development, higher education, etc.). As in the United States, the basic characteristics of Nigeria's federal system were determined by a civil war (1967–70).

Comoros is a federation of three island-states (a fourth island voted to remain a French colony). The central government controls defense, interisland transportation, foreign relations, economic planning, education, and health, while each state handles local taxation and must be consulted on all economic matters affecting the island.

After Sudan's long civil war between the North and South, it finally worked out a quasi-federal solution. Although no other region gets special attention, under the Constitution of 1973 the three southern provinces (Black, non-Moslem) jointly are permitted to choose a president who is also vice president of Sudan. The southern government is responsible for all matters except for those reserved to Sudan (such as defense, foreign affairs, currency, education, communications, and citizenship). At independence, Cameroon, Uganda, and Zaire also had federal characteristics, but these were soon abandoned in favor of unitary rule.

Indigenization   The process of replacing foreigners with nationals. All colonies faced an influx, first of foreign administrators, then of foreign entrepreneurs who set up banks, small businesses, and even large manufacturing and mining activities. After independence, former colonies found that their own pool of trained indigenous talent was so low that it seemed necessary to retain the foreign personnel merely to keep things running. However, a feeling that true independence could not exist with foreigners running many government offices as well as many local businesses rapidly seized the political leadership, and soon a cry for indigenization spread to many parts of newly independent countries. *See also* PARASTATAL, p. 98.

Significance   Except for some of the former French areas, independence saw a rapid demand for indigenization (sometimes called "Africanization") in most of Africa. Foreign administrators, police officers, and military officers were told that they would have to leave as soon as local indigenes were trained to replace them. Local bureaucrats in the ranks below the foreigners put great pressure on their governments to move the foreigners out quickly, and by 1968–70, in most of Africa except parts of former French West Africa, most aliens were sent home. The process was not always smooth. In some areas, e.g., Northern Nigeria, the local people feared that indigenization meant that distrusted fellow citizens from another region would replace foreign administrators, and in these cases foreigners were preferred. Also indigenization moved so fast in the 1960s that many unqualified indigenes moved up to very responsible positions, with a resultant collapse of efficiency. However, administrative indigenization was basically completed for most of Africa by the 1970s. It was followed by demands for business indigenization, which is still occurring in Nigeria, Kenya, Ghana, Zambia (formerly Northern Rhodesia), and Zaire (formerly Belgian Congo) and is closely related to efforts at acquiring state ownership or at least state control of foreign businesses.

Legislature That branch of government primarily concerned with the making of laws. Legislatures may exist at national, regional, or local levels. At the national level the most common form of legislatures are (1) the parliamentary, in which the legislature designates from its membership, and controls, the person to be chief executive (prime minister), and (2) the separation-of-powers type, in which the legislature must deal with an executive independent of its control (as in a presidential executive system). Modern legislatures were formed primarily out of the pressures of various interests in society to have a voice in governance. Flowing out of this interest came the rise of competitive political parties. Under such developments, legislatures came to represent interests as reflected by electoral strength. Legislative bodies thus became forums for debate and compromise of divisions in society. Many legislatures are bicameral, consisting of two houses, one representing populations (as in a house of representatives), the other representing geographical areas (as in a senate) or some special interest (as in a house of chiefs). *See also* EXECUTIVE, p. 89.

Significance Incipient legislatures as described above exist in only a few states in Africa, those attempting to run competitive democratic systems (Botswana, Egypt, Gambia, Mauritius, Morocco, Nigeria, Senegal, South Africa, and Zimbabwe). The remainder basically operate by a so-called single party or a mobilizational machine (p. 97), which greatly modifies the legislative process as described. In these mobilizational societies, the single legal organization determines laws and policies through its leader and his advisers. If there is a structure designated as a legislature, its membership is restricted to persons approved by the mobilizational leadership, and it cannot initiate legislation but merely assents to what the mobilizational leadership requests. However, if the "legislature" in this case is elected, it serves as a legitimizer for the rulers. Only three states in Africa are bicameral. Nigeria's National Assembly is divided between two equal bodies, a House of Representatives based on population, and a Senate, based on an equal representation of five members from each of 19 states. The other two bicameral states have unequal "second" houses. Botswana's Parliament has a National Assembly and a House of Chiefs (the latter must be consulted on chiefly matters). Zimbabwe's Parliament has a House of Assembly of 100 members, 80 of whom are elected from a common roll, and 20 from a White roll; and a Senate of 40 members (5 Mashona chiefs, 5 Matabele chiefs, 6 persons appointed by the president on advice of the prime minister, 10 persons chosen by Whites in the House of Assembly, and 14 persons chosen by the remaining members of the House of Assembly), which has equal powers with the House only on certain constitutional matters.

Ministry One of a group of major departments in the executive branch of government. In a parliamentary system there are a number of ministries each headed by a minister, with one person who is prime minister and chief executive of the government. Some ministers are designated members of the cabinet, which has collective responsibility for formulating governmental policies and in enforcing law.

In presidential systems, each ministry is headed by a minister (sometimes called a secretary) who is appointed by and is individually responsible to the president. However, the president may designate one person as prime minister, but in this system the latter simply coordinates the work of the ministries—the president remains firmly the dominant executive figure. Collectively, his ministers may also be called a "cabinet," but his security of office distinguishes him sharply from his ministers, who serve at his pleasure. The president is the chief determiner of policies and enforcer of law.

Almost all governments will have ministries of defense, foreign affairs, justice, and internal affairs. In the twentieth century most governments have also added ministries to deal with agriculture, labor, commerce and finance, posts and communications, and education. New states are likely also to have ministries concerned with various aspects of planning and development. *See also* DEVELOPMENT ADMINISTRATION, p. 87; EXECUTIVE, p. 89; PARASTATAL, p. 98; PLANNING, p. 99; PUBLIC ADMINISTRATION, p. 100.

Significance All states in Africa have ministers, although they are called Commissioners in Equatorial Guinea, State Commissioners in Guinea-Bissau and Zaire, and Secretaries in Libya. The number of ministries varies from a low of 8 in Comoros and Equatorial Guinea, to 30 in Guinea and 31 in Ivory Coast, with the average being 19. Ministers are political appointees, i.e., they are chosen for their loyalty to the policies of the president or (in the parliamentary system) because of their leadership in the dominant party. Under the control of each minister is the body of public administrators who carry out government policy and laws in their area of expertise. The minister's role is to pass along government policy to the heads of the bureaucracy, who pass the instructions downward to the point where the policy is implemented. Most African states have the typical ministries mentioned above in addition to one or more of the new ministries concerned with planning and development. (One exception is Libya, which has abolished its Ministry of Defense on the grounds that there is no need for the office when all citizens are responsible for the nation's defense.) Since 45 of the 51 independent states are presidential in form, most ministers serve individually at the pleasure of the chief executive. In the six parliamentary systems, efforts are made to instill in each minister a sense of collective responsibility for the policies of government, but only time will tell if the efforts will succeed.

When the ministers are considered collectively in African states, they are referred to as the "Council of Ministers" (in 22 states), the "Cabinet" (in 19 states), and a variety of names in 6 states: "Executive Council" in Benin and South Africa, "Supreme Military Council" in Equatorial Guinea, "General Popular Committee" in Libya, and "National Executive Council" in Zaire. A typical "cabinet" was the one formed in 1980 by President Hilla Limann (now deposed) in Ghana. He established a ministry for each of the following functions: Finance and Economic Planning; Defense; Interior; Foreign Affairs; Agriculture; Local Government, Rural Development and Cooperatives; Health; Transport and Communication; Works and Housing; Lands and Natural Resources; Trade and Tourism; Industries, Science and Technology; Labor, Youth and Social Welfare; Education, Culture and Sports; Information and Presidential Affairs; and the office of Attorney General. An unusual feature in some African countries is the existence of extraministerial groups used by some executives for advice. In Nigeria, besides ministers, the constitution permits the president to appoint special advisers, and President Shagari has eight. Ghana had established in 1980 a "council of state," which seemed to be interposed between the president and his "cabinet." A similar structure has also been established in four military regimes: the People's Redemption Council in Liberia, composed of 15 noncommissioned officers; the

Supreme Revolutionary Council in Madagascar, composed of 20 people, 6 of whom are high-ranking military officers; the Military Committee for National Salvation in Mauritania, composed of 15 high-ranking officers; and the Politburo in Somalia, composed of 5 high military officers. Thus, ministers advise the president, direct the enforcement of laws in their ministry, and sometimes share the ear of the executive with people they often regard as outside the executive system.

Monarchy A system of government in which a single person is head of state by virtue of inheritance or selection to the office from a royal list. If the person is a ruling monarch as well as a reigning one, he is also head of government. In history the two major types of monarchs have been regarded as absolute (who admitted to no limitations on their power except as determined by them) and benevolent (who were perceived to rule in the public interest). The trend since the beginning of the nineteenth century has been the gradual disappearance of monarchies except where the monarch (as in Great Britain) has been retained as a national symbol while other people actually run the government. *See also* EXECUTIVE, p. 89.

Significance In the last 30 years, monarchies have been abolished in Egypt, Libya, and Ethiopia, and in 1979 the self-proclaimed "emperor" of the Central African Republic was overthrown. Only three monarchies survive in Africa today. In Morocco, King Hassan still rules but is in the process of converting the system to a democratic monarchy, with competing political parties permitted to determine the composition of the legislature and with the king obligated to designate as prime minister (and therefore chief executive) the person who can command a majority of support in the legislature. In Swaziland, King Sobhuza, until his death in 1982, was a ruling monarch. At independence in 1968, the country was organized as a democratic monarchy. But in 1973 the King staged a coup and asserted his ruling authority by abolishing the constitution, banning political parties, and dismissing the legislature. He later proclaimed (without submitting the matter to referendum) a new constitution that permitted a legislature (controlled by him) to advise him on current issues and used a traditional council to advise him on Swazi traditions. In Lesotho, King Moshoeshoe II reigns but does not rule. In 1970 Prime Minister Leabua Jonathan staged a palace coup, suspended the constitution, and took over all governmental power. The king was forced into exile for a few months but was permitted to return to the country after agreeing not to take part in politics. (In Mauritius, the Queen of England is still recognized as head of state and represented by a governor-general, but effective political power is in the hands of the prime minister.)

"No-Party" System A political system that has no formal means for aggregating or articulating interests in a society. Few rulers are powerful enough to ignore completely the various interests in a society without some structure for aggregating and expressing those interests. In the absence of such a structure rulers may simply make decisions which they know are favored by special elites such as the nobility, the religious leaders, the landed aristocracy, or a clique of military officers. "One-party" systems always claim to reflect either the general will as represented by those people in the population who join the "party" or the will of workers as represented by the true believers. "No-party" systems can only claim to represent what rulers perceive and determine to be the social interests, i.e., they represent what power can impose. *See also* COMPETITIVE PARTY SYSTEM, p. 85; DEMOCRACY, p. 71; "ONE-PARTY" SYSTEM, p. 97; POLITICAL PARTY, p. 99; TABLE B-5, p. 204.

Significance At this time, the "no-party" states in Africa are Central African Republic, Comoros, Liberia, Mauritania, Niger, and Swaziland. Except for Swaziland, the "no-party" status appears to be temporary and may soon be replaced by a "one-party" system.

"One-Party" System A political system that relies on a so-called single party to aggregate and articulate interests in the society. The argument is that if interests in society are allowed freely to aggregate or collect together they will automatically clash with other interests. If only one "party" is permitted to exist, then the various interests will either have to compromise, accede to the dominant voice in the "party," or simply remain silent without an outlet for expression. The idea that there could be a single "party" in a society was developed by V. I. Lenin, who maintained that there could not be any competing interests tolerated in a society run by the vanguard of workers. Once the vanguard takes over (in the name of socialism), only one interest is legal, that determined by the vanguard. All other interests are antagonistic to the interests of the workers as defined by the vanguard and must be prohibited. Since the term *party* comes from the same root as *part,* it originally referred to the various parts of society that became identified by interests—labor, management, farmer, professional, intellectual, financial, trade, etc. It is, of course, impossible to divide anything into one part or a society into one party, so the idea of *one-party* is an anomaly. Rather than "one-party," it is more apt to refer to the kind of organization envisioned by Lenin as a "mobilization machine"—an organized structure under the dominance of a ruling elite designed to channel all interests in the society into acts and beliefs acceptable to the rulers. *See also* COMPETITIVE PARTY SYSTEM, p. 85; DEMOCRACY, p. 71; "NO-PARTY" SYSTEM, p. 97; POLITICAL PARTY, p. 99; TABLE B-5, p. 204.

98					The African Political Dictionary

Significance About 80 percent of all states in Africa operate as "one-party" systems. The Marxist states and most of the socialist states operate "one-party" systems based on ideological considerations: namely, that only a "party" of correctly motivated people can possibly guide an African society in its struggle to develop. Other dictatorships restrict the society to one "party" because they believe it is easier to control a single organization than a number of organizations all competing to gain control of the government.

Parastatal A publicly owned enterprise or corporation for engaging in primarily economic activity. Parastatals are created by socialist states for ideological reasons. Other governments set up parastatals for various reasons: to do what the private sector cannot or will not do, to nationalize a foreign-owned business that has interfered in domestic affairs, to gain an economic monopoly in a certain area (such as petroleum), to reduce the influence of a small body of private wealth, to capture profits from a neglected resource, or to control foreign trade. The parastatal (also called statutory authority, government corporation, state-owned enterprise, or public corporation) is an entity partly or wholly owned by government but separated from routine public administration. The separation from the ordinary bureaucracy is maintained in order to free the parastatal from financial and personnel controls often associated with civil service standards. The parastatal is usually freer than the civil service system in exercising management prerogatives, in hiring and firing, and in negotiating contracts. Also, the parastatal can sue and be sued, acquire and control property, and have access to funds both from government revenue and by borrowing (Gant, 1979, p. 109). *See also* PUBLIC ADMINISTRATION, p. 100.

Significance Parastatals are common throughout the world, in capitalist and mixed economic systems as well as socialist and communist systems. However, they are especially widespread throughout Africa. The most obvious forms came from the massive nationalization moves of the Marxist and socialist states (Benin, Congo, Ethiopia, Guinea, Mali, Somalia, Tanzania, Uganda, and Zambia). The governments, as early as the 1960s, took over banking and finance, transport, freehold land, hotels, import-export trades, and large industries. Other states, for nonideological reasons, took over banking and insurance, petroleum production, plantations, timber marketing, and electric enterprises (e.g., Ghana, Kenya, Nigeria, and Zaire). Some nationalization has also occurred in the following states: Cameroon, Central African Republic, Gabon, Madagascar, Malawi (formerly Nyasaland), Mali, Mauritania, Senegal, Sierra Leone, Togo, and Zaire (formerly Belgian Congo). Ironically, because of the absence of local managerial talent, many of the parastatals are still controlled by foreign staffs. Most state-owned enterprises have received a great deal of criticism: They are not as efficient as before, profits tend to decline, research and development practically disappear, and productivity goes down. South Africa, however, provides an exception to the charges: Its parastatals are efficient, make profits, and engage heavily in research and development (Phillips, 1974). Some states, in contrast to the majority, have avoided the state-ownership route, for example, Ivory Coast.

Planning The act of carefully assessing resources over a fixed time and assigning them to specific national goals, such as improved defense, education and agriculture, the building of dams for electrical power, the improvement of roads and railroads, etc. Planning as a governmental activity setting specific targets to be achieved by specific dates involving the total economic wealth of the country was first used by Chairman Stalin of the USSR. Thus, governmental planning came at first to be associated with socialist regimes. However, many developing countries now engage in governmental planning, and even modern capitalist countries, in formulating budgets, engage in considerable planning. *See also* DEVELOPMENT ADMINISTRATION, p. 87; TABLE B-4, p. 202.

Significance Most of the governments of Africa have some kind of a development plan, and most even have some kind of a ministry devoted to planning (Table B-4, p. 202). The major problem with planning in Africa is the absence of factual data. When governments do not know the exact population size and therefore the tax base, planning becomes difficult if not impossible. One economist who served as advisor to an African state entitled his book on the experience *Planning without Facts* (Stolper, 1966). Although governments continue to plan, most plans are failures, not only because of the lack of data with which to plan but also because of the vagaries of international pricing that, in a five-year period, will produce drastic shifts in the prices countries can receive for their coffee, cocoa, copper, diamonds, or oil (see Caiden and Wildavsky, 1974). If, as is true of most African countries, they must rely on imported oil, the price rise between 1974 and 1980 could destroy any plan, as it did for a great number of African states.

Political Party An organization of people with common interests who have joined together to compete in elections with other similar organizations for the right to have its candidates serve in executive and legislative (and sometimes judicial) positions in government. A political party differs fundamentally from an interest group since the latter (for example, a market women's association, a farmers' cooperative, a chamber of commerce) is organized to promote the purposes and goals of the group, and only incidentally to *influence* governmental decisions. Political parties are organized not to influence but to *make* governmental decisions. The primary challenge of a political party is for its members and candidates to tolerate an election loss and prepare for a more successful campaign at a later election. Political parties as defined here are relatively recent in history, having arisen in Western democracies in the last 200 years. A political party as defined here must not be confused with the single organization that exists in so-called one-party systems, in which the organization in control of government outlaws all competitive parties and prohibits their having any chance at governing. See also COMPETITIVE PARTY SYSTEM, p. 85; DEMOCRACY, p. 71; "NO-PARTY" SYSTEM, p. 97; "ONE-PARTY" SYSTEM, p. 97; TABLE B-5, p. 204.

Significance African states have since their independence overwhelmingly abandoned political party politics. The elimination of political parties has come primarily by coups d'etat or by a victorious ruling group merely declaring all competitive groups to be illegal. Political parties as defined here exist only in Botswana (formerly Bechuanaland), Egypt, Gambia, Mauritius, Morocco, Nigeria, Senegal, South Africa (for Whites only), and Zimbabwe (formerly Southern Rhodesia).

Public Administration The process by which governmental decisions and policies are implemented. Those who effect governmental decisions are called public administrators or bureaucrats and are distinguished from those who *make* the decisions, who are politicians. While politicians make decisions based on some perception of the public interest or their own personal interests, administrators, at least theoretically, carry out those decisions on the basis of carefully drawn rules. The rules of public administration emphasize (1) selection of administrators on the basis of skills and competency; (2) nonpartisanship; (3) fairness in applying rules; (4) the keeping of complete records and files; and (5) administrative faithfulness to the intention of the political decision makers. Public administration, furthermore, is hierarchical, with authority ranging from a clear top position downward to the lowest position. Many governments today have a civil service (or public service) commission that tests applicants for government employment, hires them, promotes them, and protects them.

The commission tends to regulate all government employment except the very top people, such as ministers. These latter are usually appointed by the chief executive directly from persons loyal to his program. Through these appointed ministers, the executive controls the major forms of public administration. However, legislators and judges often have their own administrative staffs that are under their control rather than that of the executive. *See also* DEVELOPMENT ADMINISTRATION, p. 87; MINISTRY, p. 94; PARASTATAL, p. 98; PLANNING, p. 99.

Significance In Africa there are basically two kinds of public administration: (1) the bureaucracy common to most countries, represented by ministries (or departments) of finance, justice, defense, foreign affairs, education, utilities, and communications; and (2) the bureaucracy for development with parastatals and ministries devoted to economic development, agricultural productivity, population policy, planning, research, manpower training, and foreign aid (see Table B-4, p. 202). An efficient and honest system of public administration is expensive to train, even for the first purpose and becomes especially burdensome when both purposes are pursued. That helps to explain why the bureaucracies of most African states are regarded as poorly trained, inefficient, and corrupt. There are, of course, many individual exceptions, but the constant complaint of Africans and foreigners alike is that in general the bureaucracy does not get things done or done well. Political loyalties and ethnic background are still important criteria by which many people are admitted into the system of public administration. Highly competent people all too often rise quickly through the ranks (or fail to rise quickly enough) and leave the service for more lucrative jobs. Middle and lower management levels are often staffed with only partially trained people because fully trained people in such large numbers are not available. As a result, throughout Africa, an efficient system of public administration is regarded as one of their high-priority needs. Yet there is no known way to create such a system rapidly, say in less than one or two generations, and even that requires great expenditures, unavailable in most of Africa. But the weak bureaucracy must also be explained by the fact that present-day administrators have had little experience in the top layers of administration because colonial powers used their own nationals rather than local Africans for such positions. In fact, it was not until just before independence that a few Africans were permitted into the top ranks of public administration and not until a few years after independence that the new governments could fill all top posts with indigenes. In the process, most people agree that many poorly qualified people simply moved up.

Unitary Government   A form of rule in which the center binds all people and local units equally. In unitary systems the central authority can bind all citizens and all local or regional units to its laws. Unlike federal governments, unitary governments do not have to share power with local units. However, unitary government is not the same as absolute rule. While some unitary governments, as in dictatorships, may be absolute, others, as in Great Britain or France, may place great restrictions on the powers of government. The difference is reflected in the concept in England that Parliament is supreme (it can make any law on any subject regarded as appropriate), which can be contrasted with the power of the United States Congress, which, for example, cannot pass a law on marriage and divorce because such laws are reserved to the states. Thus, unitary governments are easy to establish legally because they require only a concept of a neat hierarchy of power, ranging downward from the supreme legislature and/or executive to every citizen. Of the approximately 165 nation-states in today's world, about 153 are unitary in structure and therefore clearly the preferred way to rule among mankind. The remaining dozen are federal and contain about one-third of the world's population and almost one-half of the world's land area, indicating that unitary government may be less desirable for nations with large populations and land areas. *See also* FEDERAL GOVERNMENT, p. 91.

Significance   All the states of Africa except for Comoros, Nigeria, and Sudan are unitary in structure. Cameroon, Uganda, and Zaire (formerly Belgian Congo) were federal at independence but were transformed to unitary structures as quickly as rulers could do so. Unitary systems are easier to run than federal ones, and surely have advantages in homogeneous societies. African societies, however, are not homogeneous, and the imposition of unitary rule has meant in many states that people who have different values or customs from those who run the center must nevertheless conform to the center. African leaders justify the imposition of unitary rule on the grounds that it is the best way to mould heterogeneous people into a single nation. In any case, unitary governments are clearly the dominant form in Africa, regardless of size or diversity of peoples.

7. Political Development and Modernization

Development   Goal-directed behavior. The term *development* appears in the discussions of all countries today. Analysts divide the world into developed and developing and sometimes into overdeveloped and underdeveloped (or undeveloped). The concept of development is relative and refers basically to how states relate to the Industrial Revolution of the last 200 years. Developed countries are those of Europe, those settled by Europeans, and Japan. They are industrial (50 percent or *less* of the population is in agriculture), highly literate, homogeneous, and politically stable. Developing countries lack one or more of these characteristics. The term development, however, is frequently limited to only one aspect of development, namely economics. Thus, most people mean economic development when they use the term and usually are referring specifically to industrialization. This usage neglects the need also for development in political and social systems as a state moves from an agricultural to an industrialized base. *See also* other headings under DEVELOPMENT, pp. 103–113.

Significance   All countries in Africa must be regarded as politically, socially, and (except for South Africa) economically underdeveloped. None has yet developed a stable political system capable of doing what politics must do for a society; none has yet integrated its people into a homogeneous, literate, national mass; and none (with the exception noted) has developed its economic potential. Whether African states in general are developing or remain essentially undeveloped is part of the on-going debate among scholars.

Development: Dependency Theory   The belief that economically underdeveloped countries are dependent on the developed countries and that this dependency is the cause of their continued economic stagnation. The dependency relationship was established during the age of mercantilism, the period of the slave trade, the rise of imperialism, and the establishment of colonialism. Dependency became even greater after independence because of neocolonialism. The result is an international division of labor in which the developed countries (particularly the capitalist ones) dominate world trade and resource utilization and the underdeveloped countries are able merely to acquiesce because they lack sufficient resources to pursue independent economic policies. This dependency keeps them poor. Dependency theorists usually recommend three courses of action to escape dependency: socialism, national self-reliance, and disengagement from the world capitalist system. *See also* other headings under DEVELOPMENT, pp. 103–113.

Significance All socialist countries and many others as well voice concern with their plight of dependency. Tanzania in its 1977 Constitution spelled out specifically that its objective was "to build socialism on the basis of self-reliance." It did not go so far as to renounce all ties with capitalism, nor to drive out the multinational corporations operating there, which had numbered 59 in 1968 (Morrison, 1972, p. 155). But its leaders have joined others in blaming their poor economic growth on their country's dependency on great capitalist powers. However, one scholar has put the dependency theory—that economic dependency is associated with economic underdevelopment—to an empirical test for Africa. He collected data on 23 indicators of economic performance and correlated these with their dependence on foreign powers and found "that the proposition that economic dependence is associated with underdevelopment ... is simply not supported by the evidence" (McGowan, 1976, p. 35). Another empirical study, however, while concluding that economic "dependence does not allow for fully independent policy positions in other areas" also found that both capitalist and Marxist theories seemed unable to promise "improvements in the situation of the masses" (Vengroff, 1977, p. 630). Capitalism seems destined to produce great internal inequality, although it does appear to produce overall economic growth (ibid.). When it is noted, furthermore, that the Marxist approach, where it has been tried in Africa, does not show much economic growth or improvement in equality (except possibly in Tanzania), the dependency theory must be questioned. One can favor socialism and national self-reliance, however, on other than economic grounds, for example, by arguing that they are morally preferable, conform to traditional practices, or are easier to effect than capitalism and individualism.

Development: Economic Goal-directed behavior designed to change the economic base of society from its traditional form to a more modern form. Economic development is usually measured by steady increase in the gross national product of a country, which in turn is measured by the total goods and services. The basic problem is how to stimulate a society to increase its goods and services when it depends heavily on subsistence-level agriculture and has high rates of illiteracy, low rates of income, savings, and productivity, decentralized political structures, poor social mobility, and rudimentary transportation and communication facilities. In fact, economic development is more of a political problem than an economic one in the sense that the first question to decide is how to proceed. Capitalists insist on a free market and socialists on state ownership, while others call for a mixed system. After the basic political question has been decided, others arise: whether to emphasize agriculture or industrialization; electric power grids or steel mills; roads or railroads; mass education through elementary level or elite education through university. If the right decisions are made about taxation, borrowing money from abroad, encouraging increased production, stimulating savings, educating for the right skills, and supporting improved transportation and communication networks, then it is presumed societies will develop through stages. The first stage is a period of building resources (dams, roads, schools, mining of minerals and metals, borrowing from abroad, promoting agricultural efficiency); the second stage is a period of "take off" that constitutes a break with the traditional economic past as more and more wealth becomes available for more and more uses; and finally, the third stage of internally sustained economic growth is reached. Many scholars and politicians, however, maintain that growth that does not relieve the misery of the masses is "growth without development" and often cite Ivory Coast as an example. On the other hand, equalizing the plight of the masses and raising their standard of living slightly by bringing down the standard of living of elites, if not accompanied by a larger gross national product, produces "development without growth," and Tanzania is offered as an example (Ottaway and Ottaway, 1981, p. 44). *See also* other headings under DEVELOPMENT, pp. 103–113.

Significance Economic development in Africa ranges from meager to none (except for the White sector in South Africa, which has now reached a stage of internally sustainable growth). A few states are in the stage of building resources, but for most states it is difficult to find much evidence of significant economic development. Where some evidence exists, it is in very limited areas referred to by economists as "development islands" located in an ocean of little or no development.

Even the development islands seem to be built around single economic activities rather than many complex and interrelated activities. For example, basically agricultural activity occurs in a few such islands: on the lower Nile in Egypt, around Khartoum in Sudan, around Addis Ababa in Ethiopia, along the west coast, around Kano in Nigeria, around Lake Victoria, on the lower Congo, around Luanda in Angola, and in small enclaves in Zambia (formerly Northern Rhodesia), Malawi (formerly Nyasaland), and Mozambique. A few states, notably Algeria, Gabon, Libya, and Nigeria, have been able to import large quantities of foreign exchange for developmental purposes through sales of petroleum. Extensive and intensive mining occurs primarily in the Zaire-Zambia area and in Liberia and Guinea. Truly extensive plural economic activities involving advanced agriculture, mining, and industrial activity are limited primarily to South Africa and Zimbabwe (formerly Southern Rhodesia). The political problem for almost all of Africa is how to start a traditional, decentralized society on the road to savings and investments, literacy, upgraded skills, and a commitment to change. Even to get the process started requires foreign aid, and acquiring that is a major political challenge. Meanwhile, the gap between the rich North and the poor South continues to widen.

Development: Least Developed Countries (LLDCs)   Those countries of the world designated by the United Nations as being the least developed as distinguished from the Less Developed Countries (LDCs), and sometimes referred to as the Fourth World. In 1968 the UN General Assembly invited the Secretary-General to propose a way to define LLDCs and to recommend special measures to help them. In 1970 a committee proposed three main criteria for defining LLDCs: (1) a per capita Gross Development Product of not more than $100 per annum; (2) manufacturing representing not more than 10 percent of GDP; and (3) a literacy rate of not more than 20 percent for people over 15 years of age. By these criteria the UN was able to designate 25 countries of the world as the poorest of the poor. By December 1980 the list had grown to 31. *See also* other headings under DEVELOPMENT, pp. 103–113.

Significance   Twenty-one of the 31 LLDCs are African states: Benin; Botswana (formerly Bechuanaland); Burundi; Cape Verde; Central African Republic; Chad; Comoros; Ethiopia; Gambia; Guinea; Guinea-Bissau; Lesotho (formerly Basutoland); Malawi; Mali; Niger; Rwanda; Somalia; Sudan; Tanzania (formerly Tanganyika and Zanzibar); Uganda; and Upper Volta. Besides the three criteria listed above, these countries share other characteristics: a low rate of economic growth (whereas LDCs grew about 40 percent in the decade of the 1970s, LLDCs grew only 6 percent); exceptionally heavy reliance on agriculture with little industry; dependence on only one or two export products; embryonic health services; shortage of drinking water; low educational opportunities; very short life expectancy; and a growing gap between themselves and the LDCs, not to speak of the widening gap between themselves and the developed countries (Champmarin, 1982, p. 57). The LLDCs are especially vulnerable in today's world. The rich Western countries show little inclination, and the East European countries show no inclination, to help. The rich OPEC countries fear that they may be called on to assume some responsibility for the poorest areas. And the other Third World countries, the LDCs, fear that special recognition of the plight of LLDCs might lead to some reorganization of international aid programs that would be detrimental to them. The only positive action to date has come from the European Economic Community, which in 1981 agreed to an aid target of 0.7 percent of GNP to Third World countries and to earmark 0.15 percent of GNP to the LLDCs. Whether this meager help will have any impact may not be known for years.

Development: Neocolonialism A concept or belief that political independence unaccompanied by a break with capitalism institutes a new subservient status. Theorists of neocolonialism argue that political independence was a sham because (1) independence was granted to the small middle class who comprised the privileged class in the colony; (2) the middle class was inextricably tied to international capitalism; and (3) the imperialist countries simply worked through the indigenous capitalist class to maintain economic domination. In this context, political independence was granted with little fear in the capitalist world that any economic loss would occur. In fact, after independence imperialists continued to make investments, loans, and grants to African states that promoted the interests of imperialists and local capitalists but not of the masses. Kwame Nkrumah of Ghana, an early exponent of the idea of neocolonialism, said it was the most exploitative form of imperialism because, for those who practice it, it means "Power without responsibility," and for those who suffer from it, it means "exploitation without redress."

The multinational corporation is regarded as a prime example of neocolonialism. The foreign company, in cooperation with domestic elites, binds national policy more and more to capitalism. The foreign company, it is argued, is too powerful for a weak government to control because the company has something the government wants and needs. The multinational oil company, for example, not only has oil-mining capacity, but it also has superior managerial skills, knowledge of world marketing conditions, ability to employ local people, access to financial markets, and other things valued by the African government. This condition produces a dependency relationship for the government that restricts its ability to act internationally; for example, if it is dependent on a Japanese company for a large part of its copper revenue, a government is likely to be cautious in criticizing Japan for some Japanese action with which it disagrees.

Scholars of neocolonialism also argue that the wealth of the neocolony is frittered away by new tastes and values that support world capitalism, such as Western films, entertainment, clothing, cars, foods, fads, and other luxury goods, as well as educational exchanges, technological transfers, economic advice, and military support. The neocolonial relationship, it is further alleged, explains why so many African countries, after 20 years of "independence," have faced economic stagnation and decline, agricultural deterioration, rural emigration, and massive unemployment. External rather than internal forces, consequently, explain Africa's economic failures; neocolonialism is the root cause. Not only is the economy distorted by imperial ties, but the ability to pursue independent foreign policies is also distorted and dominated by the neocolonial relationship: Consequently, even political independence is nonexistent except in a purely formal sense. The only escape, the theorist of neocolonialism concludes, is to adopt socialism and self-reliance and to sever dependence on capitalist countries. The models for this policy are the Soviet Union, China, and Cuba. *See also* other headings under DEVELOPMENT, pp. 103–113.

Significance The theorists of neocolonialism are correct in pointing out that external factors can greatly affect the economic performance of African countries, as falling cocoa prices demonstrated in Ghana in the 1960s and rising oil prices demonstrate today in all non–oil-producing states. To base a theory on external factors alone, however, seems unrealistic. It ignores the fact that internal factors are also necessary for development, such as clearly formulated goals, commitment to savings, a willingness to sacrifice, and a healthy sense of nationalism, all weak in Africa, even in socialist states. Internal elites, furthermore, are not mere pawns of the world market, as Nigeria has demonstrated in its opposition to certain policies of the United States, to whom it sells most of its oil. African states frequently vote against the Western states in the United Nations. Internal factors, therefore, are also important.

While self-reliance has an attractive ring to it, it is questionable how far it ought to be carried if development is to occur. Many analysts argue that foreign aid is necessary for rapid development, and point out that the Soviet Union in its early years relied on much foreign assistance. To cut off ties with the West (the primary source of assistance) in the name of self-reliance may, therefore, delay development, since the Soviet Union (the alleged friend of the self-reliant country) refuses to be an alternative source of foreign assistance. The two prime examples of states that have turned to self-reliance are Tanzania and Guinea. Tanzania has had little growth since it embarked on its course of self-reliance in 1966, although there has been some lessening of inequality (p. 105). Guinea has pursued its socialist, self-reliant goals since 1958, and its economy is regarded as a failure, even by its President, Sekou Touré. In mid-1982, Mr. Touré was encouraging American private investment in Guinea, a reversal of previous policies. Except for the few states with real (chiefly mineral) wealth, the African states do not vary greatly in their economic plight, whether they are socialist or capitalist. Even the so-called capitalist states have mixed, not *laissez faire*, systems. Furthermore, those states with foreign investments, including multinational corporations, have learned how to control them through nationalization, joint venture deals, renegotiated contracts that minimize foreign impact on domestic policies, and, where necessary, expulsion.

Although the theory of neocolonialism seems plausible on its face, it has not yet demonstrated that it is a powerful explanation for Africa's plight. Most African leaders, furthermore, are reluctant to break ties with the capitalist world on a vague promise that things might improve. Finally, it should be noted that the concept of neocolonialism (like that of dependency) is a highly emotional one in Africa. Even African theorists who do not find the concept theoretically valuable nevertheless resent the reality that foreigners often influence greatly the decisions of many governments, especially the weakest ones. It is this uncomfortable relationship that has led most African countries to press for a New International Economic Order, which may free them from some capitalist restraints without throwing them in the Soviet camp.

Development: New International Economic Order (NIEO)

A perception of the world that calls for drastic change, to the benefit of poor countries, in many standards and procedures used in current international financial, trade, and aid arrangements. The NIEO is part of what is also called the North-South dialogue. Many proposals have been put forth for a New International Economic Order, one of the more grandiose coming from the conference in New Delhi, India, in January 1980 sponsored by the United Nations International Development Organization. That conference simply asked the rich countries to contribute $25 billion a year to the poor countries, to be administered by Third World countries. Other proposals for change have arisen from numerous sources and call for such things as the following: the setting up of machinery (paid for by rich countries) for guaranteeing fixed prices for the raw materials sold by poor countries; the cancellation of debts owed by poor countries to the rich; the abolition in rich countries of import duties on goods manufactured in poor countries; interest-free loans to the poor; a considerable increase in the amount of aid transferred from the rich to the poor countries; and international regulation of multinational corporations. *See also* other headings under DEVELOPMENT, pp. 103–113.

Significance The earliest concerns for "economic equality" were expressed at the Non-Aligned Summit in Cairo in October 1964, attended by 29 African states. Gradually the concern for economic equality changed to a demand by poor states for a New International Economic Order, a term in wide use by 1970. By 1980 an Independent Commission of International Development Issues, headed by the West German leader Willy Brandt, was dramatizing the need for a NIEO by noting that 80 million desperately poor people live in the southern lands, where 25 million children under age 5 die each year, and where 70 percent of the world's people subsist on 20 percent of what the world produces. While both North and South may agree on the awful plight of the South, no progress has been made toward a New International Economic Order. There is no evidence that money alone, controlled by the South's own rich elites, would alleviate the plight of the poorest. There is also the belief that the greatest chance for improving the economic well-being of poor countries rests on internally generated commitments in the poor countries. Rich countries, furthermore, have simply not shown any inclination to give such huge portions of their wealth to the poor as are demanded. To complicate matters, the poor have no bargaining chips. They cannot play the West and the Soviet bloc off against each other. The Soviet bloc will not talk about the matter, refusing even to attend conferences on the North-South dialogue. The Western powers attend conferences but pledge only tiny proportions of what the poor countries are pleading for.

Development: North-South Dialogue Communications between the rich, industrialized countries (the North) and the poor, underdeveloped countries (the South) concerning the poverty of the latter and possible ways of alleviating it. Most of the rich countries lie north of the Tropic of Cancer, while most of the poor lie south of it; hence the name of the dialogue. For the dialogue, the less developed countries (LDCs) formed the "Group of 77" in 1964 at the Geneva meeting of the United Nations Conference on Trade and Development (UNCTAD). Although the name of the group remains, membership has grown to 114 countries plus the Palestine Liberation Organization. The dialogue occurs mainly in the United Nations, but also in meetings of the Group of 77, in conferences on world trade, in forums dealing with the ocean's resources, in meetings on the proposed New International Economic Order, and other similar debating areas. The differences between North and South are startling: Although the North has 30 percent of the world's population, it has 80 percent of its wealth and income. The world's economic and military power and armament production are concentrated in the North. Ninety-eight percent of all research and development funds for technology are in the North, as are 90 percent of all industries. Most world trade occurs between and among northern countries; most multinational corporations radiate out of Western northern countries; and North America dominates world food production (Singer, 1978, p. 543). *See also* other headings under DEVELOPMENT, pp. 103–113.

Significance All of Africa (except for South Africa) is part of the South in the North-South dialogue. In fact, many African states are among the poorest in the world. Although the North-South dialogue has been going on about 15 years, the South has little to show for the effort. The North refuses to accept responsibility for the South's poverty. The South, furthermore, has suffered humiliation even from other southern countries, namely the oil-rich members of the Organization of Petroleum Exporting Countries (OPEC). Although the South supported the OPEC price squeeze on the wealthy countries in 1974, it soon found itself (except for its own OPEC members—Algeria, Libya, Nigeria, and Gabon) paying 500 percent more for its own oil imports. The increased price of OPEC oil, in fact, effectively stopped what economic development was occurring in many African countries. Thus far, the South as a whole has very little on which to bargain with (and coerce) the North. This makes the South's plight even worse because it sees its future dependent more and more only on the good will of the North, a weak reed on which to build. However, even good will is in short supply, and there is little evidence that the North-South dialogue has yet produced any benefit for the South.

Development: Political Goal-directed behavior designed to bring about a stable process in government that can provide effective leadership and legitimacy. Many political scientists emphasize the *functional* changes that must occur before a state can be said to be developing. Rather than focus on the government's institutions, they talk of the ability of the ruling elite to stimulate and control the direction and rate of change in economic growth. Other political scientists stress that *political* development is not dependent on economics but on the ability to create *governmental institutions* that can perform the political tasks needed in all societies. A developed political system has managed to do at least four things with government. First, it has centralized power and in doing so has weakened local and traditional centers of power. Centralization need not be absolute, and seldom is, in developed political systems, but when local autonomy is permitted it is not able to stop the central government from performing its role. Second, it has found some acceptable way of changing leaders peacefully. How rulers get to rule is the most important *political* question in any country. In developed polities today, the most common solution is through popular, regularized elections, although the Soviet Union provides the exception by having found a way to change rulers by choice of the top elite in the Communist Party. Third, it has created a strong bureaucracy capable of responding to new social demands. The bureaucracy is able to move with some efficiency in areas of rapid or constant change such as advanced agriculture, industrialization, transportation, education, migration, urbanization, social security, etc. Fourth, it has created ways to involve the general population in national politics so as to provide legitimacy for the government. While most politically developed societies acquire legitimacy through open, competitive and regular elections, the Soviets seem to have acquired legitimacy by their system of noncompetitive elections. Political development, therefore, is progress toward resolving the problems related to governmental centralization, peaceful selection of leaders, efficient bureaucracy, and legitimacy. *See also* other headings under DEVELOPMENT, pp. 103–113.

Significance African states are deficient in all four requirements of political development. While all are attempting to centralize power, local forces based on ethnic, language, and/or regional concerns continue to frustrate these efforts. In terms of rulers, there are only two cases (involving the exclusive White electorate in South Africa and the June 1982 election in Mauritius) where a ruling executive has been removed and replaced by the electoral process. Once a ruler gets control, he does not willingly relinquish power even when he loses an election, as happened in Sierra Leone (where the military intervened to try to keep the loser in power) and Lesotho (where the ruling Prime Minister staged a palace coup). A few rulers have died in office but all were replaced by "party" elites or military leaders. In 11 countries (Cape Verde, Djibouti, Gambia, Guinea, Ivory Coast, Malawi, Mozambique, Tanzania, Tunisia, Zambia, and Zimbabwe), the ruler who inherited power at independence is still ruling. There is, consequently, little evidence that African states can change rulers peacefully. As to bureaucracy, African states are still struggling to build an efficient, corruption-free system of public administration. Finally, most governments do not permit mass participation in politics, and of those that permit elections most do not permit free opinion or competition. Evidence for legitimacy is almost nonexistent. It should be noted, however, that eight countries (Botswana, Egypt, Gambia, Mauritius, Morocco, Nigeria, Senegal and Zimbabwe) are trying to adapt the open, competitive electoral process of democracies, but only Mauritius has demonstrated that it can remove a ruler peacefully by this method. Six countries (Algeria, Ivory Coast, Kenya, Tanzania, Tunisia, and Zambia) that do not permit the masses a voice in choosing the top ruler have nevertheless devised a method for permitting competition in legislative elections among officially approved candidates. Apart from these 14, there is little evidence of political development in Africa. However, like economic and social development, political development is a process (not an event) and may not be apparent until viewed over a period of decades or generations.

Development: Social   Goal-directed behavior designed to improve general social conditions (in contrast to the more specifically focused economic and political development). Included in the notion of social development are improved national integration and the lessening of ethnic and tribal identification, the spread of literacy, increased equality between the top and lower levels of society, longer lifespans, increased availability of health services for more and more people, improved nutrition, and a growing sense of well-being in the society. Theoretically, social developments should flow from economic and political development, although hopes for social development are usually specifically mentioned in economic and political planning. *See also* other headings under DEVELOPMENT, pp. 103–113.

Significance   While not totally absent, social development has been very meager in Africa. The low level of success in economic planning, the extensive political instability, and the exceptionally high rate of population growth have hindered any meaningful social development. The low economic growth rate for most African states is about the same as the population growth rate, meaning no improvement in general well-being for the average citizen. However, some social development is occurring in the richer of the African countries, Algeria, Angola, Gabon, Ivory Coast, Libya, Nigeria, South Africa, and Zimbabwe (formerly Southern Rhodesia).

Diffusion Theory The concepts related to the transmission of cultural characteristics from one society to another. Although the transmission can be in both directions between any two societies, the dominant pattern resulting from the Industrial Revolution has been from developed countries to developing countries. It is usually believed by scholars of diffusion that technology is the easiest thing to diffuse; that social institutions are difficult to diffuse; and that ideologies are the most difficult of all to diffuse. The reasons for these degrees of receptivity to foreign things seem clear: people generally believe they can borrow material goods (such as cars, airplanes, steel mills, electric power plants, paved highways, ballpoint pens, clothing, advanced agriculture, assembly lines, etc.) and merely benefit from them without any change in their views of themselves or the world; they hesitate to import foreign social institutions because these require changing well-known local patterns; and they strongly resist foreign ideologies because these require them to redefine themselves. Nevertheless, diffusion of all three characteristics of culture has been going on apace for centuries and is especially fast today. *See also* MODERNIZATION, p. 117.

Significance Diffusion for Africa has been a two-way affair. For hundreds of years Africa diffused its populations (unwillingly) through slavery to the Middle East and the New World. It also diffused gold and leather goods and other products to Europe, and more recently it has been diffusing oil and metals to all parts of the world. Basically, however, Africa has been the receiver of diffusions. European languages have diffused into Africa and become the official languages of most of the African states. Advanced industrial technology is spreading slowly throughout the continent, while there has been a much more rapid spread of Western tastes in such things as food, liquors, dress, and entertainment. Attempts to capture Western bureaucratic structures have been widespread, but in general political structure most states have avoided both the Western democratic patterns and the Marxist mobilizational patterns. The diffusion of ideologies has been quite mixed. The earliest diffusions were of a religious nature—the spread of Islam from the north and then the spread of Christianity from the south and the east and west coasts. Then came competitive democratic concepts followed by Marxist concepts in a few states. Socialist ideologies have been received in some states. The ideology of science has also been spreading. These ideologies have been blended with traditional ones in such a fashion that no "pure" form now exists. Africans are probably in the process of blending these diffused technologies, social institutions, and ideologies with their own traditional forms in such a way as to emerge soon with their unique, homogeneous cultural patterns, different for each state. Rapid diffusion, however, of so many foreign elements produces general social instability since there are always active receivers and active resisters of change. Thus, diffusion helps to explain the resulting political instability. (See Table B-5, p. 204).

Economic Viability   The ability, within the conditions present, to attain economic goals. Whether a country has or does not have economic viability depends on a great number of interlocking factors, such as its exploitable natural resources, population size and density, agriculture, political leadership, ability to borrow from abroad, literacy, cost of energy, level of urbanization, etc. Economists suggest that minimum requirements for economic viability in developing countries are a population size of at least 10 to 15 million people (Spengler, 1971, pp. 107–8); a reasonably low population growth rate; and vast improvements in agriculture before or accompanying early industrialization (Myrdal, 1973, p. 107; Bairoch, 1975, p. 203). Other factors that will vary greatly from country to country are the value of easily exploitable minerals, the price of energy, the size and dynamism of an entrepreneurial class, and the extent to which economic equality is spreading in the society. *See also* MODERNIZATION, p. 117.

Significance   African states do not fare well on measures related to economic viability. A few African states have vast sources of natural wealth in the form of uranium, petroleum, copper, bauxite, diamonds, and agricultural potential (including Algeria, Angola, Ethiopia, Libya, Namibia, Nigeria, South Africa, Sudan, Zaire, and Zimbabwe). Most of these are regarded as economically viable. While the other countries may have some form of potential wealth, most of them have population sizes that make economic viability questionable: Only 13 countries (Nigeria, Egypt, Ethiopia, Zaire, South Africa, Morocco, Sudan, Algeria, Tanzania, Kenya, Uganda, Ghana, and Mozambique) have populations in excess of 10 million. Furthermore, African population growth rate is now at 2.9 percent per year, making it the highest in the world, which means that the economic growth rate has to be at least 2.9 percent merely to keep even on a per capita base. The rapid growth rate has also meant that African states now have 48 percent of their population under 15 years of age or over 65; that is, almost half of the population is at an unproductive age. Also it must be noted that far from developing, African agriculture is actually declining, requiring more and more importation of foods merely to feed the populations, thus using wealth that could otherwise be spent on development. Finally, except for the oil-producing states (Algeria, Angola, Libya,

Nigeria, and Gabon), many African states have seen their development plans shattered by the 500 percent rise in the cost of petroleum since 1974. This picture raises the spectre that most African states today may not be economically viable. That awareness will certainly put great strains on the political systems as leaders and masses alike see their hopes for improved standards of living shattered.

Foreign Aid The transfer of wealth from one country to another. Foreign aid usually takes the form of economic loans, economic grants (gifts), military equipment, military training, transfer of technology, transfer of food, and the loan of technical experts, advisors, professors, and teachers. While most foreign aid is bilateral, some aid goes from the rich to the poor countries through regional organizations and global agencies under the United Nations. Such aid is not strictly one-way; some recipients of bilateral aid such as Nigeria will give of its own wealth to a regional organization such as the Economic Commission of West African States to help its neighbors. Donors give aid because they believe it is in their security, economic, and/or moral interests to do so. They believe that aid will help the recipient state to develop economically, to become or to remain politically stable, to become or remain militarily strong in its area, to become or remain friendly, and to relieve the glaring aspects of poverty. Recipient states borrow or receive aid to try to hasten economic development, to improve their military posture, and to assist them in meeting catastrophic conditions of drought, malnutrition, and disease. *See also* headings under DEVELOPMENT, pp. 103–113; ECONOMIC VIABILITY, p. 115.

Significance The obvious impact of foreign aid can be seen in Africa in the form of highways, agricultural experimentation stations, school buildings, dams, electric power grids, and military equipment. Less obvious effects of foreign aid exist in the help given in drought relief, training programs, advisors, and professors, teachers, and health personnel. Nevertheless, important as such aid may appear, it has not been enough to get economic development going. Foreign aid going to Africa has been very low and is decreasing. If, as some economists argue, foreign aid is necessary for rapid economic growth, then Africa faces the bleak prospect of slow growth, if growth occurs at all. After over two decades of capital transfers, however, African states in general find that they are more heavily indebted than at any previous time—their growth has been so low that they cannot begin to pay back what has been borrowed. One reason why Africa has received so little foreign aid in relation to the rest of the world is probably due to the unpredictable relationships it creates. After building the Aswan Dam in Egypt, the Soviets were unceremoniously thrown out later. After a deliberate effort to woo support in many African countries by vast technical aid programs, Israel found that the continent voted overwhelmingly to break off relations and join the Arab (and Arab oil) side (p. 170). It must also be noted that foreign aid is not always what it seems. The United States often "gives" credit, which means the recipient country is required to buy American goods—good for American industry and agriculture but paid for by American taxpayers through higher prices. It also means that the recipient country cannot shop for the best prices but must buy in the United States. Some countries, like Tanzania, regard these as "strings" attached to aid and refuse aid offers, or reduce the amount they are willing to accept. The uncertainties of foreign aid programs help to explain the increasing demand from African states for a New International Economic Order (p. 109).

Modernization A condition in which a culture in its various characteristics has captured the most advanced forms of technology, sociological institutions, and ideology. It is a relative term; thus, at the time of the Roman Empire, a modern society was one which had captured advanced agriculture, engaged in international commerce, was urbanized, had a state structure with at least an executive and a bureaucracy, had writing, coinage, irrigation, the wheel, and iron, and perceived the world in terms larger than the state. So today, modernization refers to states that have captured the Industrial Revolution, have built vast political, economic, and social institutions for living in a rapidly changing mechanical world, and have added the scientific view to other ways of perceiving life. As the present Industrial Revolution continues to unfold, the characteristics of modernization continue to change; for example, the computer age is now changing the way things are made (by the use of automation, which reduces the number of employees), the way mathematics is taught and learned, and the way knowledge is stored and research conducted. *See also* headings under DEVELOPMENT, pp. 103–113; ECONOMIC VIABILITY, p. 115.

Significance Modernization, though sought by every state in Africa, is terribly costly in terms of the great loss of lives, values, and traditions which occurs. As one scholar was noted, "modernity breeds stability, but modernization [the process of trying to become modern] breeds instability" (Huntington, 1968, p. 41). Another scholar stated the impact of modernization as follows: "Physical mobility released man from his native soil; social mobility liberated man from his native status; psychic mobility liberated man from his native self" (Lerner, 1959, p. 18). While modernization may look like freedom to the modernized, it may look like slavery to the traditionalist. The reasons are clear: Modernization means capturing advanced agriculture; urbanization; mass education; higher education; some form of industrialization; new commercial and financial institutions; efforts at national integration; changed local communities; the emergence of new elites and the downgrading of old; the emergence of centralized governments and the concomitant loss of local power; a penetrative bureaucracy; a monetary system; wage labor and labor unions; mass participation in public life, and so on. What one group gains in modernization another usually loses. And when the process of change is rapid or imposed, as in much of Africa, political instability results. (See Table B-6, p. 208.)

Multinational Corporation   A company that originates in one country and establishes branches in two or more foreign countries. MNCs (as they are often abbreviated) are important because of their proliferation since World War II, their wealth, and the number of foreign countries involved. To exclude small companies operating in a few countries, economists tend to define the MNC as a corporation operating in at least six countries and grossing at least $100 million a year. By this definition there are perhaps 4,000 MNCs operating in probably every noncommunist country in the world, and a few communist countries also. About one-half of all MNCs are of United States origin; the remainder are mostly of Canadian, European, and Japanese origin. About four-fifths of all MNCs operate in rich countries, and one-fifth have operations in Third World countries. MNCs open up operations in Third World countries because of easier access to raw materials, cheap labor, and new markets. Opposition to MNCs has been growing from many quarters. In the rich countries some governments complain that MNCs have become so large and powerful that they are independent forces in the world, not bound by national laws or patriotism but guided by universalist values and concerns. Labor unions in rich countries charge that MNCs export jobs and capital to the poor countries. In April 1974 the United Nations General Assembly condemned the Transnational Corporations (TNCs, the term preferred by the UN) for undue power and influence in developing countries. Poor countries have condemned the MNCs for reluctance in reinvesting their profits in the poor country where they were earned, and for co-opting the poor country's elites by involving them in MNC operations and thus dividing their loyalties between their country and the MNC. Marxist countries condemn them as greedy, money-grabbing devices of capitalist countries to steal the wealth of the poor. Finally, some scholars criticize MNCs for creating in poor countries islands of relative affluence in a sea of poverty. *See also* headings under DEVELOPMENT, pp. 103–113.

Significance Despite the broad condemnation of MNCs, they continue to be invited to set up production or distribution operations in Africa and other Third World areas. This is presumably calculated on the basis of relative benefits, i.e., that whatever harm is caused by the presence of MNCs is more than offset by the good. There is little doubt the MNCs do have effects in the countries where they operate, but some governments are learning to use the MNC for their own purposes. Richard Sklar (1975), in his study of MNCs in Zambia noted that copper mining, which was dominated by two MNCs, provided 60 percent of all government revenues and 95 percent of the total value of all exports. The rural areas were treated as a source of cheap labor, and there thus arose an area of modern technology surrounded by a stagnant rural economy. The government of Zambia finally decided to acquire a 51 percent ruling interest in order to use the MNCs for development purposes. Two new political interests resulted: The government joined with the companies against the mine workers' demands for higher pay in order to forestall similar demands in other sectors; but the government joined with the rural areas in promoting rural development and created a "community of interest" between the companies and mine workers, who saw any emphasis contrary to their interests as threatening. Many governments in Africa now attempt to gain at least a 51 percent ownership in the MNCs operating in their countries, to force the use of a high percentage of local citizens in managerial positions, and to require that some of the profits be reinvested locally.

Third World That portion of the world not committed to either the West (the so-called First World) or the Soviet bloc countries (the so-called Second World) during the period of the Cold War, revealed by professions of "neutralism" and "nonalignment." By the late 1970s the term Third World had come to be applied loosely to any poor, "southern" states and included some states (for example, Cuba, Afghanistan, Vietnam) aligned with the Soviet Union and some (for example, a number of Francophone states in Africa) aligned with France. Furthermore, China is usually excluded from the term, as are Israel and South Africa. *See also* headings under DEVELOPMENT, pp. 103–113; MODERNIZATION, p. 117.

Significance The term Third World is now used rather loosely to refer to the poor countries of the world outside of Europe and excluding China. Sometimes it seems to mean the same as "nonaligned." Some people also exclude Latin America from the term. Nevertheless, for most users of the term, it embraces all of Africa except South Africa. Even so, the term does not reflect any sense of commonality apart from the vague sharing of poverty. Furthermore, some countries rich from oil still are included in the term Third World. It therefore has all the imprecision of other terms that try to lump together some but not all of the countries of Africa, Asia, and Latin America.

8. Revolutionary and Counterrevolutionary Forces

African National Congress (ANC)—South Africa An organization formed in 1912 in the Union (now Republic) of South Africa by four Black lawyers who had studied abroad. One objective of the organization was to extend to the entire country the limited franchise that non-Whites in Cape Province held. Another aim of the ANC was to oppose all forms of discrimination based on race. The ANC grew gradually to 100,000 members by the 1950s. In 1952, the ANC chose as President-General, Albert John Luthuli (1889–1967)—Zulu chief, Christian, a follower of Gandhian nonviolence, and a man destined to win the 1960 Nobel Peace Prize. Luthuli and the ANC demanded "full democratic rights, with a franchise on the basis of universal suffrage"; full citizenship rights for all Africans; and a multiracial society. The procedure for protest was to be "in the spirit that revolts openly and boldly against injustice and expresses itself in a determined and nonviolent manner." In spite of the nonviolent character of the ANC, the organization was banned in 1960 and went into exile in Mozambique. There it has become more militant and violent, and engaged in guerrilla training and the smuggling of guns, bombs, and booby traps into South Africa. *See also* AFRIKANER, p. 35; APARTHEID, p. 35; BLACK CONSCIOUSNESS, p. 122; BOER, p. 39; GUERRILLA WARFARE, p. 126; ORGANIZATION OF AFRICAN UNITY, p. 157; PAN-AFRICANIST CONGRESS, p. 134; TERRORISM, p. 83.

Significance The ANC failed in its objectives from the beginning. Under White-established laws the limited franchise disappeared altogether, citizenship for Blacks was denied, non-Whites were forced to carry identification passes, a vast panoply of segregation laws were enacted, access by Blacks to land in their country was severely restricted, and, after 1948, the full edifice of *apartheid* laws was enacted. Passive resistance had no impact on Afrikaner decision makers. After the slaughter by police of 67 Blacks and the wounding of 186 others in Sharpeville (March 1960) and the subsequent banning of the ANC, the organization-in-exile gradually became violent, although it still espouses a multiracial society (in contrast to its offshoot, the Pan-Africanist Congress). The ANC-in-exile is currently led by the former advocate of nonviolence, Oliver Tambo. The ANC-in-exile has won financial support from liberal countries such as Sweden and the Netherlands, the Soviet bloc nations, and the Liberation Committee of the Organization of African Unity. Between 1979 and 1981, ANC guerrillas are reported to have clashed with police, attacked a police station in Soweto, caused $8 million damage to South Africa's coal-to-oil facilities, and blown up a power station. The importance of the ANC relates to its role in stimulating non-White opposition to the South African government and its *apartheid* policies, and in providing leadership for the liberation movement. Despite its failure to achieve its basic objectives, it continues the struggle.

Black Consciousness   A concept espoused in 1960 by Robert Sobukwe, founder of the Pan-Africanist Congress. Sobukwe was shortly thereafter sentenced to prison on Robben Island. He was freed in 1969, but remained a "banned" person until his death of cancer in 1978. While he was in prison, his concepts of Black Consciousness were defended by the South African Student Organization (SASO) led by the late Steve Biko. Biko couched the concepts of Black Consciousness in the terms of the Hegelian dialectic, that is, that White racism must be countered by Black racism. His words were: "Since the thesis is a White racism, there can only be one valid antithesis, i.e., a solid Black unity to counterbalance the scale. If SA [South Africa] is to be a land where Black and White live in harmony without fear of group exploitation, it will only be when these two opposites have interplayed and produced a viable synthesis of ideas and *modus vivendi*." The concept of Black Consciousness continues to be one of the issues that separates the Pan-Africanist Congress from the older African National Congress. As recently as 1977, ANC leader Oliver Tambo declared that the revolutionary movement in South Africa must adhere "to the principles and concepts of non-racialism." *See also* APARTHEID, p. 35.

Significance   Steve Biko was murdered by police, while in detention, on September 12, 1977. The White government then attempted to repress Black Consciousness. Only weeks after Biko's murder, SASO and 17 other Black organizations and one mixed organization were declared illegal; two Black newspapers and seven White ones were closed; 40 Black leaders were arrested; and a number of other people, including Whites, were banned. The killing of Biko and the subsequent harsh repression lend credence to the beliefs that Black Consciousness is spreading and a racial war threatens the White regime. On May 1, 1978, the Azanian People's Organization (AZAPO) was launched as a successor to the outlawed Black Consciousness groups. Azania is the name some Black nationalists prefer for South Africa.

Civil War A war fought within a country between two or more groups of people, usually from different geographical areas, ethnic backgrounds, or ideologies. The established government may be (and usually is) one of the groups, but in the absence of an established government the warring groups may be attempting to gain control of the society and establish a government. Where one group is the established government, the other group (or groups) seeks some political advantages that may range from special privileges (such as the right to be consulted or to appoint a particular official) to outright secession as an independent state. Unlike a coup d' etat, which is an elite phenomenon, a civil war involves a large proportion of the general population, especially in the regions of violence and in the areas of any antigovernment community. Civil wars are generally more costly for a country than international wars both in lives and economic losses. *See also* COMMUNAL INSTABILITY, p. 124; COUP D'ETAT, p. 125; INTERNATIONAL WAR, p. 155; MASS INSTABILITY, p. 129.

Significance Civil wars have occurred in the following African countries: Angola (1975–present); Burundi (1965); Chad (1965–present); Ethiopia (1955–present); Ivory Coast (December 1969); Nigeria (1967–70); Rwanda (1963–64); Sudan (1955–72); and Zaire (1960–63, 1967, January 1977, May 1978). No dissident group, however, has succeeded in toppling the established government or in gaining independence for itself. On the other hand, the southern Sudanese (Black, non-Arabic-speaking, and non-Muslim in contrast to the White, Arabic-speaking Muslims of the north) managed after 17 years of civil war to gain some autonomy for the southern provinces and to have Christianity recognized along with Islam as a religion of Sudan. In addition, English has been officially accepted as the language of the south. The struggle in Nigeria was the most notorious African civil war, and captured considerable world attention, partly because of the false charges that the Nigerian Federal Government intended to practice genocide on the dissident Igbo. The effort of Eritreans to gain independence from Ethiopia is now in its 27th year, and is thus the longest civil war. The efforts of the Polisario Front of Western Sahara to gain independence from Morocco is regarded by the Organization of African Unity (OAU) as an international war; Morocco, however, regards it as a civil war because it (Morocco) claims all of Western Sahara (the former Spanish Sahara).

Communal Instability Violence between ethnic groups or against government by a group identified by ethnic, linguistic, religious, historical, or other factors that set it apart. Communal instability differs from mass instability by its identification with a clearly defined community rather than with the general population. A civil war in which an ethnically defined group attempts to secede from the state (as the Igbo did in Nigeria's Civil War, 1967–70) is one form of communal instability. Another form is the rebellion in which a community seeks, through violence, some special relationship for itself with government. For example, between October 1964 and November 1967, the Lumpa Church of Alice Lenshina fought the government of Zambia for the right to practice faith healing and to forbid its members from participating in political affairs. The church was banned and, after many deaths, finally defeated. (Many of its members fled into exile in Zaire.) A third form of communal instability is known as *irredentism*, which is the effort to unite certain people and territory in one state with another on the grounds that they belong together. For example, in the present Somali-Ethiopian war, Somalia is trying to seize and incorporate the Ogaden area of Ethiopia and its Somali-speaking people. Interethnic violence that is not directed against government also constitutes a form of communal instability (as documented by violent clashes between Mende and Temne workers in Sierra Leone during December 1968). (Cf. Morrison, et al., 1972, p. 124.) *See also* CIVIL WAR, p. 123; COUP D'ETAT, p. 125; MASS INSTABILITY, p. 129; POLITICAL VIOLENCE, p. 134.

Significance Communal instability has been widespread in Africa. At least 37 cases of communal instability exist in at least 19 countries (See Table B-6, p. 208). Many factors account for the spate of communal instability: the revival of precolonial antagonism between groups; group frustration at what is perceived to be unfair treatment by government; group fears of being dominated by another group; group resentment at having its territory divided by colonial powers. Since the conditions that stimulate communal instability persist, continued communal violence can be expected.

Contagion Effect The emulation in one country of something that has already occurred in another. It is similar to the "domino thesis," a doctrine that maintains: If one country falls to a certain ideology, other nearby countries will also fall. In Africa the contagion effect is occasionally used to explain a rash of military takeovers. According to this view, if a military coup is successful in one country, military men in nearby countries will be tempted to overthrow their government.

Significance It is difficult, if not impossible, to demonstrate the contagion effect of military coups in Africa. Table B-6 on page 208 provides some clues. In the 10 years embracing 1952 through 1961 there were 7 coups or attempted coups, for an average of .7 per year. In the decade embracing 1962–71, the number increased to an average of 3.4 per year, and in the decade 1972–81, to 5.6 per year. However, it should not be concluded that previous successful coups inspired the later coups or attempted coups. While some coup leaders have claimed they were inspired by successful efforts in other states, the underlying causes for coups in most cases are found in general political instability. The increase in the number of coups per year is probably better explained by: (1) the increased number of states; (2) the political instability in many states; and (3) the fact that 10 states have had 3 or more successful coups, and 21 have had 3 or more successful or attempted coups, indicating that the greatest instability has occurred in a fairly large number of specific countries. Thus, the contagion effect, if it exists at all, operates only in selected states.

Coup d'Etat The overthrow or sudden alteration, usually by violence, of an existing government by a group of citizens. The term comes from the French and means "blow against the state"; it is often abbreviated simply to *coup*. A coup is always an elite activity in that it is staged by a small group with access to weapons or to military support. Coups tend to be divided into two types: military or palace. A military coup involves the seizure of government by military persons of any rank. A palace coup involves the seizure of government by people who are already ruling: They suspend the constitutional process and attempt to rule without restraints, which requires the acquiescence if not the approval of the military. Thus, in the palace coup, the ruler entrenches himself in power; while in the military coup, the coup makers remove the ruling executive either by killing, imprisoning, or exiling him or by refusing to let him return home if he is already outside the country (as happened in Ghana in 1966, Uganda in 1971, and Nigeria in 1975). Coup makers intend to run the government or appoint those who will run it. While perpetrators of coups d'etat may have radical, conservative, or reformist objectives, some seem to have no objectives other than the seizure of power. *See also* CIVIL WAR, p. 123.

Significance   The first coup d'etat in Africa (following World War II) occurred in Egypt when military men under General Naguib and Colonel Abdul Nasser ousted the king in 1952. The first coup in Black Africa occurred in Zaire, September 14, 1960. It was followed in the 1960s by coups in 13 African countries and by mid-1982, the total number of coups d'etat in Africa had reached 62 in 30 countries (see Table B-6, p. 208). Most coups in Africa have been of the military type, but palace coups have also occurred in Uganda (February 22, 1966), Lesotho (January 30, 1970), Swaziland (April 12, 1973), Seychelles (June 6, 1977), and Upper Volta (February 8, 1974).

Guerrilla Warfare   War waged by irregular groups against established governmental forces or occasionally against other irregular forces. Guerrilla warfare is usually fought in rural or isolated parts of a country by local inhabitants who know the terrain well. Guerrillas are often farmers or traders, indistinguishable from other indigenes; but at times, often at night, they come together to attack regular troops, to bomb buildings (such as police offices, power stations, and other government structures), terrorize a target community, or otherwise destabilize government. While guerrillas usually exist in remote and mountainous areas of their own country, they also often establish military bases in nearby countries friendly to their cause. They tend to survive by living in areas where they have the sympathy of the local people, who may feed them, keep them informed, and refuse to divulge information about them. Guerrillas hope to wear down their opponents' resistance by constant harassment of a "strike and run" nature. *See also* CIVIL WAR, p. 123.

Significance   Guerrilla warfare has become widespread throughout Africa. African National Congress guerrillas from South Africa now operate against South Africa from bases in Mozambique. Pan-Africanist Congress guerrillas operate against South Africa from Tanzania. Guerrilla bands now exist to fight the governments of Angola, Burundi, Chad, Djibouti, Egypt, Ethiopia, Libya, Malawi (formerly Nyasaland), Morocco, Mozambique, South Africa, Sudan, Tunisia, Uganda, and Zaire (formerly Belgian Congo) and possibly Central African Republic, Congo, Equatorial Guinea, Ghana, and Guinea. Guerrilla warfare seems to be an effective way of harassing a government and has contributed to vast changes, such as the liberation of Angola, Mozambique, and Zimbabwe. Some guerrilla movements, however, are quite small and seem unable to do more than keep the government alert.

Independence Movements Organizations formed to seek the independence of colonies from European rule. The French regarded their colonies as permanent, indivisible parts of France; the Belgians had vague concepts of ultimate independence in perhaps 200 or 300 years; and the British thought in vague terms that colonialism was temporary. World War II was the watershed after which independence movements emerged to challenge European colonialism. The independence of India in 1947 is often regarded as a catalyst for later movements. By 1950, in British West Africa, political parties had formed and were demanding independence as one of their goals. In fact, in Black Africa, the first successful independence movement was initiated by the Convention People's Party (CPP). The CPP, led by Kwame Nkrumah, won independence for Ghana in March 1957. Parties operating as independence movements were slower to form in French West Africa, although the Democratic Party of Guinea led by Sekou Touré won independence for Guinea in 1958. In the colonies of East and Southern Africa with White settlers, independence movements had to compete not only for independence for the colony but also against the demands for special privileges sought by the White settlers. In the Belgian Congo (now Zaire), the first significant independence movement did not make its impact felt till 1956, only four years before independence was actually granted. Clandestine independence movements began in Portuguese colonies in 1953 (Angola) and 1955 (Mozambique); after 1957, they emerged in Angola as the MPLA, FNLA, and UNITA, and in Mozambique as FRELIMO. Independence, however, was not won until 1975. SWAPO is an independence movement still operating in Namibia. For dates of independence of African states, see p. 204.

Significance After World War II independence movements spread throughout Africa. They sprang up in cultural or ethnic organizations, in newly formed political parties, in the cities, and among the educated. Surprisingly, the movements gained independence for most areas with little or no violence. The main locations for violence were in Algeria against the French; in Angola, Mozambique, and Guinea-Bissau against the Portuguese; and in Rhodesia (Zimbabwe) against the White settlers. The independence struggle in Namibia is still unresolved. Independence movements after World War II now appear to have been part of the vast movement to end the age of imperialism. They evolved as the means to pressure Britain, France, and the other colonial powers to grant independence quickly. Independence movements undoubtedly ended colonial rule earlier than the European powers had intended. In some cases, particularly in the Portuguese areas, they were critical in the achievement of independence.

Maoism   A version of Marxism, espoused by Mao Zedong (formerly written in English as Mao Tse-tung) of China, that stresses: internal self-reliance, the use of peasants in guerrilla warfare against colonial and capitalist regimes, the inevitability of armed struggle in producing social change, reliance on rural and peasant support in transforming society, a new international economic order, rejection of Soviet support for peaceful coexistence with capitalism, and emphasis in the early stages of social reconstruction on doctrinal purity (redness) over economic development (expertness). Maoism became the basis for open antagonism between China and the Soviet Union (the latter claiming a more accurate understanding of Marxism). It led China into conflict with the Soviets in the competition for support in the Third World. *See also* CHINESE POLICY IN AFRICA, p. 176; MARXISM, p. 74; SOVIET POLICY IN AFRICA, p. 185; THIRD WORLD, p. 119.

Significance   In Africa, Maoism has been remarkably benign. From their earliest contacts with independent Africa, the Chinese have seemed more interested in countering Soviet influence than in pushing doctrinal Maoism. They have not demanded doctrinal purity in supporting African causes. Chinese aid programs have been mainly economic, often accompanied by experts and skilled workers, and have benefitted conservative as well as radical states: Algeria, Cameroon, Egypt, Gabon, Gambia, Ghana, Guinea, Kenya, Morocco, Niger, São Tomé and Príncipe, Tanzania, Zaire, and Zambia. Under Mao, China supplied money and about 15,000 workers to build the Tan-Zam Railroad (known also as Tazara) from Dar es Salaam to Zambia. Following Mao's death, China sold military equipment to Egypt, after the latter broke relations with the Soviet Union. To counter Soviet support for the MPLA in Angola, China supported UNITA and FNLA and thus found itself on the side of South Africa and the United States. During the struggle for Zimbabwe, the Soviets supported Joshua Nkomo and ZAPU; China, in turn, supported Robert Mugabe and ZANU (p. 176). When Somalia and Sudan severed relations with the Soviet Union in 1977, China applauded. In fact, it is not clear what Maoism means in relation to Africa. Four years after Mao's death (1976), the Chinese were still invoking Mao to warn Africa of "Soviet socialist-imperialism" as "their gravest menace" (Legum, 1979, p. C 15). On the other hand, in contrast to Mao's insistence on continued armed struggle, China now stresses the importance of stability, apparently on the assumption that instability invites Soviet meddling. Furthermore, not even during Mao's ascendancy did the Chinese attempt to impose doctrinal purity in Africa even though it was a key precept in China. Finally, most leaders in Africa who deal with China cannot be said to be Maoist, and the few who may be, seem merely to be Marxists who lean toward China rather than the Soviet Union.

Mass Instability Violence against government involving elements of the general population seeking some change in policy, officeholders, or constitutional form. Mass instability differs from elite instability in which a small group with access to military force or the acquiscence of the military attempts to change government. It also differs from communal instability, which involves an ethnically or regionally defined group. Mass instability, therefore, involves a random or generalized distribution of interests in the society that seeks to change government by revolts and revolutions. An example of mass instability occurred in Sudan, October 20–30, 1964, when the judiciary and civil service called a general strike. Teachers and students joined the protest, and all began to fight the military. After 36 people had been killed and it appeared the revolt might spread, the military government abdicated. *See also* CIVIL WAR, p. 123; COMMUNAL INSTABILITY, p. 124; COUP D'ETAT, p. 125; POLITICAL VIOLENCE, p. 134; REVOLUTION, p. 135.

Significance In spite of its success in Sudan in 1964, mass instability (as defined here) in Africa has been rare and generally unsuccessful in attaining its goals. In Table B-6, p. 208, 20 cases of mass instability are identified as opposed to numerous cases of elite instability (in coups and attempted coups) and communal instability. This indicates that when members of the general population feel sufficiently frustrated with government and resort to force, they join with others with whom they identify ethnically or regionally rather than with the general citizenry.

Mercenary A person hired to serve in a foreign army, or one who for pay attempts by violence to influence a foreign political or military situation. Examples of the first definition include private American citizens who fought on the side of UNITA in Angola in 1974–75 for pay or men from southern Sudan who were hired by Uganda's Idi Amin to serve in his army in the 1970s. An example of the second definition was the group of 44 Whites, operating from South Africa on November 27, 1981, who tried unsuccessfully to overthrow the government of Seychelles. Mercenaries are generally despised because they appear to have no values apart from greed, glory, hatred, or love of adventure and danger. For these reasons, the term mercenary is used with considerable imprecision. An OAU report, for example, charged that the people who invaded the Benin airport in January 1977 were mercenaries composed of White men and citizens of Guinea and Benin who had been trained in Morocco and Gabon. The report does not identify the mercenaries' source of pay nor what interests they represented; the Benin government charged that they were in the pay, not of a government, but of an ex-president of Benin. The UN Security Council, in Resolution 419 of November 24, 1977, condemned the Benin invasion, also without connecting the invaders to any source of pay, although references to France, Ivory Coast, Togo, and Senegal (as well as Morocco and Gabon) turned up in the UN investigation. The whole episode is still largely a mystery. Bob Denard, the mercenary who led the attack, said later (August 1978) that the episode was not a coup attempt but a slap in the face of President Kerekou of Benin for having insulted President Bongo of Gabon. To confuse the concept of mercenaries further, China has charged that the Cuban troops in Angola are mercenaries in the pay of the Soviet Union. However, since they were regular troops in the Cuban army, they cannot accurately be described as mercenaries.

Significance Small groups of foreigners with unclear sources of pay have threatened African governments from time to time, notably Guinea (1970), Benin (1977), Togo (1977), and Comoros (1978). More traditionally defined mercenaries, however, were hired to defend colonial regimes in the Portuguese territories, and the White government of Rhodesia hired mercenaries to try to stave off majority rule. Mercenaries were also used by Zaire (formerly Belgian Congo) in its early years of turmoil (1960–65), and by both sides in Nigeria's civil war. Most (but not all) mercenaries operating in Africa have been Whites, and this has led African governments to suspect that the home governments of the mercenaries were clandestinely supporting their nationals in efforts to delay independence, overthrow some African governments, and/or support racism in the southern part of the continent. Probably the two most notorious mercenaries are the Frenchmen Bob Denard (also known as Gilbert Bourgeaud), who appears to be prospering in Comoros (whose President owes his office to Denard's overthrow of the previous president), and Col. Mike Hoare, who, after earlier notoriety in Zaire, led the abortive attack (from South Africa) on Seychelles in 1981.

Militarism A theory, belief, or practice, often called "praetorianism," in which the armed forces seek to influence or dominate the political life of a country. Militarism has a very weak theoretical base, and in almost every case it is better understood by examining the practices of military men than in searching for philosophical statements. What the practice shows is that many military men believe they have a duty to do more than defend the state; they claim a right to defend a particular form of government. In this light, they may seek to influence governmental decisions or even to exercise a veto over them. In its extreme form, militarism is demonstrated by the behavior of armed forces personnel in overthrowing a government and then either (1) installing a government favored by the military rulers or (2) running the government directly. Why militarism occurs is not agreed upon by scholars. Political analysts hold that it results from (1) the natural contempt army officers have for politicians; (2) the glorification of violence; (3) the low level of political participation in the general public; (4) the failure of democratic principles to "take hold" in a society; (5) the absence of any effective counterbalancing forces to the army (such as public opinion, respect for law, a powerful church, or a possessive ideology); and (6) chaotic social conditions that only an armed force can control. *See also* COUP D'ETAT, p. 125.

Significance   Militarism has spread throughout Africa since 1952. Since World War II, 27 countries have been subjected to military rule. Military seizures of power have generally been justified by the perpetrators on the grounds that the deposed rulers had become corrupt, incompetent, insensitive to popular interests, or neglectful of modern needs. While some instigators of military rule have been high-ranking officers, others have been middle-level officers, and some have even been noncommissioned officers (as in Liberia in 1980). Military rule is quite vulnerable because the principle that justified the original military takeover can be invoked by any nonruling military group to stage its own overthrow. Consequently, many countries have endured a series of military regimes (see Table B-6, p. 208). The prevalence of military rule in Africa is partly explained by two interrelated facts: governments are weak, and armies, no matter how small, represent the only disciplined force. These factors also help to explain the ease and frequency of military coups.

Militarism: Development Thesis   The theory or belief that military intrusion into politics is directly related to the stage of political, economic, or social development. The argument proffered by the development thesis is that states that attempt to develop rapidly are more prone to military rule than those (as in Western cultures) that develop more slowly. Thus, in the early stages of rapid change, political participation is low, public consensus on change is weak, effective political parties capable of reflecting and compromising interests are weak or nonexistent, and traditional values and behaviors are constantly challenged and shattered. In such a context, the thesis argues, there is a high likelihood that military people, being the only organized, well-armed group, will intervene to eliminate what they regard as intolerable politics. Thus, the thesis suggests that low levels of political participation and consensus are correlated with high levels of military intervention. Conversely, as societies attain higher levels of political participation and consensus, the incidences of military intervention should decline. The thesis does not argue that military regimes are able to develop a society politically and economically; it claims only that when politics fails the army is likely to intervene. *See also* MILITARISM, p. 130; MILITARISM: GUARDIAN THESIS, p. 132.

Significance The development thesis of militarism seems to offer an explanation for the spate of military governments in Africa. Every instance of military intervention has occurred in a country attempting to deal with the issues of rapid development. This may, however, be merely a temporary fit between theory and political condition. Recently in Latin America a number of military interventions occurred in the most developed countries (Argentina, Brazil, Chile, and Uruguay), considerably weakening the development thesis. Thus, military intervention in Africa may not be related primarily to stages of political or economic development, but perhaps to the guardian thesis or the fact that military forces are better organized than governmental institutions. The development thesis is weak also in not dealing with the question of how political development is to occur if the military prohibits experience in politics. Furthermore, since military rule is conceived as temporary, the thesis is faulty in not offering an explanation as to when and under what circumstances military regimes should relinquish power to civilians again.

Militarism: Guardian Thesis The theory or belief that the proper role of the army is to defend the constitutional system from violations by either the civilian rulers or revolutionary groups. Under the guardian thesis, the military, especially high-ranking officers, claim to know what the constitutional system is and what violates it. Thus officers (rather than political competition, political parties, the electoral process, legislators, the judiciary, or the executive branch) become the guardians of the system, able at their discretion to intervene and set things right. The thesis maintains that military intervention should be brief and that government must be returned to civilians as soon as possible. *See also* MILITARISM, p. 130; MILITARISM: DEVELOPMENT THESIS, p. 131.

Significance The guardian thesis has been used in Africa during every military coup that was justified on the grounds that its purpose was (1) to eliminate political corruption or (2) to restore true democratic government. These two reasons have been used more frequently than any others to justify military coups against civilian governments. However, those coups designed to change the political system (as in Egypt, 1952; Libya, 1969; or Ethiopia, 1974), or the overthrow of one military group by another (as in Benin, Dec. 1965; Ghana, 1979; or Nigeria, July 1966) could not be explained by the guardian thesis. In the first case, the purpose was to destroy not preserve the established system, and in the second, the situation involved conflicts between military groups (rather than military agreement on a guardian role). The guardian thesis is weak in that it cannot explain what in the training of officers uniquely equips them to be the guardians of the political system.

Military Rule Government by military personnel (1) who acquire the power to rule by a coup d'etat or, in the case of an international war, by defeating the armed forces of a state, and (2) who maintain their military identification while ruling. Under military rule the top official in the government may be designated by some title that reflects his military role as, for example, Chairman of the Provisional Military Administrative Council (Ethiopia), Head of the Supreme Military Council (Ghana, 1975–79), Chairman of the Military Committee for National Salvation (Mauritania), President of the Supreme Military Council (Niger), or Head of the Federal Military Government (Nigeria, 1966–79). Others may attempt to cloak the military connection by such appellations as Head of the People's Redemption Council (Liberia) or President of the Supreme Revolutionary Council (Madagascar). Still others hide the military connection altogether and use the simple title of president, such as: Algeria, Burundi, Congo, Equatorial Guinea, Mali, Rwanda, Somalia, Sudan, Togo, Uganda (1971–79), Upper Volta, and Zaire. In Libya, Colonel Qaddafy calls himself General Secretary. While military rule always means that military men, in control of the coercive might of the army, are the ultimate makers of government policy, it need not mean that military personnel man every important office. Although military officers may serve as ministers of government, and be appointed to head parastatals (such as government-owned railroads), universities, or special commissions, the more common pattern is for the military rulers to appoint civil servants to run most government offices and to select ex-politicians to head offices that entail intimate contacts with the general population. By these means, military rulers seek to gain popular acquiescence or even support for their rule.

Significance Twenty-seven African states have, since 1952, come under military rule for a time. Some military rulers have eventually turned government back to civilians (Nigeria, Ghana, Sierra Leone), while others have attempted to politicize the military rule itself and to develop nonmilitary symbols for their rule (as in Egypt) in hopes of changing the system gradually from a military to a civilian one. The major pattern, however, seems to be indefinite incumbency, primarily because it is easier for the military to take over a civilian government than it is to create one. In addition, once military rule begins, there is a natural reluctance for the officers involved to give up their prerogatives and perquisites of office.

Pan-Africanist Congress (PAC) An organization in the Republic of South Africa that broke away from the African National Congress in 1958. Led by Robert Sobukwe, the Pan-Africanist Congress emphasized blackness rather than multiracialism, a Pan-African nation rather than the South African nation, and greater militancy than had been used by the ANC. Sobukwe called for work stoppages and asked Africans to burn their identification passes. He called for a mass rally on March 21, 1960, to stage a collective burning of passbooks. At Sharpeville, police shot into the crowd and killed 67 people and wounded 186. (Even though he was not part of the PAC, Chief Luthuli of the African National Congress burned his card when he heard of the slaughter.) In April of that year, the government banned the PAC along with the ANC. The PAC went underground and also began to operate in exile in Botswana. Sobukwe was sent to the infamous Robben Island prison in 1960, was released but "banned" in 1969, and died of cancer in 1978. *See also* AFRICAN NATIONAL CONGRESS, p. 121; AFRIKANER, p. 35; APARTHEID, p. 35; BLACK CONSCIOUSNESS, p. 122; BOERS, p. 39; GUERRILLA WARFARE, p. 126; ORGANIZATION OF AFRICAN UNITY, p. 157.

Significance The Pan-Africanist Congress-in-exile has engaged in training guerrillas and staging sabotage and terrorist raids into South Africa. Its leadership, however, has remained seriously divided. Although the Liberation Committee of the Organization of African Unity recognizes the PAC as a liberation force, it has received little support from African leaders except Qaddafy of Libya and, until his ouster in 1979, Amin of Uganda.

Political Violence Action by an individual, a group, or a government that inflicts damage on people for political purposes. The methods of political violence include: assassination, massacre, torture, destruction of property, incarceration, terror, riots, rebellions, strikes, coups d'etat, civil wars, and revolutions. Political violence is used by individuals and groups in order to influence and/or control government, and by governments in order to maintain control.

Significance The extent of political violence in Africa is partially revealed in Table B-6, p. 208. Not shown in the table are plots, conspiracies, alleged coups d'etat, demonstrations, secret arrests, mutinies, and political imprisonment. The existence of political prisoners has become widespread in Africa. A political prisoner is a person not otherwise guilty of violating law who is arrested on suspicion that he/she opposes the government, has spoken against the government, or may in the future oppose the government. The number of political prisoners in Africa is unknown and may range from fewer than a dozen or so in a country like Zambia to a few hundred in Guinea or a few thousand in Libya. Amnesty International, in the last ten years, has documented the existence of political prisoners in Cameroon, Central African Republic, Equatorial Guinea, Ethiopia, Guinea, Kenya, Liberia, Libya, Mali, Morocco, Sierra Leone, Somalia, South Africa, Tanzania, Zaire, and Zambia. Some political prisoners, sometimes called prisoners of conscience, are merely detained indefinitely without charges or trials, but in some countries (e.g., Libya, Mali, South Africa, Uganda, and Zaire) political prisoners have been tortured, bayonetted, clubbed, or shot to death. A new element of political violence has shown up in a 1980 report of Amnesty International, which documented cases involving 17 African states where refugees were forcibly returned home and then were arrested, tortured, or murdered while in custody (Legum, 1981, p. A98).

Revolution A major transformation of political, economic, and/or social principles and institutions in a state resulting from the overthrow of an established political system. A vast transformation that occurs without a political overthrow of government (as when many states in the past 100 years changed from agricultural to industrial societies) is not usually called a revolution, but an example of evolution. The major models for political revolution in the modern world are the American (1776), French (1789), and Russian (1917) Revolutions. A revolution, unlike a coup d'etat, has considerable support from the general population and involves ideological commitments on the part of the revolutionaries for major changes in the holders of governmental powers, the structure of government, and the purposes and goals of government.

Significance In one sense, all African states are revolutionary. Every society that has changed from a colony to an independent state has undergone a major transformation, although in Africa the overthrow of European rule in most cases was so free from violence that some analysts question whether the process was revolutionary at all. In fact, many of the states now under indigenous rulers have simply continued policies initiated by the colonial power (e.g., Ivory Coast), and therefore the term *revolution* seems somehow inappropriate. Many leaders do not consider their regimes revolutionary even though the change from colonial to independent status meets this definition. On the other hand, all states in Africa born of violence claim to be revolutionary. Other states not born of violence, but which have adopted socialist goals, regard themselves as revolutionary (although in Africa, capitalist goals are just as revolutionary and can be just as transformative of society). The term *revolution* becomes vague in such contexts because leaders, without any overthrow of government, simply evolve new goals that are then labeled revolutionary. Julius Nyerere's 1977 Constitution specifically states that the leadership goal is "to bring about a socialist revolution in Tanzania." In a parallel development in 1977 in Libya, the General People's Congress stated that it "confirms the march of the revolution led by Col. Muammar al-Qaddafy, the revolutionary leader, toward complete People's Authority" (Legum, 1979, p. C111). Thus, it is possible in Africa to claim that the revolution has already occurred by the transformation from colonial to independent status and that the revolution involves merely a transfer of rulers; it is equally possible to say that the revolution is an on-going process of social transformation led by elites with a vision and blueprint for methods to achieve it.

Secession Withdrawal of a people and the territory they occupy from a state to form an independent state or to join another state. People attempt to secede from a state in order to chart their own destiny and establish or maintain their own beliefs, language, and customs or to join others who share them. They seek to be ruled by members of their own group or from their own region. They may also attempt to secede in order to establish a different kind of political or economic system. Civil wars usually stem from secessionist objectives. Secessionist movements that have resulted in violence occurred in: the Katanga (now Shaba) region of Zaire (formerly Belgian Congo), the southern region of Sudan, the Igbo ("Biafra") region of Nigeria, the Eritrean region of Ethiopia, the Ogaden region of Ethiopia, the Ewe region of Ghana, the Agni region of Ivory Coast, the Somali region of Kenya, and the western region of Uganda. *See also* COMMUNAL INSTA-

BILITY, p. 124; CIVIL WAR, p. 123; GUERRILLA WARFARE, p. 126; POLITICAL VIOLENCE, p. 134.

Significance The fear of secession probably haunts African leaders more than anything else. In sub-Saharan Africa, few states are free from the threat of a secessionist movement. No secessionist movement has yet succeeded in its objectives, largely because state leaders have moved swiftly to suppress them and have garnered the support of other African leaders. The belief exists that if just one existing state is torn apart by a successful secession, it may portend the dissolution of many other states. In such an eventuality, chaos and suffering on an unprecedented scale would sweep through the continent.

9. Intra-African Law, Organization, and Relations

African Defense Force A proposed military organization for Africa. At the inaugural meeting of the Organization of African Unity (OAU) in 1963, President Kwame Nkrumah of Ghana proposed an "African High Command to ensure the stability and security of Africa." He added that the only way Africa could be a nuclear-free area independent of foreign military intervention was by creating "a common defence force with a common defence policy." In spite of Nkrumah's plea, the Charter of the OAU failed to provide for a defense force, and merely pledged its members' "cooperation for defence and security." Since the founding of the OAU, numerous proposals have been made to set up some kind of common security or defense force, presumably to deal with liberation problems and to replace foreign troops now in Africa dealing with intra-African conflicts. No progress has been made to date on setting up such a collective security system. *See also* ORGANIZATION OF AFRICAN UNITY, p. 157; POLITICAL SECURITY COUNCIL, p. 161.

Significance The concept of an African defense force faces the same objections as collective security forces in the United Nations: In a world of sovereign, independent, territorial states, common values, interests, and goals must be very closely shared before states will agree to create a force uncontrolled by them individually. African states are no more united in their common dealings with the world about them than are other members of the UN. Some Francophone states welcome French troops on their soil, while other African states welcome Cuban and Soviet forces, and still others eschew all foreign military involvements. Ideological commitments divide the continent on many issues where a common defense force might operate, e.g., in the Morocco-Polisario conflict. No state is willing today to commit its forces in advance to deal with some unforeseen conflict, for example, a clash between socialist and capitalist states. Inability to agree on some common defense force and policy, however, means that individual states will continue to pursue their own defense policies, which will likely also continue to involve extra-African countries.

President Julius Nyerere in 1978 reported that some European states were discussing the possibility of helping Africa set up a Pan-African security force. He angrily denounced the move as nothing more than the attempted "domination of Africa," a "new insult to Africa and Africans." Either Africa will set up its own peace force "or there will be no Pan-African force." He supported the idea of an African high command but then lamented that: "It is highly unlikely that the Organization of African Unity meeting [in July] at Khartoum will be able to agree unanimously on the creation of such a military force, or—if it did—that it would be able to agree unanimously on which countries to ask for support if that was needed." President Nyerere's lamentations capture the essence of the problems associated with a common defense plan for Africa.

African Development Bank (ADB) A multilateral, regional bank set up in 1964 to promote economic development in Africa. Headquartered in Abidjan, Ivory Coast, the bank was sponsored by the UN Economic Commission for Africa. All African states except South Africa are members. The original authorized capital stock was $250 million, but has grown to $1.2 billion. However, paid-up subscriptions by 1980 were only $300 million, stemming from the inability of many African states to pay their subscribed share. Although African states had wanted to keep the bank exclusively African, they have now agreed to admit non-African members (under rules that retain African domination of decisions). *See also* ARAB BANK FOR ECONOMIC DEVELOPMENT IN AFRICA, p. 175.

Significance Like all regional banks, the ADB was formed to promote regional interests through loans to support specific projects. Most loans, about 90 percent, have been made to support programs in transportation, new industries, and local banks, agriculture, power, water supply, and sewerage systems. By having their own regional bank, African leaders can make decisions on what is to be supported, based on African interpretation of needs. However, as many as 22 non-African countries may now join since membership was opened. This may mean more capital, but it may also mean, in spite of the best intentions of African members, non-African influence on decisions.

Boycott Refusal by one country to buy products from another country, or internally, refusal to buy products from a company or business. Internationally, a boycott may be instituted by a government that refuses to grant import licenses for products from the boycotted country, or it may be private with individuals refraining from buying products from the boycotted country. Individuals may also boycott specific companies (such as Nestlé) rather than all products from a country. See also BYRD AMENDMENT, p. 175; EMBARGO, p. 148.

Significance Africa's concern for the use of the boycott was revealed at the Addis Ababa meeting in 1963, which created the Organization of African Unity (OAU). The conferees passed a resolution unanimously that: "*Asks for an effective boycott* of the foreign trade of Portugal and South Africa by (a) prohibiting the import of goods from those two countries; (b) closing African ports and airports to their ships and planes; (c) forbidding the planes of those two countries to overfly the territories of all African states." In 1965–66, African states persuaded the United Nations to boycott all products from Rhodesia. A universal boycott can be devastating for the boycotted country. The boycott on Portugal and South Africa has never been universal, so it has had only minimal impact. The boycott on Rhodesia was nearly universal and is believed by many to have played a significant role in bringing down the White regime there. Because of its success in Rhodesia, African states are pressuring the United Nations to place a boycott on South Africa, with the hope that it will not only bring a resolution to the Namibia issue but to *apartheid* also. African states themselves have placed a boycott on sports events involving South African teams, and most other countries of the world cooperate with the boycott in various ways. Ironically, however, despite a continent-wide boycott (except for neighboring states) of trade with South Africa, that country exports more and more food and manufactures every year to independent African states. It is known, for example, that South Africa is the largest supplier of goods to Botswana (formerly Bechuanaland), Lesotho (formerly Basutoland), Malawi (formerly Nyasaland), Mauritius, Mozambique, Swaziland, and Zimbabwe (formerly Southern Rhodesia), and is a major source of foreign goods for Zaire (formerly Belgian Congo) and Zambia (formerly Northern Rhodesia). South Africa itself claims to sell to 47 independent African states but refuses to divulge the names. In contrast to international boycotts, South Africa has also begun to face internal boycotts of some importance. In 1980–81, Black students, parents, teachers, churches, and social organizations staged a boycott against segregated schools and sporting events. During the boycotts, 50 people were killed and 1,000 arrested. Indications are that this may only be the beginning of the massive use of the internal boycott against the White regime.

Coordinating Committee for the Liberation Movements of Africa (African Liberation Committee or ALC) A committee established in 1963 at the founding of the Organization of African Unity (OAU) to support liberation movements by providing them financial and military aid. A headquarters was established in Dar es Salaam with a secretary-general. The original members of the committee were Algeria, Egypt, Ethiopia, Guinea, Nigeria, Senegal, Tanzania (formerly Tanganyika and Zanzibar), Uganda, and Zaire (formerly Belgian Congo). The OAU designated May 25 as African Liberation Day. It also stipulated that member states would receive "nationalists from liberation movements" in order to give them training "in all sectors" (Article I, section 14 of OAU Resolutions, 1963). In 1963 the Algerian guerrilla movement had just won a long battle for independence from France. However, Portugal had reiterated its determination to hold on forever to Angola, Mozambique, and Guinea-Bissau; South Africa offered no encouragement for the early independence of Namibia; and while independence for Malawi (formerly Nyasaland) and Zambia (formerly Northern Rhodesia) seemed imminent, that for Zimbabwe (formerly Southern Rhodesia) seemed quite remote. Besides these areas, another dozen islands and enclaves were under colonial rule with little planning for their ultimate independence. In setting up the Liberation Committee, therefore, the OAU members were stating a commitment to use violence to erase the last vestiges of intransigent colonialism on the continent. *See also* AFRICAN NATIONAL CONGRESS, p. 121; GUERRILLA WARFARE, p. 126; INDEPENDENCE MOVEMENT, p. 127; PAN-AFRICANIST CONGRESS, p. 134.

Significance In 1963, African states were by no means in agreement on the question of encouraging violence. Influential leaders like Kwame Nkrumah of Ghana and Tom Mboya of Kenya supported the concepts of nonviolence espoused by Mahatma Gandhi. By 1963, however, India had taken Goa by force and the Algerians had used violence to drive out the French. These victories plus the intransigence of Portugal and South Africa turned the tide in favor of armed violence. The Front for the Liberation of Mozambique (FRELIMO) began to operate out of southern Tanzania in 1963 and continued its fight until victory was won in 1975. In Angola, three major groups formed to fight for independence: the Popular Movement for the Liberation of Angola (MPLA), the National Front for the Liberation of Angola (FNLA), and the National Union for the Total Independence of Angola

(UNITA). In 1964 the ALC threw its support behind Holden Roberto, leader of the FNLA, but switched in 1974 to supporting the MPLA, led by Agostinho Neto, because South Africa gave aid to FNLA. As the Zimbabwean denouement unfolded, the Liberation Committee supported both factions of the Patriotic Front, one led by Robert Mugabe and one by Joshua Nkomo. Today, the ALC supports the fight of the South West African People's Organization (SWAPO) for Namibian independence. As the noose has tightened around South Africa, support is now being given to the African National Congress and the Pan-Africanist Congress, both guerrilla movements seeking to overthrow the White-dominated government. In the Western Sahara, the Liberation Committee supports the Polisario against Morocco. It refuses, however, to support the Eritrean fight for independence from Ethiopia, on the grounds that existing states must not be dismembered. The shift from nonviolence to violence has paid off so far for the OAU, although there is now some apprehension that as South Africa is backed into a corner the conflict there may break out into a major, possibly racial, war.

Diplomatic Relations The act whereby two states recognize each other and exchange diplomatic personnel. By establishing diplomatic relations with another state, a government intends to communicate with it by exchanging persons with designated diplomatic ranks. The highest-ranking diplomat is known as an ambassador (or if sent from the Vatican, a papal legate or nuncio; or between Commonwealth countries, a high commissioner); below the ambassador are (1) the envoy extraordinary, minister plenipotentiary, and papal internuncio; (2) minister resident; and (3) chargé d'affaires. Ambassadors and ministers are accredited from one head of state to another, whereas the chargé d' affaires is accredited to the foreign minister. The official residence abroad of an ambassador is an embassy, of a minister a legation. Diplomatic relations provide a personal link between the chief executives of two countries. The diplomat abroad becomes the eyes and ears of his country for observing and reporting on matters of peace and war, on matters of mutual interest between the two countries, and on matters of economic, political, military, or social interest to his government. He is also the voice of his government to the host government, constantly alert to represent his government's position on any and all issues in international relations. In order to protect diplomatic personnel, a body of diplomatic privileges and immunities has been developed in international law. Thus a country, to assure the security of its own diplomats and their records abroad, grants privileges and immunities to foreign diplomats and their records. The privileges and immunities include freedom from arrest (for any offense) and from search and seizure of any records. (Iran's violations of these privileges by making hostages of diplomatic personnel in 1979–81 won it world disapproval.) If a diplomat misbehaves, the only recourse a host government has is to declare him *persona non grata* (unacceptable) and order him to leave. However, since governments value diplomatic relations with others, they are usually careful to send discreet, prudent persons abroad to represent their interests. See also INTERNATIONAL LAW, p. 150; THIRD WORLD, p. 119.

Significance Because diplomatic relations provide valuable information about the world, African states, on gaining independence, moved to take advantage of this old practice. However, the expense of opening an embassy abroad and staffing it with up to a few dozen people is very great for poor countries. Consequently, African states have been selective in establishing diplomatic relations (see Table B-7, p. 214). Of the approximately 165 states in the world (including the Vatican) only Algeria, Egypt, Ethiopia, Nigeria, and Tunisia have established relations with at least 100 of them. At the other end of the scale are São Tomé and Príncipe, Equatorial Guinea, and Comoros, which have diplomatic relations with 31, 26, and 24 states respectively. South Africa has only a few more at 37, which is not due to the heavy expenses of maintaining embassies abroad but to its pariah status. It has relations with only one African state, Malawi (formerly Nyasaland), and has no relations with any Second World state and few with non-African Third World states. Table B-7 also shows that about one-third of the diplomatic relations of African states are with other African states; about 30 percent with First World states; about 17 percent with Second World states; and almost 20 percent with the other (non-African) Third World states. In June 1982, Ghana announced it was closing one-fourth of its embassies, including those in Uganda and Zambia (formerly Northern Rhodesia), because of costs. Other states may follow suit as their economies worsen. Many African states utilize their United Nations delegations to negotiate agreements and carry on other forms of diplomatic activities as a means of keeping costs down.

Domestic Jurisdiction The power or authority recognized by international law for a state to define and regulate certain conditions and activities exclusively by its own laws. Domestic jurisdiction is specifically recognized as a principle by the United Nations in Article 2, paragraph 7 of the Charter: "Nothing contained in the present Charter shall authorize the United Nations to intervene in matters which are essentially within the domestic jurisdiction of any state or shall require the Members to submit such matters to settlement under the present Charter; but this principle shall not prejudice the application of enforcement measures under Chapter VII." The Charter, however, does not define domestic jurisdiction. This means that each state may declare what is in its domestic jurisdiction unless the international community rules otherwise. All states jealously guard their right to define citizenship and passionately reject any attempt of outsiders to intervene in what they claim to be a matter of domestic jurisdiction. Nevertheless, the UN has passed resolutions condemning the way South Africa defines and treats its citizens, leading some people to argue that certain types of mistreatment of citizens come under *international* rather than domestic jurisdiction. When the Security Council placed an embargo on sales of arms to South Africa in 1977 because of its "violence against the African people," it based its authority to deal with this matter on Chapter VII of the Charter, which deals with threats to the peace. As noted above, the domestic jurisdiction clause specifically grants the United Nations the right to intervene in matters of domestic jurisdiction when Chapter VII conditions exist. Thus, at least in the case of South Africa, the way a state treats its citizens is no longer a matter of domestic jurisdiction. Nevertheless, states unanimously proclaim that some matters belong to their domestic jurisdiction, such as the type of government they prefer, the leaders they have, the economic systems they follow, their definition of citizenship, their interpretation of human rights, and in general all social and economic matters. Even so, the South African embargo now provides precedent for the principle that *any* activity inside a state that is regarded as a threat to the peace may cease to be a domestic matter and come under international jurisdiction, at least if the permenent members of the Security Council agree. *See also* BOYCOTT, p. 141; EMBARGO, p. 148; INTERNATIONAL LAW, p. 150; INTERNATIONAL ORGANIZATION, p. 152; INTERVENTION, p. 156; ORGANIZATION OF AFRICAN UNITY, p. 157; REFUGEES, p. 162.

Significance African states have been as devoted to the principle of domestic jurisdiction as other states. Although the Charter of the Organization of African Unity (OAU) does not use the words "domestic jurisdiction," the second principle on which it is founded is the "non-interference in the internal affairs of states." Like the UN Charter, the OAU Charter does not define "internal affairs." In practice, however, the African states have made it clear that racism and colonialism are not matters of "internal affairs," and they have thus freely intervened in states over these matters. They were not in agreement, on the other hand, on whether Idi Amin's internal terrorism was a matter of domestic or international jurisdiction, and many condemned

Tanzania for invading Uganda and removing Amin. Furthermore, African states made no move to stop the Tutsi genocide of Hutu in Burundi in 1972, or the mass slaughter of hundreds of thousands of citizens under Macias Nguema in Equatorial Guinea and Jean-Bedel Bokassa in the Central African Republic. Nor have African states moved to condemn internal conditions that have forced millions of people to flee their homes as refugees. Thus, except for conditions they define as racist or colonial, African states (like others) make no effort to restrict a state's treatment of its own citizens. Devotion to the principle of domestic jurisdiction helps to explain why little progress has been made internationally on questions of human rights.

East African Community (EAC) The now-defunct organization created by Kenya, Tanzania (formerly Tanganyika and Zanzibar), and Uganda on June 1, 1967, to coordinate communications, finance, commerce, industry, and social and research services. Actually, these functions had been performed since 1961 (before independence) as the East African Common Services Organization, and the EAC seemed but an auspicious development for continuing the earlier intimate association. All three states had been ruled by Britain, and by independence several interterritorial institutions were already in place. So promising were the prospects, including the possibility of bringing in other East African states, that the treaty of 1967 was signed for 15 years. Ironically, the EAC tore apart by December 1977. Part of the difficulty was political: Idi Amin of Uganda was anathema to Julius Nyerere of Tanzania, and Jomo Kenyatta of Kenya barely tolerated him. But economic factors were the main cause for the dissolution. Kenya's superior manufacturing capacity gave it advantages over its two partners. Kenya emphasized capitalistic, while Tanzania emphasized socialistic norms. Under Amin, Uganda's economy became less and less viable. Suspicions became more and more open. Finally, in January 1977, the jointly-owned East African Airways failed and was grounded. In February, Nyerere charged that Kenya treated Tanzania and Uganda as poor relations, and then in a dramatic move closed the border between Kenya and Tanzania (largely because tourists were going to Nairobi and visiting Tanzania from there on one-day excursions that benefitted Kenya much and Tanzania little). By the end of 1977, commonly owned units in each country were incorporated into the national economy and the EAC died. *See also* AFRICAN-CARIBBEAN-PACIFIC COMMUNITY, p. 172; ECONOMIC COMMISSION OF WEST AFRICAN STATES, p. 147; INTERNATIONAL ORGANIZATIONS, p. 152; ORGANIZATION OF AFRICAN UNITY, p. 157; REGIONALISM, p. 163.

Significance The experience of EAC dramatizes the difficulty of meaningful regional cooperation of basically poor states that are at uneven levels of development. Each to a large extent was competing for national advantage in each area. Political and ideological factors were always at the front. The goodwill and trust necessary for intimate cooperation, even among older states, often are generations in building, and such cooperation among newly independent, highly nationalistic, and suspicious states would have been unusual. Personal animosities among Amin, Kenyatta, and Nyerere merely exacerbated the situation. The challenge for other regions seeking close cooperation is to see if they can learn from the failure of ECA.

Economic Community of West African States (ECOWAS)

An organization formed by a treaty signed in Lagos in May 1975 to promote trade, self-reliance, and cooperation in West Africa. All 16 West African states belong. The organization consists of the Authority of Heads of State and Government, which meets annually, the Council of Ministers, which meets as needed, a tribunal to interpret the treaty, and an executive secretary. Headquarters is in Lagos. The first concerns of ECOWAS have been trade liberalization, a transportation network, currency convertibility, industrial and agricultural cooperation, and the prospects for a common defense pact. *See also* AFRICAN-CARIBBEAN-PACIFIC COMMUNITY, p. 172; INTERNATIONAL ORGANIZATIONS, p. 152; ORGANIZATION OF AFRICAN UNITY, p. 157; REGIONALISM, p. 163.

Significance ECOWAS is the boldest effort to date in Africa to effect regional cooperation on a grand scale. In some ways, West Africa seems an unlikely candidate for close relations. With 16 states, it is the largest of any region. Half of all the people live in Nigeria, a feared and distrusted giant to many of the other states. In fact, Nigeria provides one-third of the ECOWAS budget, and controls 60 percent of the trade in the region and two-thirds of the GNP. Nine of the 15 countries are French-speaking, and most of them are closely involved in organizations among themselves or with France that are competitive with ECOWAS. Five of the remaining states are English-speaking, and two are Portuguese-speaking. ECOWAS emerged, however, because Nigeria continued to press for it and because Francophone states, especially Senegal, began to realize that some kind of cooperation among these 16 interlocked states could be ultimately beneficial to all. The African-Caribbean-Pacific Community (ACP), furthermore, had thrown Francophone and Anglophone states together in what looked like potential advantages. Mutual suspicions may continue for some time, but if ECOWAS begins to show some successes, and Nigeria continues to avoid intervention in other states' affairs, then this organization may become a model for other regions of Africa.

Embargo A government edict prohibiting citizens from trading with another country. An embargo may be applied to certain goods, such as arms, or it may apply to all goods. The objective of an embargo is to inflict enough pain on the target country that it changes its behavior to a form more suitable to the embargoing countries. *See also* BOYCOTT, p. 141.

Significance From the time of independence, most African states have embargoed all sales to South Africa, and until recently, to Portugal and Rhodesia. African sales to South Africa have never been large enough to have much of an impact on that country. Consequently, the OAU began a campaign in 1970 to pressure the United Nations to call for an embargo against South Africa of all goods or at least all arms sales. A voluntary embargo had been approved as early as 1963. Finally, on November 4, 1977, the Security Council (with the approval of all the permanent members, China, France, the United Kingdom, the United States, and the Soviet Union) agreed to a mandatory embargo of all military arms to South Africa. Secretary-General Kurt Waldheim called it an historic occasion, the first time ever that the UN had taken action under Chapter VII of the Charter, dealing with threats to the peace. African states thus have precipitated a bold new venture for the UN, but it is doubtful that it will be important in resolving the crisis in South Africa. The embargo has been largely a failure. There was evidence that in 1980 such odd accomplices as the United States, the Soviet Union, India, France, Denmark, South Korea, and Botswana (formerly Bechuanaland) were all involved in arms trade with South Africa in violation of the embargo. Furthermore, there was evidence that the embargo, far from weakening or coercing South Africa, had driven it to greater self-sufficiency. It now produces armored cars, tanks, planes, mortars and medium artillery, patrol boats, heavy-armor steel, chemical weapons (including teargas and napalm) and most types of ammunition, bombs, fuses, and propellants. On the grounds that many countries violate the embargo and that South Africa has now become self-sufficient, President Reagan's Assistant Secretary of State for African Affairs, Chester Crocker, recommended in 1981 that the United States not sever all ties with South Africa in the field of nuclear cooperation (see Legum, 1982, pp. B806–07). Thus, it is possible that the embargo has contributed to making a more powerful South Africa.

Front-Line States The five African states (Angola, Botswana, Mozambique, Tanzania, and Zambia) regarded as being on the "front line" in the struggle to bring about an independent Zimbabwe (formerly Southern Rhodesia) under Black majority rule. Front-line presidents began meeting in 1976 and agreed on certain principles in dealing with the Rhodesia/Zimbabwe struggle, namely that Britain should continue to rule the area as a colony until majority rule was guaranteed, and that the two guerrilla armies (one led by Robert Mugabe, the other by Joshua Nkomo) must continue to cooperate. Often joined by Nigeria (as the great power in Africa), the front-line states maintained a basically solid front on these principles until independence for Zimbabwe was won in 1980.

Significance The intransigence of the front-line states is regarded by many as (1) forcing the rival guerrilla factions to cooperate and thus focus their activities on the White regime, and (2) maintaining a solid front that was able to wear down the regime to the point that it yielded on the major demands of Blacks. Based on that success, the OAU in June 1980 recognized another group of front-line states related to Namibia (namely Angola, Botswana, Mozambique, Zambia, and Zimbabwe) by calling on all peace-loving states to assist those states in their "struggle against the racist Pretoria regime."

Homelands in South Africa Areas in South Africa set aside as "independent states" for Black ethnic groups. The White government in South Africa, rather than attempt to integrate its various peoples, decided in 1959 that "Bantu peoples" formed separate nations and ought to have their own states. The government began thereafter to designate reserved areas that would then gradually become independent nations. About 13 percent of South Africa, much of it very poor land, was set aside for over 70 percent of the population. Ten separate Homelands (or Bantustans as they were once called) were envisaged for what were regarded as ten distinct Black nations. The objective of the White rulers was reiterated in 1978 when the new Minister of Plural Relations (formerly Bantu Administration) asserted that when the resettlement into Homelands is completed, "there will no longer be a Black man in SA who has South African citizenship." Blacks were thus defined as foreigners in their own land. Blacks who refuse to migrate to "their" Homeland can be forced to go (if the White community does not have some use of their work). The first Homeland was Transkei (composed of Xhosa), declared "independent" by South Africa on October 26, 1976, followed by Bophuthatswana (composed of Tswana) on December 6, 1977, Venda (composed of Venda) on September 13, 1979, and Ciskei (composed of Xhosa) on December 4, 1981. *See also* APARTHEID, p. 35.

Significance Not a single country in the world has recognized the so-called independent states created by South Africa. The United Nations Security Council has said that the pronouncements of independence were totally invalid. The Organization of African Unity (OAU) has regularly condemned the concept of independence as spurious. Black South Africans are rejecting the concept of Homelands more than ever, and movements have been formed to stop the appearance of any more of the targeted "states." If no state in or outside of Africa recognizes the independence of so-called Homelands, then their status as independent states is tenuous. If Black South Africans can stop the further spread of these peculiar creations, then White South Africa will surely be forced to reconsider the entire operation. So far, the existence of these "Homelands" has made little or no contribution to racial harmony in the country. In any case, these entities are not yet part of the world of independent, sovereign states because they are merely creations of, and controlled by, the dominant White minority of South Africa.

International Law The system of rules on the rights and duties of states in their mutual relations. International law is based on the concept that all states are independent, sovereign, and equal and that they create law in their interactions with each other. All states seem to agree that any treaty they sign binds them to observe it, and treaties, therefore, constitute a source of international law. The United Nations, in setting up the International Court of Justice, states that besides treaties three other sources of international law exist: (1) international custom, (2) "the general principles of law recognized by civilized nations," and (3) judicial decisions and the teachings of "qualified publicists" of the various nations. The UN Charter, furthermore, lists seven principles that control the organization, principles that are presumed to be international law since the Charter is itself a treaty, thus binding all members. The principles assert (1) the sovereign equality of all members; (2) that all members will observe the obligations spelled out in the Charter; (3) that all members will settle their international disputes peacefully; (4) that all members will refrain from the use of force against the territorial integrity of any state; (5) that all members will assist the UN when it is taking preventative or enforcement action; (6) that the UN may force nonmembers to comply with these principles; and (7) that nothing in the Charter permits the UN to intervene in the domestic affairs of any state except in taking enforcement measures under Chapter VII. *See also* ORGANIZATION OF AFRICAN UNITY, p. 157.

Significance International law has not loomed large in African international relations. In fact, unlike the United Nations' Charter, international law is not mentioned in the Charter of the Organization of African Unity (OAU). The OAU Charter, however, in its preamble, does affirm adherence to the principles of the UN Charter as well as the principles of the Universal Declaration of Human Rights. But the OAU also listed seven principles, three of which differed considerably from the UN (see p. 158 for a description of the OAU principles). The OAU principles condemned all forms of international support for political assassinations; declared absolute dedication to the emancipation of all colonies in Africa; and asserted the principle of nonalignment. There may yet be one principle not mentioned above which is superior to all others, namely, opposition to all racism. In fact, the African states may be in the process of building a hierarchy of international law customs that control only African states. The hierarchy appears to involve these standards: (1) the illegality of all racism; (2) the illegality of all colonialism; (3) the sanctity of boundaries inherited at independence; and (4) the right of self-determination to peoples. Opposition to racism is more important than opposition to colonialism, as was shown when African states demanded that Britain reseize Rhodesia when the White regime declared it independent; or when South Africa's incursions into Angola were condemned by the OAU as racist aggression but no condemnation followed the Somalia aggression on Ethiopia or Tanzanian aggression on Uganda (the distinction between the first and the second two being the matter of race). Africans do not hesitate to intervene in the internal affairs of South Africa, even to supporting anti–South African guerrillas, presumably on the grounds that racists have no rights. Further down in the hierarchy, opposition to colonialism is more important than the right of self-determination, as shown by OAU resolutions demanding that Mayotte be joined to Comoros in spite of the overwhelming (99 percent) preference of Mayotte's population to remain joined with France, a right granted to Mayotte's population in Article 76 of the UN Charter. Respect for national boundaries is more important than the right of self-determination as shown by African support for Ethiopia against the Eritrean demands for independence. The right of self-determination, however, *is* supported for the Polisario against claims by Morocco that it ought to control the former Spanish Sahara (that is, the Polisario claim does not dismantle an existing state). Thus, international practice and custom may be building for Africa an international law that downgrades the principle by which African states themselves became independent, namely the right of self-determination. Finally, the international law recognized by African states may not be the same as that recognized by the rest of the world.

International Organization A formal structure transcending national boundaries setting up an institution capable of making decisions and carrying on day-to-day activities. Public international organizations are formed by treaties between or among states, such as the Charter of the United Nations or the Charter of the Organization of African Unity. Private international organizations are formed by agreement between or among national private organizations, such as Rotary International, and are known as Non-Governmental Organizations (NGOs). International organizations arose in the West in the late nineteenth century to permit two or more independent states to pursue some common aim without requiring national leaders always to be present. Such common aims might be the operation of a customs union or a canal or a bank. International organizations have flourished since World War II, there now being probably a few thousand in the world. *See also* ECONOMIC COMMUNITY OF WEST AFRICAN STATES, p. 147; ORGANIZATION OF AFRICAN UNITY, p. 157; REGIONALISM, p. 163.

Significance International organizations have become very important for African states. The varieties of African involvement in such organizations can be seen in the following breakdown of types, purposes, and membership.

Universalistic International Organizations
1. United Nations Organization, created to promote world peace. All 51 independent African states belong.
2. UN-created organizations:
   a) Economic Commission for Africa (ECA), to facilitate African economic development.
   b) Food and Agricultural Organization (FAO), to promote training, research, and experimentation in food production.
   c) International Bank for Reconstruction and Development (IBRD or World Bank), to make loans to finance capital and other investments.
   d) International Development Association (IDA), to make loans on bases more generous or more flexible than the World Bank.
   e) International Finance Corporation (IFC), to encourage private enterprise.
   f) United Nations Development Program (UNDP), to create local organizations for capturing wealth through better use of human and natural resources.

g) United Nations Educational, Scientific and Cultural Organization (UNESCO), to advance educational, scientific, and cultural relations.
h) United Nations High Commissioner for Refugees (UNHCR), to promote the welfare of refugees (see p. 162).
i) World Health Organization (WHO), to promote health.

International Organizations with Mixed African and Non-African Memberships

1. African Development Bank (ADB, see p. 140).
2. Arab Bank for Economic Development in Africa (BADEA, see p. 175).
3. Arab League, to promote the cause of Arab-speaking peoples (see Africa and the Middle East, p. 169). Membership includes the states of the Middle East plus the African states of Algeria, Djibouti, Libya, Mauritania, Morocco, Somalia, Sudan, and Tunisia.
4. The Commonwealth, to facilitate consultation and expression of views among certain states related to British colonialism. African states constitute the largest bloc of members and include Botswana (formerly Bechuanaland), Gambia, Ghana (formerly Gold Coast), Kenya, Lesotho (formerly Basutoland), Malawi (formerly Nyasaland), Mauritius, Nigeria, Seychelles, Sierra Leone, Swaziland, Tanzania (formerly Tanganyika and Zanzibar), Uganda, Zambia (formerly Northern Rhodesia), and Zimbabwe (formerly Southern Rhodesia). *See also* ANGLOPHONE AFRICA, p. 173.
5. European Economic Community (EEC), to promote development needs especially by permitting agricultural goods from the African, Caribbean, and Pacific states (ACP, see p. 172) to enter EEC markets duty free. Membership includes the 10 states from Europe plus 63 ACP states. Forty-three sub-Saharan states belong, whose entry was facilitated by the first Lomé Convention in 1976 and the second Lomé Convention in 1981.
6. The Franc Zone, to provide convertible currency. Besides France, 13 Francophone states (see p. 180) belong: Benin, Cameroon, Central African Republic, Chad, Comoros, Congo, Gabon, Ivory Coast, Mali, Niger, Senegal, Togo, and Upper Volta.

International Organizations with Exclusively African Membership

1. African and Mauritian Common Organization (OCAM), to promote economic, social and technical development. Membership includes Mauritius and Rwanda and the former French colonies of Benin, Central African Republic, Ivory Coast, Niger, Senegal, Togo, and Upper Volta.
2. Customs and Economic Union of Central Africa (UDEAC), to promote customs and economic cooperation. Membership includes the

former French colonies of Cameroon, Central African Republic, Congo, and Gabon.
3. Economic Community of West African States (ECOWAS, see p. 147).
4. Entente Council (Conseil de l'Entente), to promote economic coordination. Membership includes the former French colonies of Benin, Ivory Coast, Niger, Togo, and Upper Volta.
5. Niger Basin Authority, to promote the development of the Niger River area. Membership includes Benin, Cameroon, Chad, Guinea, Ivory Coast, Liberia, Mali, Niger, Nigeria, Sierra Leone, Togo, and Upper Volta.
6. Organization for the Development of the Senegal Basin, to promote the development of the Senegal River area. Membership includes Mali, Mauritania, and Senegal.
7. Organization of African Unity (OAU, see p. 157).
8. Southern African Development Coordination Conference (SADCC, see p. 166).
9. West African Economic Community (CEAO), to promote trade and regional economic cooperation. Membership includes the former French colonies of Ivory Coast, Mali, Mauritania, Niger, Senegal, and Upper Volta.

At least 100 other international organizations have partial or exclusive African memberships. They are concerned with such varied subjects as timber, livestock, education, professional associations, arts, religion, health, transport, and others. While some are bilateral, most are multilateral in membership. It can thus be seen that international organizations are beginning to play a role in Africa, stimulated among other things by the desire to gain strength by joining with others. It must be emphasized, however, that African involvements with international organizations are overwhelmingly economic in focus; all leaders are wary of anything that might restrict political freedom.

International Relations   The relations among states. International relations includes bilateral as well as multilateral relations. It deals with areas as complex as international law and international organizations. It includes foreign policies, treaties, diplomacy, regional interests, and wars. It embraces, literally, all the myriad ways that states of the world can and do deal with each other. *See also* DIPLOMATIC RELATIONS, p. 143; INTERNATIONAL LAW, p. 150; INTERNATIONAL ORGANIZATION, p. 152; INTERNATIONAL WAR, p. 155; INTERVENTION, p. 156.

Significance African states at independence joined the world of international relations. They joined the United Nations and began to work in its numerous agencies. They formed their own regional organization, the Organization of African Unity (OAU). They established diplomatic relations with many states, primarily on the basis of their concept of national interest and the ability to pay, but (except for Malawi) refrained from establishing relations with South Africa. They formulated foreign policies, and then sought ways to coordinate them so as to give them added weight. Constituting about one-third of the membership of the United Nations, African states try as often as possible to vote as a bloc and thus shape UN resolutions. They sign friendship treaties, fight wars, intervene, and promote peace as other states do. African states today are fully engaged in the international relations of the world, as fully engaged as they want to be or can afford to be.

International War War between two or among three or more independent states. International war differs from a civil war in that in the former organized national forces are fighting each other while in the latter the protagonists may be a national army against a break-away army or even irregular forces, or may entail conflict between irregular forces seeking to gain control of an area. It is not always easy, however, to distinguish between the two types of war. Morocco claims that the Polisario resistance in Western Sahara constitutes a civil war in the territory claimed by Morocco, while the Organization of African Unity (OAU) regards it as an international war between two states, Morocco and the Republic of Sahrawi (as the Polisario movement calls the former Western Sahara). *See also* CIVIL WAR, p. 123; POLISARIO FRONT, p. 160.

Significance Numerous international wars, some quite brief, have occurred in Africa. One study in 1972 (Morrison, et al., 1972, p. 156) found that 140 acts of external aggression had occurred in Africa by 1965, although this terminology did not require evidence of the actual use of violence. Some government-directed border clashes occurred between Ghana (formerly Gold Coast) and Togo (1957–63) over Ewé irredentism; and between Somalia on one hand and Ethiopia and Kenya on the other sporadically during the 1970s over Somali irredentism. A four-day war was fought by Libya and Egypt (July 21–24, 1977). Border clashes have been reported from time to time between Algeria and Morocco, and between Gabon and Equatorial Guinea. Full-fledged international wars were fought between Ethiopia and Somalia, February 1977–March 1978; and between Tanzania and Uganda, November 1, 1978–May 29, 1979. Given the number of states in Africa and the elite dissatisfaction in many of them with their boundaries, it is surprising that so few international wars have occurred.

Intervention An act by one state that attempts to influence internal developments in another state. Intervention is condemned by all states, yet few states will refrain from intervening in other states when their interests call for it. Some states have been known to try to influence the outcome of elections in other states, but most intervention is much less blatant and comes about by the condemnation by leaders of one state of actions that occur in another. Sometimes leaders will refrain from openly condemning other governments but induce the government-controlled media to do so. The ultimate intervention is the use of force. If the government, however, welcomes or invites the foreign intrusion, as with Cuban troops in Angola and Ethiopia, or Libyan troops in Chad in 1979, most scholars do not regard this as intervention (see Aluko, 1981). *See also* BOYCOTT, p. 141; EMBARGO, p. 148; INTERNATIONAL LAW, p. 150.

Significance The Charter of the Organization of African Unity (OAU) was founded on the principle of "non-interference in the internal affairs of states," and supported as well the United Nations' condemnation of intervention. Nevertheless, African states have constantly intervened in racist and colonial situations, not only by verbal denunciation but by overt support for guerrilla violence against states that are recognized members of the world community. On issues involving racism and colonialism, African states have been almost universal in their assertion of the right to intervene, a right also practiced by other states in the world in defense of their interests as defined by themselves. Other kinds of intervention include the criticisms by many states of the ties former French colonies maintain with France, and criticisms of Malawi (formerly Nyasaland) because it continues to trade with South Africa. Military intervention by African states includes the invasion of Ethiopia by Somalia, of Uganda by Tanzania, and of Chad by Libya.

Lusaka Manifesto A statement issued by the Organization of African Unity (OAU), meeting in Lusaka, Zambia, in 1969, dealing with African objectives in southern Africa. The Manifesto asserted that the opposition of African states to the various administrations in southern Africa was not because the rulers were White. Rather: "We are hostile to them because they are systems of minority control which exist as a result of, and in the pursuance of, doctrines of human inequality. What we are working for is the right of self-determination for the people of those territories." The Manifesto then proclaimed that: "We are not talking racialism when we reject the colonialism and apartheid policies now operating in those areas...."

Significance The Lusaka Manifesto had at least five objectives: (1) to make it clear that African leaders were not anti-White and thus racist in their opposition to *apartheid*; (2) to make it equally clear that Whites born and raised in southern Africa were also Africans and entitled equally with other Africans to live there; (3) to leave no doubts in the eyes of the world what African hopes and intentions for southern Africa were; (4) to appeal to the rest of the world, particularly to democratic regimes, to join them in pursuing just goals; and (5) to urge international cooperation in removing the scourge of *apartheid* peacefully before it broke into open violence. Unfortunately, the Manifesto was basically ignored for a decade, by which time nonpeaceful moves to change the conditions in southern Africa were well under way. In the meantime, however, the United States Secretary of State, Henry Kissinger, while visiting Lusaka on April 25, 1976, publicly accepted the principles of the Lusaka Manifesto. His acknowledgment heralded the belated efforts of the Western nations to deal with the Zimbabwean (p. 167) and Namibian (p. 182) questions.

Organization of African Unity (OAU) The organization formed in Addis Ababa by 30 African states on May 25, 1963, to promote African interests. As Black African states began to gain their independence after 1957, it appeared that they might gravitate to two antagonistic poles in defining intra-African interests. One bloc of states became known as the Casablanca Group as a result of a conference held in the Moroccan city in January 1961. Pushed largely by President Kwame Nkrumah of Ghana (formerly Gold Coast), this bloc affected a radical stance and spoke strongly of the need for political unity in Africa. Members of this bloc were the provisional government of Algeria, Egypt, Ghana, Guinea, Mali, and Morocco. The second bloc met in the Liberian capital in May 1961 and became known as the Monrovia Group, embracing 19 states. Its leaders were President Tubman of Liberia, Prime Minister Balewa of Nigeria, and Emperor Haile Selassie of Ethiopia. This bloc was regarded as more conservative and emphasized economic cooperation rather than political unity, as well as noninterference in internal affairs, and respect for territorial boundaries. Thus, the Addis Ababa meeting called for some compromises, but managed finally to get the support of both groups.

The principles of the OAU Charter reflect primarily the interests of the Monrovia Group: the sovereign equality of all states; noninterference in the internal affairs of states; respect for the sovereignty and territorial integrity of each state; peaceful settlement of disputes; condemnation of political assassination and subversive activities in other states; dedication to the independence of all African territories; and nonalignment with any blocs. The Charter sets up machinery for a continuing organization: an Assembly of Heads of States and Governments; a Council of Ministers; and a General Secretariat. After signing the Charter, the conferees at Addis Ababa then passed a number of resolutions pleasing to the Casablanca Group, particularly the resolutions to set up a coordinating committee to support liberation movements on the continent (see p. 142), and supporting nonalignment. Other resolutions condemned *apartheid*, called for independence for existing colonies on the continent, supported general disarmament, and agreed to set up a committee to deal with economic barriers. Only three independent African states failed to attend the conference: Morocco because of the presence of Mauritania, which Morocco claimed; Togo because of its suspicions that President Nkrumah had been involved in the January 1963 assassination of Togo's President Olympio; and South Africa because it was not invited. *See also* AFRICAN DEFENSE FORCE, p. 139; GUERRILLA WARFARE, p. 126; INTERNATIONAL ORGANIZATION, p. 152; POLISARIO FRONT, p. 160; POLITICAL SECURITY COUNCIL, p. 161; UNILATERAL DECLARATION OF INDEPENDENCE, p. 167.

Significance Fifty states (all of the independent states except South Africa) are now members of the OAU. Since its founding, the OAU has created a number of commissions, committees, and organizations: the Arbitration Commission; the Scientific, Technical and Research Commission; the Coordinating Committee for the Liberation Movements of Africa (p. 142); the African Civil Aviation Commission; the Organization of African Trade Union Unity; the Pan-African News Agency; the Pan-African Postal Union; the Pan-African Communications Union; the Supreme Council for Sports in Africa; the Union of African Railways; the Center for Linguistic and Historical Studies by Oral Tradition; the Joint Regional Food and Nutritional Commission for Africa; the Economic, Social, Transport and Communications Commission; the Education, Science, Culture and Health Commission; the Defense Commission; the Labor Commission; and the Commission on Refugees. It has supported liberation movements, including guerrilla activities, which led to the independence of Angola, Mozambique, and Zimbabwe, and continues to support guerrillas fighting for the independence of Namibia.

With almost unanimous agreement, OAU members tend to vote as a bloc in the United Nations on issues involving South Africa. They excluded South Africa from the Economic Commission for Africa (ECA) and UNESCO, and (except for vetoes cast by the United States, Great Britain, and France) would have expelled South Africa from the United Nations. They have spearheaded a drive for an arms embargo against South Africa and are attempting to get UN approval for a complete boycott of the country. The OAU is now supporting the African National Congress and the Pan-Africanist Congress as guerrilla movements aimed at transferring rule in South Africa to the majority.

In 1980, the OAU held the first African Economic Summit devoted to the idea that Africans have to solve their own economic problems rather than depend on the goodwill of others. It adopted the "Lagos Plan of Action," which envisages by the year 2000 self-sufficiency in food, the formation of regional economic communities to be followed by an African Economic Community, and internally self-sustained economic development. Also in 1980, the OAU circulated for ratification the African Charter on Human and People's Rights. The Charter was prompted by the recognition that, while OAU members had been quick to condemn violence, torture, and murder when committed by Whites in southern Africa, they had remained silent when these same violations of human rights were committed by members of the OAU.

In spite of these accomplishments, the OAU has faced a number of failures. In 1965 only ten states carried out the OAU resolution to break relations with Great Britain over its refusal to take action on the Unilateral Declaration of Independence by Rhodesia. It was sharply divided in 1976 over the question of whether to support the MPLA in Angola, and finally won a majority support for that faction only after South Africa intervened on the opposing side. The OAU has been helpless in dealing with the serious problems related to the conflict between Ethiopia and Somalia, the Nigerian Civil War, the war between Morocco and the Polisario, the Libyan occupation of Chad, the Shaba invasions in Zaire, the split between the two factions in the Patriotic Front in Zimbabwe, and Tanzania's invasion of Uganda. Because it has no enforcement machinery, the OAU is especially weak in dealing with violence between states. While some of the factions in the OAU are due to the differences between militant and conservative states, others are due to the differences between Black and Arab-speaking states. While Black African states support Ethiopia in its conflict with Somalia as well as its civil war with Eritrea, all of the Arab-speaking states except Libya support Somalia and Eritrea. Further, many Black African states are now threatening to reestablish ties with Israel, broken off as a gesture of friendship for the Arab states (and also in hopes of getting financial help from the oil-rich Arab states).

The greatest challenge to the survival of the OAU, however, occurred in 1982 and had not been resolved as this book went to press. The immediate cause of the rift was the Morocco-Polisario war. By February 1982, 26 members (a bare majority of the 50-member OAU) had recognized Polisario. This led the OAU Secretary-General, Edem Kodjo (of Togo), to admit Polisario to membership without a formal vote of the organization. Morocco and 18 others objected to this act as unconstitutional and stated their intention to boycott any OAU meeting at which Polisario representatives would be present.

The nineteenth annual meeting of the OAU was scheduled to meet in Tripoli, Libya, on August 5, 1982. Only 28 heads of state attended, 6 short of a quorum, thus aborting the meeting. Those who boycotted the meeting said it was because of the presence of representatives of Polisario. Other reasons given, however, included the reluctance of some leaders to attend a meeting in which, by custom, the host, Colonel Gaddafy, would automatically be chosen as chairman of the OAU for 1982–83.

A second major effort was made in November 1982 to hold the summit meeting, but it also failed to gain a quorum. Numerous heads of state voiced a further displeasure, namely, their anger at Colonel Qaddafy for refusing to allow Chad's new president, Hissene Habré, to attend. No resolution is obvious at this time, and the future of the OAU is uncertain. In the meantime, President Daniel Arap Moi of Kenya, elected chairman for 1981–82, continues as the spokesman of the organization.

Polisario Front   Acronym for the Spanish term *Frente Popular para la Liberacion de Sakiet el Hamray y Rio de Oro* (Popular Front for the Liberation of Sakiet el Hamray and Rio de Oro), a guerrilla organization operating in Western Sahara. The Western Sahara, a phosphate-rich territory of about 50,000 people, was formerly a Spanish colony known as Spanish Sahara. In 1974 Spain announced its intention of withdrawing from its colony. Morocco and Mauritania each reiterated its claim to the area, and in September 1974 agreed to partition Western Sahara between them. In 1973, however, Polisario had been formed to seek independence for the territory. In October 1975, the International Court of Justice rejected the claims of both Morocco and Mauritania. Morocco then sent troops across its border into the disputed territory. Spain, in haste, signed an agreement with Morocco and Mauritania on November 14, 1975, granting the area to the two claimants, which they immediately partitioned as agreed upon. Polisario rejected these moves, and guerrilla warfare began. In February 1976, Polisario declared the formation of the Saharan Arab Democratic Republic (SADR). Algeria became the main backer of Polisario, supplying it great quantities of arms and sanctuary as needed within its borders. By 1978 Polisario brought Mauritania to its knees, and the latter renounced all claims to the southern part of the area. Morocco continues to press its claim, and battles rage frequently between the guerrillas and the Moroccan army. By mid-1982, neither camp seemed able to win an outright victory, and neither was ready to compromise. *See also* ORGANIZATION OF AFRICAN UNITY, p. 157.

Significance The question of independence for the Western Sahara has seriously divided Africa. As early as February 1977, the OAU had recognized Polisario as a legitimate guerrilla movement. By July 1980, a bare majority of OAU members recognized Polisario as the government of SADR. However, when Morocco and other states threatened to walk out if SADR were admitted to membership, the decision on admission was postponed. In February 1982, a crisis in the OAU occurred when its secretary-general decided to seat the SADR representatives. Morocco and 18 members of the OAU left in protest. The crisis stems from two things: the questionable legality of the way the Polisario representatives were seated, and the strong feelings on the two sides over the conflict between Polisario and Morocco. A bare majority of the OAU (26 members) supports Polisario, while at least 19 support Morocco. While the OAU may be threatened by such divisions, the worst threat may be Big Power confrontations. Russian tanks are now flowing through Algeria to Polisario camps, while American equipment is being used by Morocco. No resolution of the conflict is in sight.

Political Security Council A new agency of the Organization of African Unity (OAU) proposed to be created by amending the Charter. The Political Security Council would have extraordinary powers to bind members on policy, particularly those related to threats to the peace. The concept of a security council has been raised frequently in the OAU but has failed to win much support. Those who support the idea model their proposals after the Security Council of the United Nations, which has a membership smaller than the total membership of the organization, can meet quickly to deal with emergencies, and has powers to bind all states in certain circumstances. The proposal has little chance of being implemented because the African states disagree over its composition and powers. *See also* AFRICAN DEFENSE FORCE, p. 139; ORGANIZATION OF AFRICAN UNITY, p. 157.

Significance The proposed Political Security Council in the OAU has foundered on the question of representation. The large states insist that they must be permanent members of any such council, and most of the large states also insist that they be granted a veto power. Thus, the same characteristics that cripple the UN Security Council, but protect the Great Powers from majority resolutions, block African efforts to set up more powerful machinery in the OAU.

Refugees Persons who flee from an area to escape some danger. The danger may be some natural catastrophe (such as drought) but more likely is internal political conflict and occasionally foreign incursion into the refugee's country. Refugees, by fleeing their own state, place themselves at the mercy of some alien state and government. If they are lucky, they may be cared for in settlement camps, but in Africa most are left to fend for themselves. Many countries of asylum in Africa are among the world's poorest and consequently hardly able to shoulder the extra burden of refugees. The problem is exacerbated if the host government and the country from which the refugee flees attempt to maintain friendly relations, because governments often regard refugees as fugitives.

Significance It is now certain that the greatest refugee problem of recent times is occurring in Africa, the worst since World War II and overshadowing even the plight of the "boat people" of Southeast Asia. Half of all refugees in the world are African. Yet it is a problem that most of the world has ignored. African governments, however, have been aware of the problem since the OAU established an *ad hoc* Commission on Refugees in 1963. But even African governments mistakenly assumed at first that refugees were primarily the products of White-minority governments in southern Africa. In the 1970s it became clear that while some refugees were fleeing Sahelian drought, and some were fleeing White-minority regimes, most were fleeing Black governments, and Black-minority regimes as in Burundi. The greatest number of refugees were escapees from the conflicts in the Horn, Chad, Burundi, Rwanda, Sudan, and Zaire (formerly Belgian Congo). While there is no doubt about the seriousness of the problem, the exact number of refugees is unknown. In 1981, estimates varied from three to six million. The Emergency Committee for African Refugees of the Phelps-Stokes Fund of New York in 1982 estimated that ten countries each harbored over 100,000 refugees as follows: Ethiopia, 1,811,000; Somalia, 1,540,000; Zimbabwe, 660,000; Sudan, 490,000; Zaire, 400,000; Uganda, 377,000; Cameroon, 266,000; Burundi, 234,000; Tanzania, 150,000; and Nigeria, 110,000. Another eight countries (Angola, Algeria, Djibouti, Zambia, Gabon, Rwanda,

Swaziland, and Lesotho) grant asylum to numbers ranging from 73,000 down to 10,000.

The problems of dealing with refugees are especially complex in Africa. For example, a country like Zaire harbors an estimated 400,000 refugees and needs help in caring for them. On the other hand, Zaire is itself the home from which an estimated 250,000 refugees have fled to neighboring states. Another complexity arises from the fact that many refugees engage in guerrilla activities against their home government from the sanctuary of the host country. The OAU has now agreed that refugees are prohibited from using arms except when attacking White-minority-ruled countries. Another problem that has recently come to light is the fact that many states are forcing refugees back to their country of origin, where they are being imprisoned, tortured, and murdered. Amnesty International documents cases for 17 member-states of the OAU. In April 1981, the Organization of African Unity and the United Nations High Commissioner for Refugees jointly sponsored the International Conference on Assistance to Refugees in Africa to try to find solutions to this grave world tragedy. Forty-five countries pledged financial support, over half coming from the United States, but the amount pledged is a mere fraction of need. The Soviet Union and Eastern European countries boycotted the conference. In 1967 the OAU established the Bureau for the Placement and Education of African Refugees but found that a decade later the Bureau had consumed millions of dollars and helped few refugees. An investigation by the OAU in 1978 attributed the failure to incompetence and mismanagement. If Africa is unable and the world is unwilling to solve the African refugee problems, and if political instability continues to increase, then it can be expected that the numbers and plight of refugees will mount. (See Legum, 1982, p. A94–103; and *African Research Bulletin*, Vol. 18, No. 4 [April 1–30, 1981], p. 6010.)

Regionalism   A consciousness and loyalty to a distinct area smaller than the whole. If Africa is perceived as a whole, then regionalism involves any portion of it that is smaller than the entire continent and associated islands. Since Africa is the second largest continent, filled with great diversities of peoples, experiences, and values, regionalism must probably be regarded as a natural development. Scholars have thought of Africa in regional terms for decades, using for purposes of analysis such terms as Central (p. 3), East (p. 3), Indian Ocean (p. 7), North (p. 8), Southern (p. 15), and West (p. 17). Africans also have thought in regional terms for a number of reasons and objectives. The French (see p. 180) and English (see p. 173) languages have been the bases for some regional groupings. The Arabic language and Islam provide the basis for the Arab League (p. 169). Geographical contiguity explains such organizations as ECOWAS (p. 147) or SADCC (p. 166). Historical and colonial ties explain a regional organization like the Southern African Customs Union, to which Botswana (formerly Bechuanaland), Lesotho (formerly Basutoland), Swaziland, and South Africa belong and from which all benefit. In the hopes of forming a federation of Kenya, Uganda, and Tanganyika, Julius Nyerere suggested that independence for his country (now Tanzania) be delayed, but his plan was not adopted. Subsequent efforts to establish a viable East African Community (p. 146) also failed. In 1961, the French-speaking states of Cameroon, Central African Republic, Chad, Congo, and Gabon formed a customs and economic union (UDEAC, from the French acronym). Regional organizations have been formed to establish a common airline, Air Afrique, or to exploit a common river such as the Senegal, or to set up a customs union among Algeria, Morocco, and Tunisia. In fact, to date a large number of regional arrangements have been made on the continent, and regionalism may become even more important than it is. *See also* INTERNATIONAL ORGANIZATION, p. 152; ORGANIZATION OF AFRICAN UNITY, p. 157; PAN-AFRICANISM, p. 78.

Significance Regionalism is in conflict with most concepts of Pan-Africanism. Although a few Pan-Africanists think of the ultimate union of the continent only after states have first united by region, most of the early Pan-Africanists saw anything less than a continent-wide unification as something akin to balkanization (that is, the act of breaking up an area into smaller units). Pan-African thinking thus pushed for such general organizations as the OAU (p. 157) and the ADB (p. 140). Regionalism, however, responded to different pressures, one being the vastness and diversity of the continent, the other being the need for each state's leaders to act in what they regarded as the national interest. Regionalism, located between nationalism and Pan-Africanism, is much more pragmatic and more focused on immediate problems than Pan-Africanism, which tends to operate at the level of the lowest common denominator.

Sanction A punishment meted out to a violator of international law by a group of nations. Sanctions are usually of three kinds: diplomatic, usually involving the breaking of diplomatic relations; economic, usually involving boycotts and embargoes; and military, usually involving demonstrations and blockades but possibly including the ultimate sanction, attack by land, sea, and air forces. *See also* BOYCOTT,

p. 141; COORDINATING COMMITTEE ON LIBERATION MOVEMENTS, p. 142; EMBARGO, p. 148; INTERNATIONAL WAR, p. 155.

Significance African states have recognized the importance of sanctions since at least the founding of the OAU in 1963. At that time, the states present in Addis Ababa pledged themselves to coordinate "measures of sanction against the Government of South Africa." They also called on all governments having diplomatic relations with South Africa to break them. Boycotts and embargoes were also instituted against South Africa, Portugal, and Rhodesia. The OAU went so far as to establish a form of military sanction through support of guerrilla warfare against racist and colonial regimes. The sanction has been freely used in Africa, but it is not known whether it will be used after racist and colonial regimes are removed.

Shaba Conflicts Two invasions of Zaire (formerly Belgian Congo) from Angola by ex-Zairean gendarmes. The Zaireans are from the former Katanga region now called Shaba Province. They fled the Shaba area in 1964 when Mobuto seized power, and crossed the border into Angola. At the time, their goal appeared to be the secession of Katanga from Zaire. In Angola they were permitted by the Portuguese rulers to organize and plan for military excursions against Zaire, provided they supported the Portuguese fight against the freedom fighters. Apparently they supported the Portuguese until the Salazar dictatorship was overthrown, then they switched to supporting the MPLA. On March 7, 1977, the first Shaba invasion occurred, but it is not clear whether the goal was merely the secession of the mineral-rich Shaba Province or the overthrow of the Mobutu regime of Zaire. The invaders called themselves the Front for the National Liberation of the Congo (FNLC; Congo was the former name of Zaire). The FNLC leaders denied they were either Katangese or secessionists—rather they claimed to be revolutionaries from the Congo (Zaire) determined to overthrow Mobutu. Zairean soldiers proved so inept that Mobutu was forced to call on non-African foreign powers to save the government. The United States, Belgium, France, China, and South Africa sent supplies, matériel, and food, and France used its aircraft to ferry in Moroccan soldiers. Thrust back into Angola, the FNLC regrouped and attacked again on May 11, 1978. Although the Zairean army was just as inept as in 1977, the FNLC army also disintegrated after a few days. In the chaos, widespread killings of both Blacks and Whites occurred in Kolwezi, and many Europeans (mostly engaged in mining activities) were taken hostages. At Mobutu's invitation, 400 French Foreign Legion paratroopers were flown in. They captured Kolwezi, rescued most of the European population, and drove the rebels into Angola and Zambia. When French (and some Belgian) troops left, Moroccan, Ivory Coast, Senegalese, and Togolese troops formed a new force to prop up the Zaire regime. Angola subsequently took steps to prevent any further incursions from its territory. *See also* INTERVENTION, p. 156.

Significance The Shaba conflicts constitute more than a secessionist movement, although that is enough to frighten most African leaders, who do not want to encourage their own secessionist groups. The great significance of the Shaba invasions is its international implications. Mobutu charged that Angola's MPLA and Cuban troops, supported by the Soviet Union, trained and financed the FNLC, although this was denied by the accused. The U.S. charged that Cuban troops were behind the FNLC, although it appears most likely to have been East Germans. In any case, non-African powers plus four African states intervened in the conflict, which again revealed the weakness of the OAU in such cases. Further, it now appears that Mobutu survives only because of foreign support, certainly not because he has built an efficient army. The vulnerability of Africa to foreign intervention is simply illustrated again by the Shaba conflicts. Most African leaders are caught in a bind: They have little respect for what they regard as the corrupt Mobutu regime that must call on foreign governments to help him survive, and they fear to give any support to a movement that might be secessionist.

Southern African Development Coordination Conference (SADCC) An international organization of nine Black states formed in Tanzania (formerly Tanganyika and Zanzibar) in 1979 to reduce the area's dependence on the Republic of South Africa. Members of SADCC are Angola, Botswana (formerly Bechuanaland), Lesotho (formerly Basutoland), Malawi (formerly Nyasaland), Mozambique, Swaziland, Tanzania (formerly Tanganyika and Zanzibar), Zambia (formerly Northern Rhodesia), and Zimbabwe (formerly Southern Rhodesia). In its first two years SADCC had attracted $670 million. One of its priorities is apparently to reorient the transportation patterns in the area to reduce dependency on routes through South Africa.

Significance The Southern African Development Coordination Conference is apparently beginning to think in terms of the lengthy period of chaos that may occur as South Africa is forced eventually to grant citizenship rights to its non-White majority. The chaos may be considerably circumscribed if planning is begun now rather than when it occurs. African states now seem to have little hope that a transition to majority rule will occur without considerable and prolonged violence. SADCC may help to plan for the worst and thus ease some of the resultant problems (Anderson, 1981, p. 673).

Unilateral Declaration of Independence (UDI)   The act by a colony of declaring itself independent of the ruling power without the approval of the ruling power. A UDI should be contrasted with a bilateral (two-sided) agreement by which most states acquired independence. For example, in 1959 the United Kingdom and Nigerian leaders signed an agreement that if, after a national election were held in December 1959, the new legislature asked for independence, the United Kingdom would grant it on October 1, 1960. A unilateral (one-sided) declaration comes about because a bilateral agreement is rejected by the governing power.

Significance   The UDI has been used three times in Africa. The first occurred in 1965 when the White minority regime of Ian Smith declared the independence of Southern Rhodesia from British rule. Neither Britain nor any other country recognized the UDI. African states, in fact, insisted that Britain use force to regain control so that independence could later be granted by bilateral agreement to the Black majority. Fifteen years later, in 1980, such a bilateral agreement was reached. The guerrilla leaders of Guinea-Bissau declared independence unilaterally in September 1973, an action recognized by Portugal (the ruling power) on September 10, 1974. The political leaders of Comoros also made a UDI on July 6, 1975, which was subsequently recognized by France for three of the islands but not for Mayotte, the fourth island, which had voted by a 99 percent majority to remain with France.

10. Africa and the World

Africa and the Middle East The relations of African states and the states of the Middle East (generally defined as Turkey, Iran, and Afghanistan on the north and all states southward to the Red Sea and Gulf of Aden). Geographically, Africa and the Middle East are contiguous. In terms of religion, Islam predominates in all of the Middle East except Israel, and in the northern half of Africa, as shown in the accompanying map. Arabic is the major language of the Middle East except for Turkey, Iran, Afghanistan, and Israel, and in Africa is the major language in Mauritania, Morocco and Western Sahara, Algeria, Tunisia, Libya, Egypt, and Northern Sudan. The Arab League, formed in 1945 to promote Arab unity, included Egypt from the beginning and gradually came to include nine African states as they became independent. Egypt was expelled in 1979 for signing the peace treaty with Israel. The other African members of the Arab League are Mauritania, Morocco, Algeria, Tunisia, Libya, Sudan, Djibouti, and Somalia (the latter two do not speak Arabic).

As the Black African states begin to gain independence, therefore, they faced a situation in which much of Africa had already established relations with the Middle East. The first question to puzzle Black leaders was the full meaning of the concept of Pan-Africanism. Some leaders, often referred to as radical, such as Kwame Nkrumah of Ghana (formerly Gold Coast), Sekou Touré of Guinea, and Julius Nyerere of Tanzania (formerly Tanganyika and Zanzibar), thought the term should include *all* African states, the Arab-speaking no less than others. Other Black leaders, often regarded as conservative, tended to distrust Arab-speaking states and looked more to the south than to the north. They recalled that when the northern states were seeking their independence in the mid-1950s, Moroccan leaders had said that

"Moroccan independence is incomplete as long as the entire Arab Maghreb is not independent" (Zartman, 1966, p. 2), which seemed to them to have left out all of Black Africa (see p. 39). When the Organization of African Unity (OAU) was formed in 1963, however, all African states (including those of the north but excluding South Africa), were parties. Nevertheless, North Africa tended to be distinctly separate from sub-Saharan Africa during the 1960s, if for no other reason than that most of the sub-Saharan states established ties with Israel. In fact, most of them welcomed and utilized Israeli aid and technicians for many valuable projects—road building, construction, technical training, loans, etc. Even Nigeria, which has a plurality population of Muslims, welcomed Israeli help (Phillips, 1964, pp. 82–84). By early 1973, however, a dozen Black African states (Burundi, Chad, Congo, Ethiopia, Guinea, Ivory Coast, Kenya, Mali, Niger, Tanzania, Uganda, and Zaire—formerly Belgian Congo) had broken relations with Israel. One scholar argues that this mixture of radical and conservative states broke with Israel for the following reasons: (1) Israel's fanatical, exclusive Zionism was remarkably parallel to fanatical, exclusive *apartheid*; (2) Israel had refused to allow American Jews who were Black to immigrate to Israel; (3) Israel may have participated in Amin's overthrow of President Obote of Uganda; and (4) a belated awareness that North Africans are "brothers" and deserve Black African cooperation (Mazrui, 1977, pp. 135–45).

The major turning point came in October 1973, when the Organization of Arab Petroleum Exporting States (OAPEC) announced its intention to use oil as a weapon against Israel. It promised that all states that supported the Arab cause against Israel would be guaranteed oil supplies, and those that suffered from price increases would be helped. All but four (Lesotho, Malawi, South Africa, and Swaziland) of the remaining African States that had not already done so broke diplomatic relations with Israel. The OAPEC then offered $700 million to offset the quadrupling of oil prices, which came quickly in 1974. The OAU criticized OAPEC for offering too little and for bypassing the African Development Bank (p. 140). Even so, the Black African states voted with Arab states in the General Assembly of the UN to declare Zionism a form of racism (p. 190).

Tensions, however, remained high in the region until the Afro-Arab Summit in Cairo, March 7–9, 1977. The Ghana representative bitterly assailed the Arabs: "We expelled hundreds of Israelis from Ghana who were helping our country, organizing and training our air force and army. We were promised assistance by the Arabs. The OAU as a whole was promised this assistance. We waited. However, nothing or little came...." (Legum, 1979, p. A47). Tanzania criticized the Arabs for thinking in terms of a few million dollars and demanded aid of at least

$2.2 billion. Finally the Arabs were persuaded to offer $1.45 billion over a five-year period (less than what the Arabs loaned to Pakistan alone). The summit conference closed with an agreement to seek closer arrangements for joint actions and passed resolutions condemning racism, colonialism, and Zionism.

The OAU continued to criticize Arab aid as too little, as controlled by Arab countries rather than the ADB, and as going primarily to Muslim and/or Arab-speaking countries. Relations worsened when Egypt was expelled from the Arab League. When the Arab League also asked the OAU to exclude Egypt from OAU–Arab League relations, the OAU refused and said that Arab quarrels should be kept out of Africa. Plans for a second Afro-Arab Summit have been postponed, and the future of Africa–Middle East relations is unclear. *See also* ARAB BANK FOR ECONOMIC DEVELOPMENT IN AFRICA, p. 175; ZIONISM AS RACISM, p. 190.

Significance As long as the OAU thinks in terms of all of Africa, Arab League states must also be members; and as long as the African states that are also members of the Arab League continue to think in terms of Africa, they must be members of the OAU. It seems clear, nevertheless, that Arab League African states and Black African states do not perceive Middle East problems in the same way. Arab League states tend to hope for the demise of Israel and its replacement by an Arab-controlled Palestine. Black states seem to agree that Israel is here to stay but has an obligation to agree to a home for the Palestinians. Furthermore, since Egypt, not only an African state but an Arab state, has recognized Israel, many Black African states are now suggesting that diplomatic relations should generally be restored with Israel. In fact, Nigeria said that the only thing delaying such a recognition was not Arab sensitivities but Israel's ties with South Africa. Tanzania has said that relations would be restored if the Palestinians were given a homeland. Ghana, Ivory Coast, and Liberia have talked of restoring relations, and in May 1982 Zaire did so. The OAU Heads of State meeting in 1980 not only refused to expel Egypt, but refused to condemn the Camp David accords, which led to the Egypt-Israeli peace treaty. If Israel ceases to unite Black Africa with North Africa on Middle East questions, will there still be an African voice on Middle East questions? Some people believe the African dependence on Arab oil money would still unite the African states. That point is now becoming questionable as the Arab states begin to express dismay and disgust at what they see as unbridled corruption in Black African states that siphons off most aid dollars before they get to the aid target. African relations with the Middle East are unstable, centered primarily on the one hand in Israel and on the other in petrodollars and opposition to *apartheid*. As long as North Africa looks to the Middle East, the possibility of strong divisions in the OAU exist. For the present, opposition to *apartheid* and colonialism seems to be the only thing on which Africa and the Middle East are in complete agreement.

African-Caribbean-Pacific Community (ACP) An organization of 63 developing countries of Africa, the Caribbean, and the Pacific areas formed to promote the economic development of its members through affiliation with the European Economic Community (EEC). The EEC consists of 10 states (Belgium, Denmark, France, West Germany, Greece, Ireland, Italy, Luxumberg, Netherlands, and the United Kingdom), and 43 of the 63 ACP states are African (including all states of Africa except the five of North Africa and Angola, Mozambique, and South Africa). The relationship between ACP and EEC was established by two treaties signed in Lomé, Togo, in 1975 and 1979 and referred to as Lomé I and Lomé II. The location of the convention and the overwhelming dominance of African states attest to the central role of Africa in the relationship. The basic objective of the treaties is to establish trade relations with the EEC favorable to the ACP. Especially important to the ACP are agreements on export stabilization, industrial cooperation, and financial and technical cooperation. The treaty provides a formula that guarantees export markets for ACP products as well as aid entitlements to each ACP member. Zimbabwe, for example, the newest member, is entitled to over $200 million in aid over the five-year life of Lomé II. *See also* various entries under DEVELOPMENT, pp. 103–113; INTERNATIONAL ORGANIZATIONS, p. 152; NEOCOLONIALISM, p. 107.

Significance Before Great Britain joined the EEC, only the former French states of Africa had formal relations with the European Community. In fact, many of the Anglophone and radical states charged that relations with the EEC constituted neocolonialism. After Great Britain joined the EEC, the African states buried their differences, formed the ACP, and jointly negotiated the Lomé conventions. Lomé I was signed with euphoric hopes that it marked the beginning of the New International Economic Order (p. 109). However, it turned out that EEC members saw it not as a beginning but as a regularization of trade arrangements. Lomé II was signed with more realistic expectations. Nevertheless, the Lomé conventions are important to Africa. Over 50 percent of all African exports go to Europe, most of which, thanks to Lomé II, enter duty-free. Also, 55 percent of all African imports are from Europe. Furthermore, because of Lomé II, African states maintain a favorable balance of trade with the EEC (that is, they sell more than they buy).

African Group African member-states of the United Nations (except for South Africa) that caucus as a group and attempt to present a united front on issues and to promote African interests. The African Group caucuses regularly on all issues of importance to Africa. The Group, furthermore, has been recognized by other states as a channel of communication. For example, in working out a plan for resolving the Namibia issue, the African Group was frequently consulted by the "contact" group of five Western powers (the United States, Great Britain, France, Canada, and West Germany). The Group is now sufficiently established that the OAU can issue instructions to it on how to proceed in UN deliberations (for example, the OAU in its 1980 resolutions on Namibia instructed the African Group how to proceed if South Africa remained negative). The African Group has also found that by combining its strength with other regional groups, it can even change behavior in the UN. By combining with Arab and Asian states, it was able to get the UN Charter amended to guarantee regular representation to Africa in the Security Council, the Economic and Social Council, the International Court of Justice, and the Secretariat. In trade-offs with Middle Eastern states, it has voted against Israel in return for Arab votes against South Africa. Its 50 votes constitute the largest group in the UN, and when its members are in agreement, they become a formidable bloc if combined with some other regional group.

Significance The establishment of an African Group Office at the UN Headquarters in New York was both a symbol of Africa's hope of presenting a united front on world issues and a structural center for gathering and coordinating individual African state positions in order to try to obtain such a united front. In fact, on issues of colonialism and racism, the African Group probably has as much coherence as any group in the UN. It must be recognized, however, that African states are divided on many issues (ideology, political forms, economic systems, ties with Great Powers, boundary questions), and will not in the foreseeable future be able to present a united front on all international issues. Nevertheless, the African Group in the UN has already become a force to be reckoned with on issues on which its members agree.

Anglophone Africa The states in Africa where English is widely spoken. All of the Anglophone states of Africa, except for Liberia (which was never a colony) and parts of Cameroon and Somalia, were former colonies of Great Britain. English (often with one or two other languages) is an officially recognized language in Botswana (formerly Bechuanaland), Cameroon, Gambia, Ghana (formerly Gold Coast), Lesotho (formerly Basutoland), Liberia, Malawi (formerly Nyasaland),

Mauritius, Nigeria, Seychelles, Sierra Leone, Somalia, South Africa, Swaziland, Uganda, Zambia (formerly Northern Rhodesia), and Zimbabwe (formerly Southern Rhodesia), and is widely spoken in Egypt, Kenya, Sudan, and Tanzania (formerly Tanganyika and Zanzibar). As these colonies became independent, one of their concerns was whether and to what extent special relations should be maintained with the former metropole (ruling center). One attraction for the Anglophone states was the Commonwealth, an international organization formed around Britain, composed of former colonies. Commonwealth membership not only provided special tariff advantages in trade, it provided certain visa and passport privileges to citizens traveling in other Commonwealth countries. Members also were more likely to receive aid from Britain than were non-Commonwealth states. Equally important was the large international forum that Commonwealth meetings provided. At these annual meetings, all members may express their opinions about any and all matters. Conclusions reached at the conference are not binding; nevertheless the forum is regarded as a valuable way to press opinions, to defuse tensions, or to speak to the world with a rather loud voice. After all, the Commonwealth, besides Great Britain, includes India, Pakistan, Bangladesh, Malaysia, Canada, Australia, New Zealand, and smaller states, as well as the following states of Africa: Botswana, Gambia, Ghana, Kenya, Lesotho, Malawi, Mauritius, Nigeria, Seychelles, Sierra Leone, Swaziland, Tanzania, Uganda, Zambia, and Zimbabwe. Thus the term *Anglophone* is in Africa somewhat more inclusive in scope than the term *Commonwealth*, since English is widely spoken also in the non-Commonwealth states of Cameroon, Egypt, Liberia, Somalia, South Africa, and Sudan. Nevertheless, somewhat carelessly, the term Anglophone often is used as if it were synonymous with the Commonwealth. *See also* FRANCOPHONE AFRICA, p. 180; HISPANOPHONE AFRICA, p. 181; LUSOPHONE AFRICA, p. 181.

Significance The 21 Anglophone states contain 58.7 percent of Africa's population, making English the most pervasive of the European languages. The 15 African states in the Commonwealth make up almost one-third of the states of Africa and 35 percent of the population. The Commonwealth provides a vehicle not only to share views among themselves but with other Third World countries, the leading one being India. It also allows them to continue to put pressure on Britain as needed for solving African problems, as in Zimbabwe up to 1980, and in Namibia and South Africa today. While the Commonwealth states and Britain do reach agreements on issues (for example, the Zimbabwe issue when Whites still ruled), they differ on many other points. The African states resent deeply Britain's heavy trade relations with South Africa and British failure to bring about Namibian independence. Also bothersome is Britain's refusal to abandon the Indian Ocean island of Diego Garcia (a military base) to Mauritius. Finally, Britain's own declining economy has meant a sharp reduction of its aid to African states, which goes primarily to the Anglophone states. However, without Britain the Commonwealth would cease to exist. Whether the Anglophone states in Africa could forge another organization that could unite their voices is unknown. Thus, as it stands today, Anglophone means largely but not exclusively Commonwealth, and Commonwealth means primarily British concerns (but not British domination), or concerns with Britain. (See Map A-4 on p. 197.)

Arab Bank for Economic Development in Africa (BADEA)
A bank formed by the Arab League in 1973 to aid members of the OAU, except those that are also members of the Arab League. Headquarters is in Khartoum, Sudan. BADEA was created at the time the non-oil-producing states of Africa were beginning to face the devastating quadrupling of oil prices. By 1980, the 18 Arab states had subscribed $738 million (over $500 million coming from four states: Saudi Arabia, Libya, Kuwait, and Iraq). African priorities mainly determine the purposes of grants and are primarily concerned with infrastructure, agriculture, industry, and energy. Some BADEA funds have been channeled into the African Development Bank (ADB), and about $9 million has been given to the southern African liberation movements. *See also* AFRICA AND THE MIDDLE EAST, p. 169; AFRICAN DEVELOPMENT BANK, p. 140.

Significance While accepting all the assistance they can get, Black African states have been critical of BADEA. They claim that (1) the amounts donated are too small as compared to the need; (2) the Arab states ought to channel their aid through the ADB, which (unlike BADEA) has Black Africans on the Board of Directors; and (3) the Arab states prefer to channel aid through national institutions and to selected countries rather than through multinational institutions like BADEA, which distributes its pittance to all states. BADEA, therefore, has not yet served to bridge the gap between Black Africans and Arab Africans.

Byrd Amendment An amendment to a law in the United States that prohibited the President from observing the UN boycott on Rhodesia (now Zimbabwe). The amendment, named after Senator Harry Byrd (Independent, Virginia) was approved by the U.S. Congress in 1971 and, in practice, applied only to chrome. The law said in effect that as long as chrome could be purchased from a communist country (meaning the Soviet Union) it could be purchased from any (meaning specifically Rhodesia). Congress justified its action on the grounds that Rhodesian chrome was cheaper than Soviet chrome, and, besides, the UN itself had documented over 100 violations of the UN boycott. The Byrd amendment was finally repealed in March 1977. *See also* CLARK AMENDMENT, p. 177.

Significance The Byrd amendment was a violation of the UN Charter and of the law of treaties. The United States had agreed to the Security Council boycott of Rhodesian goods in both 1966 and 1968, and President Johnson had issued the proper decrees to make the sanctions enforcible in the United States. Thus, the Byrd amendment appeared to be an effort by a Great Power to weaken the United Nations and international law. Equally important was the fact that the Byrd amendment was a direct slap at African states. The UN sanctions had been imposed on Rhodesia because of the UDI (p. 167) declared by the White minority. For the United States to lift the sanctions, therefore, was regarded as racist. Even the conservative Zimbabwean nationalist leader, Abel Muzorewa, charged that the Byrd amendment was "the worst blow we have suffered from any quarter." Under the leadership of President Jimmy Carter, however, Congress repealed the Byrd amendment in 1977, and helped to usher in an improved era of relations between the United States and Africa.

Chinese Policy in Africa Chinese objectives and methods of action in Africa. China's policy toward Africa has in large part been determined not by African problems primarily but by China's own struggles with the Soviet Union. At times, it appears that China supports any country that does not support the Soviet Union. Thus, when Russia supported the MPLA in Angola, China sided with the FNLA and UNITA and found itself in league with the United States and South Africa. When Russia supported Nkomo in Zimbabwe (formerly Southern Rhodesia), China supported Mugabe, but in this case wound up on the winning side. When Somalia broke with the Soviets, China embraced it. Nevertheless, it is too simple merely to say that China's policy is the opposite of Soviet policy. A remarkable parallel in terms of the countries to which each is willing to send technicians exists. (See Table B-8, p. 216.) China's policy, furthermore, seems to be taking on some definite form that allows for considerable discrimination among issues. While it opposes Soviet "hegemony" as an effort to destabilize the continent, it also recognizes that some conflicts are strictly between African states, and it regards White rule in South Africa as dangerous to peace. China refuses to take sides on disputes strictly limited to Africa. On South Africa, it seems to believe that armed struggle is inevitable. In fact, one scholar has said that China's African policy is to "encourage conventional relations, warn of Soviet ambitions, sharply indict South African minority rule, urge regional and national stability, and yet support calls for a new international economic order and a new basis for world political affairs" (Larkin, 1982, p. A153). What seems surprising to many people is that China's policy seems overwhelmingly committed to stability, a goal it openly supported in 1980, leaving people to wonder if it no longer supports armed struggle as a general principle.

Significance China's policy in Africa has been cautious and not flamboyant, and has generally been well received in Africa. Leaders ranging from conservative to radical have accepted invitations to visit China, and in 1980 alone delegations visited that country from Togo, Benin, Senegal, Tunisia, Morocco, Mauritania, Algeria, Zimbabwe, Mozambique, Tanzania (formerly Tanganyika and Zanzibar), Kenya, Burundi, Madagascar, Seychelles, Mauritius, and Djibouti. African leaders also remember that, when other nations refused, China helped Tanzania and Zambia (formerly Northern Rhodesia) build a railroad from Dar es Salaam to Zambia, thus providing landlocked Zambia with an outlet to the ocean without going through South Africa or the then-colonies of Mozambique or Rhodesia.

Clark Amendment An amendment to a United States' law forbidding arms supplies to any insurgent group in Angola without the express approval of the U.S. Congress. Named after the senator who sponsored the amendment, Dick Clark of Iowa, the embargo was passed in 1975 at the height of the civil war in Angola between the ruling MPLA on the one hand and UNITA and FNLA on the other. U.S. Secretary of State Henry Kissinger wanted to continue to send arms to the anti-MPLA forces because the MPLA had received aid and/or military forces from the Soviet Union and Cuba. The U.S. Congress, partly as a backlash to the disastrous consequences of involvement in Vietnam and partly out of respect for the OAU, which at the time recognized all factions, approved the Clark amendment and thwarted any further overt help to the anti-MPLA forces. In his first year in office in 1981, President Reagan called for the repeal of the Clark amendment on the grounds that it interfered with executive freedom to conduct foreign relations. He denied that he planned to give military aid to UNITA, as some people charged. Nevertheless, Congress failed to repeal the Clark amendment in 1981, and President

Reagan has not reopened the matter. *See also* BYRD AMENDMENT, p. 175; EMBARGO, p. 148.

Significance Black Africans welcomed the Clark amendment as a sign that the United States may realize that Africans must be left free to solve African problems. They were willing to concede that Cuban troops had moved into Angola by August 1975 to defend the MPLA, but that South African troops had intervened also to support FNLA and UNITA. When all other powers are willing to leave Angola alone, they argued, then the Cubans will be asked to leave. The Clark amendment thus appeared to be a sane step toward the objective of an Angola free from the threat of foreign intervention.

Cubans in Africa Cuban citizens in Africa for military or economic purposes. In the early 1970s, Cuba began to offer a few technicians to "revolutionary" countries such as Somalia and Guinea. Its main involvement with Africa, however, came in 1975 in Angola during the weeks preceding independence. It appeared likely that the MPLA would win control of an independent government, but during the summer of 1975, the United States, China, and South Africa began to support the FNLA and UNITA. Russia had been supporting the MPLA, but rather perfunctorily, many thought. Fidel Castro of Cuba decided, at the request of Dr. Agostinho Neto, leader of the MPLA, to send troops to help his Marxist friends. Independence came for Angola on November 11, 1975, but the civil war continued, and Cuba has kept its troops there. As the conflict intensified in 1977 between Somalia and Ethiopia, Cuba decided also to send troops to that area, switching its earlier support of Somalia to Ethiopia. It is now believed that Cuba has about 19,000 troops in Angola and 16,500 in Ethiopia, with another 1,700 scattered in Equatorial Guinea, Guinea, Guinea-Bissau, Mozambique, and possibly others. Since Cuba is a poor country, and since the Soviet Union subsidizes it at the rate of $2 million per day, it is presumed that the Soviets are underwriting Cuban involvements in Africa. Although Cuba's involvements are mainly military, it also has a number of technical experts in Africa, scattered over nine countries. For estimates of the number of Cubans in Africa, whose role in contrast to other Communist powers is far more military than technical see Table B-8, p. 216. *See also* SOVIET POLICY IN AFRICA, p. 185.

Significance African states in general were apprehensive about the stationing of Cuban troops in Angola, but they became far more tolerant when it was learned that South Africa had sent troops into eastern Angola to help the anti-MPLA forces of the FNLA and UNITA.

They became even more tolerant when Cuban troops were sent to Ethiopia. Although the OAU has condemned all non-African forces and military bases as foreign intervention, it has accepted, somewhat reluctantly, the Cuban troops on the grounds that (1) they were invited by recognized governments, and (2) in the Angola case at least they were supporting a government recognized by the OAU, and one fighting against racism and colonialism. Since Cuba is itself also a developing country and a large portion of its population is Black, Cuba has seemed more of a comrade than a puppet of a Great Power. Furthermore, Cuba shows no interest in establishing permanent military bases in Africa or of benefitting economically. Its reward seems to be strictly ideological. Consequently, Cuba must be credited with having pulled off quite a victory for itself and for its friends by the way it was able to intrude into Africa without strong opposition.

Divestiture in South Africa The act of disposing of financial interests in South Africa. The primary demands for divestiture of all foreign manufacturing or financial interests in South Africa have come from the Organization of African Unity (OAU), private groups in the United States (churches, college students, labor unions, Black Americans), and certain Blacks in South Africa. In June 1980, the Council of Ministers of the OAU reiterated its appeal to Western countries to withdraw their investments from South Africa. Private groups in the United States have called on the government to embargo American investments in South Africa. Their more dramatic efforts, however, have been in pressures they have placed on American manufacturing and financial institutions voluntarily to divest themselves of interests in that pariah country. Even groups of stockholders in specific American companies have forced votes in stockholder's meetings on the question of divestiture. In South Africa itself, the question of foreign divestiture has split Black groups because, it is argued, the first people to be hurt through unemployment if businesses fail would be Black workers. Many Blacks follow the lead of the late Chief Albert John Luthuli, the Nobel Peace laureate, who issued a simple plea in 1959—"Boycott Us." Others say they do not want to pay the awful price of unemployment with little hope that conditions will then improve. *See also* SULLIVAN PRINCIPLES, p. 187.

Significance Many groups calling for divestiture believe that the impact would be so devastating as to bring the downfall of the White-ruled regime. There is little evidence for such a belief. China and Cuba, which faced massive divestitures in the early 1950s and 1960s, respectively, were not brought down by such action. Other supporters of divestiture see it as a symbolic act of friendship for African interests, as a source of at least some pain to South Africa, and as a moral statement of opposition to *apartheid*. Some see it as a way of condemning international capitalistic activity. Many American blacks see it as a way to dramatize the plight of black people suffering the worst kind of racial discrimination in today's world. The OAU sees divestiture as further evidence of Western support for its cause. In strictly practical terms, however, the call for divestiture has not been successful; the aggregate amount of foreign capital in South Africa increases each year.

Francophone Africa The states in Africa where French is widely spoken. Most of the Francophone states were former French colonies, the exceptions being Burundi, Rwanda, and Zaire (formerly Belgian Congo). French (often with one or two other languages) is an officially recognized language in Benin, Burundi, Cameroon, Central African Republic, Chad, Congo, Gabon, Guinea, Ivory Coast, Mali, Mauritania, Niger, Rwanda, Senegal, Togo, Upper Volta, and Zaire. France, as former metropole (ruling center) and as preserver of the French language, sought from the beginning to maintain some form of community between itself and the Francophone states. At first, this included economic and military aid to the former colonies (except for Guinea, which had rejected France's offer of community in 1958). French aid, in fact, has kept some states (for example, Chad and the Central African Republic) from collapse. France has done much to promote French language and culture. The Franc Zone embraces France and 13 French-speaking former colonies. France has also created the Agence de Cooperation Culturelle et Technique, which includes France, Canada, and the Francophone states of Africa and is known as Francophonie. In further efforts to promote French language and culture, France has installed two powerful new radio stations, one in Morocco and one in Gabon. It has also sponsored a series of French-African summit conferences that now include some non-French speakers. France does not, however, belong to all Francophone groups in Africa: French-speaking states have formed groups without France, such as the Economic Community of West Africa (Ivory Coast, Mali, Mauritania, Niger, Senegal, and Upper Volta), the Entente Council (Conseil de l'Entente), which includes Benin, Ivory Coast, Niger, Togo, and Upper Volta, and other groups of French-speaking states. *See also* ANGLOPHONE AFRICA, p. 173; HISPANOPHONE AFRICA, p. 181; LUSOPHONE AFRICA, p. 181.

Significance The Francophone states of Africa have used the French language to maintain close ties with France and to establish ties between and among themselves. The ties with France have been so close (except for a few former colonies) that many other states of Africa accuse them of being neocolonies of France. French troops were stationed in Chad until 1979, and a military base exists in Senegal. Despite the criticisms, the French-speaking states use their common language to maintain closer relations with France than with any other powers, and with each other to look at common problems and attempt to agree on some issues. Even French-speaking Zaire, which was a Belgian colony, has established close relations with France. One real payoff for Francophone relations with France has been France's willingness to provide aid. In fact, French foreign aid is restricted almost exclusively to former French colonies, which means in Africa the Francophone states. Recently, however, France has enlarged its focus to include other states that seem willing to accept French culture and language. For example, in the 1980 French-African summit in Nice, invited states included (besides the Francophone ones) Cape Verde, Guinea-Bissau, Mauritius, São Tomé and Príncipe, Sierra Leone, and Somalia. It seems clear that the French language movement, spurred by Francophone African states as well as France, has an organizational zeal not present in the Anglophone states. Twenty-four states in Africa (almost half) are Francophone, embracing about one-third of the population of the continent. See Map A-4, p. 197.

Hispanophone Africa Those states in Africa where Spanish is widely spoken. These states are the former colonies of Equatorial Guinea and Western Sahara. *See also* ANGLOPHONE AFRICA, p. 173; FRANCOPHONE AFRICA, p. 180; LUSOPHONE AFRICA, p. 181.

Significance The two Hispanophone states in Africa together contain only about 360,000 people, constituting the smallest population in Africa in which a European language is widely spoken. The two areas are not contiguous, and no movement (such as exists in Francophone Africa) exists to promote a wider use of the foreign language. The language does, however, tie the countries to Spain, and good relations exist between Spain and the Hispanophone states. See Map A-4 on p. 197.

Lusophone Africa Those states in Africa where Portuguese is widely spoken. These states are all former colonies of Portugal and include Angola, Cape Verde, Guinea-Bissau, Mozambique, and São Tomé and Príncipe; Portuguese is one of the official languages. *See also*

ANGLOPHONE AFRICA, p. 173; FRANCOPHONE AFRICA, p. 180; HISPANOPHONE AFRICA, p. 181.

Significance The five Lusophone states contain only about 20 million people and are widely scattered—no two of them are contiguous. All became independent in 1974 or 1975, but there is little evidence to date that the common language will be a vehicle for pulling them together in some form of international organization. The common language, however, does tie them to Portugal, and in spite of the violence of the independence movements in these states, good relations now exist between Portugal and the former colonies. See Map A-4 on p. 197.

Namibia Issue The question of how Namibia shall gain independence. Namibia is the former South West Africa, which was a German colony until World War I. After the defeat of Germany, South West Africa was assigned by the League of Nations to be a Class C Mandate of South Africa. A Class C Mandate was to be governed as an integral portion of the mandatory's territory, with no promise of ultimate independence, but under the responsibility of the League of Nations. League responsibility meant that the mandatory had to report regularly on its rule of the mandate. The League of Nations ceased to exist in 1946 and was replaced by the United Nations, whose Charter set up an International Trusteeship System "for the administration and supervision of such territories as may be placed thereunder by subsequent individual agreement" (Article 75). Article 77 stipulated that League of Nations' mandates were among the territories to be placed under the UN Trusteeship System. All mandatory powers except South Africa placed their mandates under UN Trusteeship supervision. South Africa argued that Article 75 referred to such territories as "may" be placed under Trusteeship, which, it said, did not bind South Africa but merely gave it the opportunity to place South West Africa under UN Trusteeship if it chose to. South Africa said it did not choose that course of action but preferred to incorporate South West Africa as an integral part of South Africa. The first session of the General Assembly refused to agree with the integration plan and asked South Africa to place the former mandate under UN Trusteeship. In the second session, the General Assembly again sought trusteeship status for the territory but seemed to acknowledge that there was no legal obligation on South Africa to grant such.

For almost 20 years, the General Assembly continued to implore the Republic of South Africa to place South West Africa under the trusteeship system. Finally, with an enlarged General Assembly resulting from the spate of new African members, that body in 1966 declared that the General Assembly had jurisdiction over South West Africa. In 1971, the International Court of Justice ruled that South Africa's presence in South West Africa, now known as Namibia, was illegal. The Pretoria regime refused to acknowledge either the General Assembly claim or the World Court opinion. Gradually there has developed a guerrilla force known as the South West African People's Organization (SWAPO), which operates out of Angola and seeks the liberation of Namibia. In 1977, a UN "contact group" was formed by the United States, Great Britain, France, Canada, and West Germany, to put pressure on South Africa to grant independence to Namibia.

In 1978 the UN Security Council passed Resolution 435, calling for a program leading to independence, including the installation of a UN force on the Angola border to replace the departing South Africans. At first, it appeared that South Africa might actually grant independence by the end of 1981, due to its belief that it could install a non-SWAPO government under its control and also to its fear that the "contact group" was losing patience with it. Its position hardened as it became clear that in a free election SWAPO was likely to win, and Reagan's election in the United States was interpreted as an easing-off of pressures from the "contact group." The year 1981 passed without Namibian independence. President Reagan, who seemed to be pro–South African, nevertheless pushed for a resolution of the Namibia issue. By the end of 1981, the "contact group" had managed to reach a common front with SWAPO, the front-line states (p. 149), and Nigeria on the matter. The common agreement calls for a popular election, a unitary state based on a multiparty system, protection of civil rights, and the UN peace-keeping force as envisaged in UN Resolution 435. Whether South Africa can be persuaded remains to be seen. *See also* LUSAKA MANIFESTO, p. 156.

Significance The issue of Namibia, more than any other except *apartheid,* unites Africa. Not only do African states see South African machinations as blatant efforts to extend *apartheid* but they see them as moves to maintain a colony on the continent. They are certain, furthermore, that South Africa can only be persuaded to grant Namibia independence by pressures from the Great Powers, especially the United States. Experience to date seems to support the African position. On the success or failure of the "contact group" may hang Africa's next move in southern Africa.

Nonalignment An attitude or policy of independence or neutralism in relation to the Cold War, particularly toward the United

States and the Soviet Union. Nonalignment means not only that states refuse to enter into treaties of alliance with either of the Superpowers, but also that they insist on pressing for coexistence between states with different ideological systems. The nonaligned are overwhelmingly from the Third World, and while the term *nonaligned* once seemed to mean "poor," today it includes the oil-rich OPEC countries.

Significance Reaction to nonalignment at first appeared to divide many of the newly independent African states. Radical states (for example, the Casablanca Group—see p. 157) demanded nonalignment, while conservative states (for example, the Monrovia Group—see p. 157) were tolerant of alignments. These differences were resolved, however, with the formation of the Organization of African Unity (OAU—see p. 158) in 1963, in which one principle was the "affirmation of a policy of non-alignment with regard to all blocs" (Article III, paragraph 7). At first nonalignment was regarded in positive terms as permitting a country to define its own national interests and to concentrate on solving its own pressing problems of modernization and national integration without getting involved in Big Power conflicts. Internationally, nonalignment has helped to undermine the rigid bipolarity of the Cold War period of the 1950s. Gradually, however, the concept of nonalignment has changed from avoidance of Big Power Politics and attention to domestic problems to efforts to make the concept deal with various alleged evils. The Non-Aligned Summit in Havana in 1979, for example, stated that nonalignment meant: "the struggle against imperialism, colonialism, neocolonialism, *apartheid*, racism, including Zionism, and all forms of foreign aggression, occupation, domination, interference or hegemony, as well as Great Power and bloc policies" (Legum, 1981, p. A 54). Furthermore, these efforts to change the meaning of nonalignment show up in the conflicts between and among nonaligned states. Many countries view the relations of Ethiopia and Cuba with the Soviet Union as alignment rather than nonalignment. The Arab-bloc states seemed to put a new meaning on nonalignment when they tried to expel Egypt from the nonaligned movement for signing a peace treaty with Israel. The other African states generally sided with Egypt. Scholars now see the nonaligned movement as gradually weakening as the bipolar period of the Cold War wanes, as ideological differences split the nonaligned states, and as areas such as Africa focus more and more on African solutions to African problems. Finally, some scholars note that the nonaligned movement had great leadership at first in men like Nasser, Nehru, Nkrumah, Sukarno, and Tito, but today possible leaders seem far more interested in domestic affairs. Thus, the future of nonalignment as a concept is uncertain.

Rescue at Entebbe The rescue by Israel of hostages held at Entebbe, Uganda, by airline hijackers. The hijackers seized the plane, released non-Israelis, and eventually landed at the Entebbe airport in July 1976. They demanded the release of prisoners in Israel. One of the hostages, an elderly woman named Dora Bloch, became ill and was removed to a hospital. President Idi Amin of Uganda seemed unable and unwilling to help. Suddenly Israeli commandos landed at Entebbe, killed the hijackers, freed the hostages, and flew back to Israel with the loss of one soldier. Mrs. Bloch was removed from the hospital and murdered, reportedly on Amin's order.

Significance While the world at large was thrilled at the daring operation by tiny Israel, African leaders were embarrassed at the ease with which a small but developed country could intervene in an African state. The OAU, at the Heads of State and Government Summit at Port Louis, Mauritius, July 2–4, 1976, bitterly condemned the "Israeli aggression on Uganda." The resolution even asserted that the aggression "results from the policy of cooperation between Israel and SA [South Africa]," although the relation of the rescue operation to South Africa was not explained. The resolution further charged that the rescue mission thwarted "the humanitarian efforts made by the President of Uganda to have the hostages released." Finally, the resolution called on the UN to take action under Chapter VII (dealing with threats to the peace) and sent condolences to the president and people of Uganda. No references were made to the danger faced by the hostages while in Entebbe or to the murder of Mrs. Bloch. While some leaders privately expressed pleasure that the hostages had been rescued, in their official capacities they could only express indignation at the helplessness not only of a sovereign state but of the OAU itself. What added an ironic twist to the whole affair was that 26 African states eight months before the rescue had voted in the UN to declare that Zionism is a form of racism (p. 190).

Soviet Policy in Africa Soviet objectives and methods of action in Africa. The Soviet Union has no deep historical connections to any part of Africa. Its own history of violent revolution and its own evolution of Marxism in the form of Leninism-Stalinism played no role in the spate of independence movements in the 1950s and 1960s. Its attitude toward Africa up to the mid-1970s was one of cautious disdain. It did side with Patrice Lumumba in the early Congo (now Zaire) crisis in 1960; it sided with the Nigerian Federal Government in its civil war with Biafra; it established close ties with Abdul Nasser's Egypt; it supplied some advisors to Guinea and Ghana in the early 1960s; it established some ties with Somalia in the early 1970s, which gave it by 1974 naval and air reconnaissance facilities to bolster its Indian Ocean activities; and it scattered technicians here and there. The early Soviet policy was especially cautious and low-key, except for the massive Aswan Dam project in Egypt. Nevertheless, the Soviet Union invariably supported the African states in their policies related to colonialism or racism since this cost it nothing and paid off in good will. It has attempted to offer policies to counter Western influence, and it has tried to contain Chinese influence. Two separate conflicts in the 1970s—in the Horn and in the liberation struggles against the Portuguese—brought about a more active policy and a deeper involvement. In 1975 the Soviets supported the MPLA in Angola, even to the point of supplying military advisors and supporting the use of Cuban troops. In 1978 the Soviets switched their support from Somalia to Ethiopia, supplied the latter with military advisors, and supported the use of Cuban troops there. It now sponsors military advisors to at least 7 countries and economic and technical personnel to at least 20. See Table B-8, p. 216 for 1978 estimates of Soviet and East European (of the latter, mainly East German) involvements in Africa. *See also* CHINESE POLICY IN AFRICA, p. 176; CUBANS IN AFRICA, p. 178; INTERVENTION, p. 156; MARXISM, p. 74; UNITED STATES POLICY IN AFRICA, p. 187.

Significance African states have been placed in a bind by Soviet intervention. A cardinal principle of the Organization of African Unity (OAU) is "non-interference in the internal affairs of states," and a common policy has been one of "African solutions to African problems." Yet today the Soviet Union and its allies have about 36,000 military personnel in Africa. (See Table B-8, p. 216.) The bind comes from the facts that (1) Soviet intervention is always at the invitation of the host government; (2) the African governments involved are supported by the OAU in their conflicts; and (3) the Soviet Union always supports the African position on matters involving racism and colonialism. While many African leaders have expressed hope that foreign military forces will soon leave the continent, there seems to be little incentive to press for Soviet withdrawal in Angola until Namibia has gained its independence. Tolerance of Soviet intervention in Angola seems to make it easier to tolerate intervention in Ethiopia. On the other hand, the emergence of a number of states avowing Marxism has created a condition of potential camaraderie for the Soviets. Some of the few Marxist states in Africa have openly voiced their commonality of interests. How close these ties may become is uncertain because (1) African states, including Marxist ones, are jealous of their independence, and (2) they recall the heavy-handedness of Soviet involvement in such places as Guinea, Egypt, and Sudan, which resulted in their expulsion. At the moment, however, Soviet policy has won it much support, ranging from open endorsement to grudging acceptance.

Sullivan Principles   A set of principles involving fair labor practices toward Blacks in private U.S. businesses operating in South Africa. The principles were created in 1977 by Reverend Leon Sullivan, a Baptist minister in Philadelphia, the first Black member of the Board of Directors of General Motors. He proposed that American firms employing Black workers in South Africa agree to a set of principles that would commit the companies to (1) improve the wages, working conditions, and fringe benefits of Blacks, (2) promote Blacks to positions of management, and (3) recognize representative Black trade unions. By 1980, 130 U.S. companies (out of approximately 350) had subscribed to the Sullivan Principles, representing about 75 percent of all employees on U.S.-company payrolls in South Africa. The objective of the principles is not only to thwart the effects of *apartheid* but to put pressure on the South African government to ease *apartheid* rules or else to discipline the offending companies and risk their pulling out of the country. Under President Carter, the U.S. State Department openly supported the Sullivan Principles as a way of producing peaceful change in South Africa. *See also* DIVESTITURE IN SOUTH AFRICA, p. 179–180.

Significance   Many people, including Blacks in South Africa, leaders of African governments, and various Americans, have opposed the Sullivan Principles. By 1980, the opposition had become strong. Blacks in South Africa told Mr. Sullivan personally that his code only sustained *apartheid*. Mr. Sullivan himself made a blistering attack on companies that had not subscribed to the code and on those that had but were weak in enforcing it. He even called on Congress to force American companies to observe the principles (there is little evidence that Congress plans to do so). African reaction in general was expressed in June 1980 by a resolution of the OAU Council of Ministers that found measures such as "the Sullivan Principles harmful to the liberation struggle, regardless of the argument that such measures are purported to be designed to create a possible constructive role for foreign investment in South Africa." Considering the intensity of opposition to the Sullivan Principles, the lukewarm support American companies give to them, and the apparent reluctance of Congress to give them the force of law, it seems unlikely that they will have much effect in South Africa.

United States Policy in Africa   American objectives and methods of action in Africa. Having had no colonies in Africa, American historical involvement in the continent was slight compared to that of European countries. In fact, pre-independence involvement was primarily of three kinds. Most significant was the fact that Africa is today the ancestral home of over 25 million American citizens whose forebears arrived as slaves. During the period of the slave traffic, however, the government of the United States was little concerned with or involved in Africa. The major exception to this observation, and the second kind of involvement, resulted from an enclave in West Africa that was settled by American ex-slaves beginning in 1816. By 1847 these settlers had proclaimed the state of Liberia, which was recognized by, and thereafter came under the protection of, the United States in 1862. The third involvement resulted from the fact that Americans like Thomas Jefferson, Abraham Lincoln, and Franklin Roosevelt had become heroes to early African nationalists.

These tenuous contacts hardly prepared the United States to develop a policy for dealing with Africa. As the explosion of independence occurred in 1960, John Kennedy was elected President. He supported the independence movement and even the movement for nonalignment. By insisting that the Congo (now Zaire) crisis of 1960–65 should be settled through the UN, he probably curtailed Soviet influence in the area. His Peace Corps was basically well received in Africa, where it contributed to the spread of education. His successor, President Lyndon Johnson, won African approval by supporting the UN boycott of Rhodesia, and African disapproval for waging the war in Vietnam. President Nixon's policy was one of disinterest, accompanied by Congress' repeal of the boycott on Rhodesian chrome. In Angola, President Ford backed the same forces as South Africa and won the fear and distrust of Africa. President Jimmy Carter got the boycott of Rhodesian chrome restored and defused much African hostility through the judicious use of Andrew Young as his ambassador to the United Nations. Through statements made by Young and Vice President Walter Mondale, Carter made it clear that majority rule in South Africa was an objective of the United States.

Carter's successor, President Ronald Reagan, while opposing *apartheid*, seems to have softened American pressures for change. On the other hand, his administration seems to be pressing for a Namibian solution the front-line states (p. 149) and Nigeria can accept. In mid-1982, the U.S. Department of State said that the basic policy toward southern Africa included the following: (1) a negotiated settlement of the Namibian issue based on UN Security Council Resolution 435 (p. 183); (2) an end to the conflict in Angola and withdrawal of Cuban combat forces; and (3) "a careful policy of constructive engagement, encouraging the government and other elements in South African society to move away from *apartheid* toward peaceful change."

A concern on the other end of the continent from South Africa is Libya, which Chester Crocker, Reagan's Assistant Secretary for African Affairs, calls "a leading Third World arsenal of Soviet-supplied hardware." Between the extreme north and south, Crocker has stated that the United States is committed to help "bring the poorer African nations more into the mainstream of the free market economy which is the soundest and surest way to growth." In fact, Reagan's policy seems to be to emphasize private investment, bilateral aid over multilateral, concern for security, a lack of concern for what is regarded as mere African rhetoric, and special attention to select countries. The select countries are Egypt, Sudan, Somalia, Kenya, Zimbabwe (formerly Southern Rhodesia), Nigeria, and Liberia; however, Reagan has proposed some new recipients for U.S. economic aid: Senegal, Botswana, Djibouti, Gabon, and Rwanda. See also CHINESE POLICY IN AFRICA, p. 176; SOVIET POLICY IN AFRICA, p. 185.

Significance African states as a whole entered independence with a reservoir of good will toward the United States. At the organizational meeting of the Organization of African Unity (OAU), the African states expressed "deep concern" over "racial discrimination" against people of African origin in the United States but also added an expression of "appreciation for the efforts of the Federal Government of the United States of America to put an end to these intolerable malpractices...." This view contrasts strongly with the 1981 OAU condemnation of "the unholy alliance" between Washington and Pretoria, the "baseless hostility toward Angola," and the effort "to misrepresent the nature of the colonial conflict in Namibia as one of global strategic consideration." President Reagan just as harshly criticized the OAU's failure to condemn Libya's invasion of Chad.

In spite of what may appear to be intolerant positions, African states generally do not appear to be strongly anti-American. While Libya has little use for the United States, Egypt and Morocco maintain close relations, and Algeria maintains formal ties. In West Africa, Nigeria maintains a love-hate relationship with its largest buyer of oil, ever wary of an American tilt toward South Africa. President Shagari made an official visit to Washington in 1980. Liberia, in the wake of its coup d'etat, continues its traditional ties. In East Africa, Kenya maintains cordial relations. From southern Africa, the Marxist President Mugabe of Zimbabwe made a visit to Washington in 1980, and formal relations are maintained by Mozambique. Angola's leaders have indicated they would like closer relations, but the United States has refused to recognize the country because of the presence of Cuban troops. In fact, just as it can be argued that Africa must deal mainly with the West because of its historical ties with the West and the inability of communist states to replace those ties, so it can be argued that Africa must maintain ties with the United States, the predominant Western power.

On the other hand, the United States must maintain ties with Africa, since it has a growing involvement on the continent. Part of that involvement is in the form of aid and entails a considerable investment in good will on the part of the United States. In 1981, the Department of State reported that Western aid going to sub-Saharan Africa totaled $9 billion, 10 percent of which came from the United States. Furthermore, the Department said, of American bilateral aid to numerous African countries, 72 percent was for economic development and 28 percent for military assistance, in contrast to Soviet aid, which is overwhelmingly military and to very few countries. American involvement, however, consists of more than aid. It is now particularly dependent on petroleum from Nigeria, and to a lesser extent from Algeria; and is dependent on cobalt, chromium, manganese, and platinum from central and southern Africa. In fact, in 1980 Nigeria had become the eighth largest trading partner of the United States in terms of total transactions (after Canada, Japan, Mexico, West Germany, the United Kingdom, Saudi Arabia, and France). U.S. private investments are increasing in many African countries, and are even being actively sought in such socialist states as Guinea, Mali, and Mozambique. Thus, the United States and many countries of Africa are becoming interdependent, and relations between them must become governed by mutuality of interests. This means that the United States must become more alert to African interests than it has been in the past. Especially important in future relations will be African perceptions of American commitments to eradicate racism and colonialism from the continent. To the extent that America does not perceive these as of the greatest concern to African leaders, strains will remain between the two sides.

Zionism as Racism A concept asserted by the General Assembly of the United Nations that Zionism is "a form of racism and racial discrimination." Zionism is a theory or movement for setting up a Jewish homeland in Palestine. It was always asserted by believers in Zionism, and by international scholars as well, that the concept is nationalistic. While it has a religious base, it is not coterminous with Judaism, since there are many Jews who are not Zionists (who do not advocate a homeland for Jews in Palestine). It also has linguistic characteristics, since Hebrew is the preferred national language. But it is difficult to connect the term with racism, since racism refers to genetic features, and Jews are not genetically distinguishable from millions of non-Jews. *See also* AFRICA AND THE MIDDLE EAST, p. 169; RACE, p. 12; RACISM, p. 13.

Significance The UN resolution declaring that Zionism is a form of racism grew out of two frustrations, that of the hatred Arabs have for the state of Israel, and the hatred Africans have for *apartheid* and White-minority rule in South Africa. These two frustrations finally merged to produce the resolution on Zionism, growing out of continued close relations between the governments of Israel and South Africa. In an earlier resolution in 1973, the UN had condemned the "unholy alliance between South African racism and Zionism" (Resolution 3151, December 14, 1973). In 1975 the OAU Heads of State and Government, meeting in Kampala, asserted that "the racist regime in occupied Palestine and racist regimes in Zimbabwe and South Africa have a common imperialist origin" (Resolution 77, July 27–August 1, 1975). It was thus only one further step to declare that Zionism is a form of racism, and a resolution to that effect was presented to the UN in December 1975. The resolution, however, was highly divisive. It passed in the UN by a vote of 72 for, 35 opposed, and 32 abstaining. Twenty-six African states, including the 9 members of the Arab League, supported the vote, but 17 African states (all in Black Africa) either voted against or abstained. Since many Black states are considering re-establishing diplomatic relations with Israel, it is not clear how they plan to reconcile the UN vote with their renewed relationship.

APPENDIX A: MAPS

A-1 *Countries and Major Geographical Areas of Africa*
A-2 *African States that Have Had One or More Successful Military Coups since 1945*
A-3 *Muslim Majorities and Large Muslim Minorities*
A-4 *Predominant European-Language Areas of Africa*

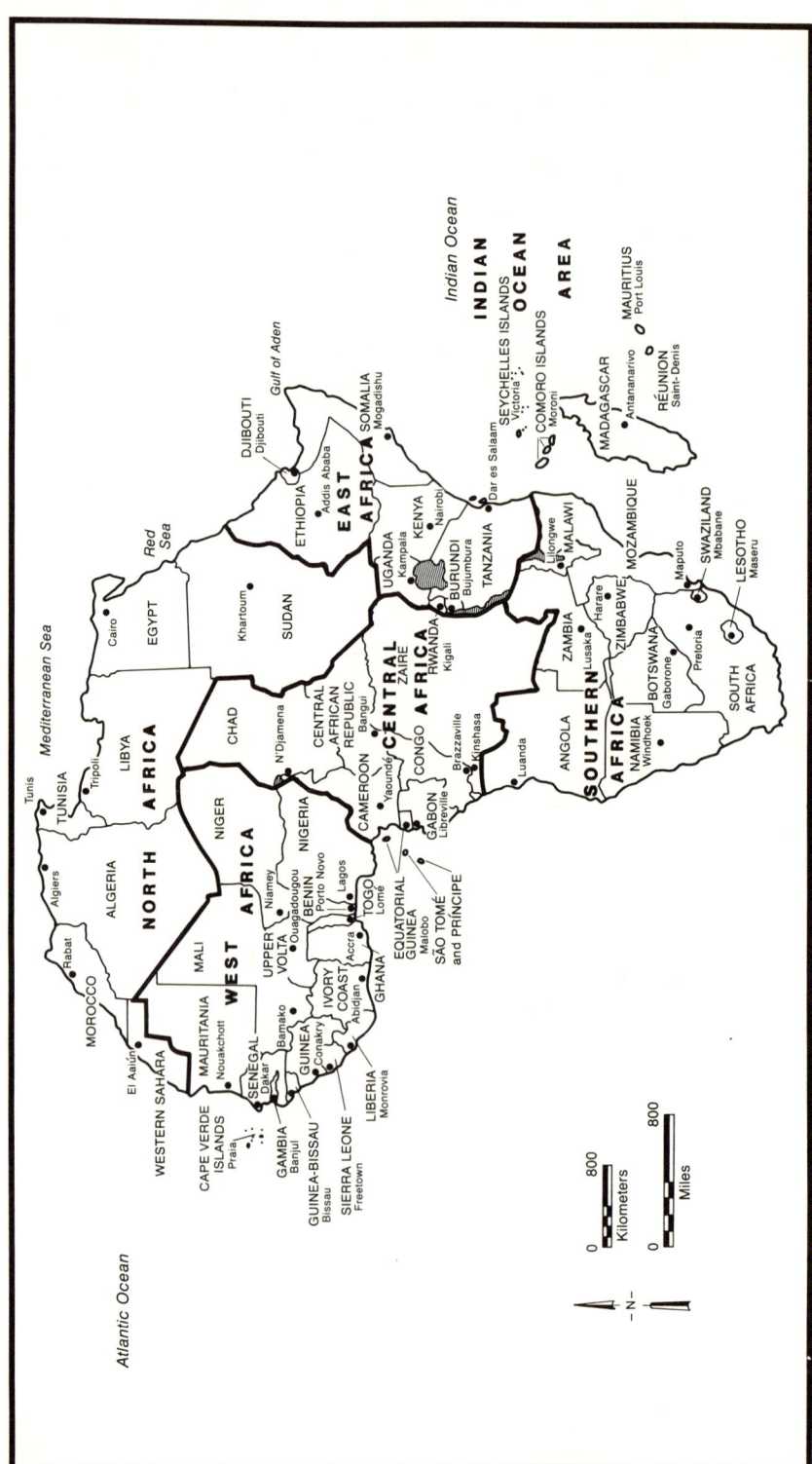

Countries and Major Geographical Areas of Africa

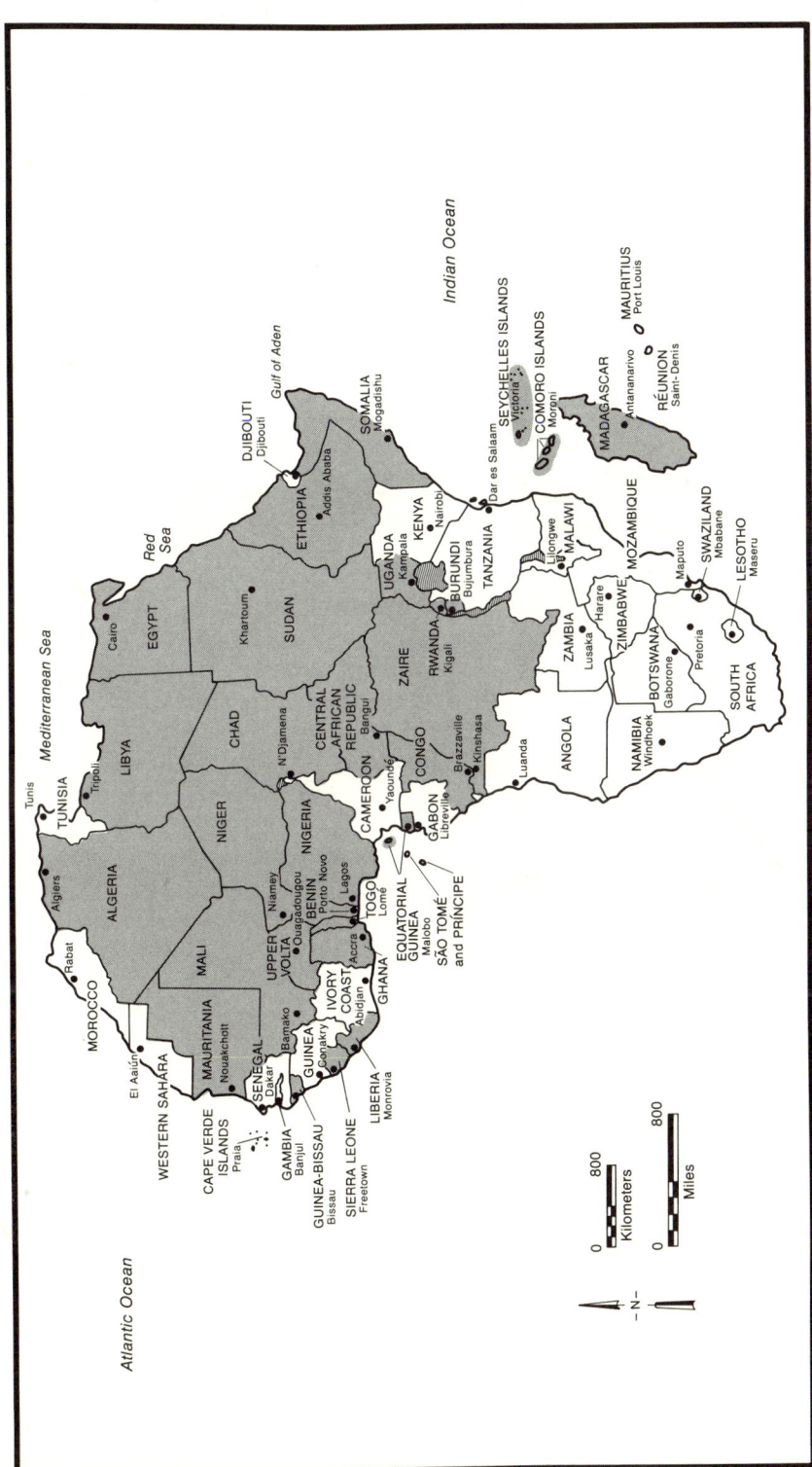

African States that Have Had One or More Successful Military Coups since 1945

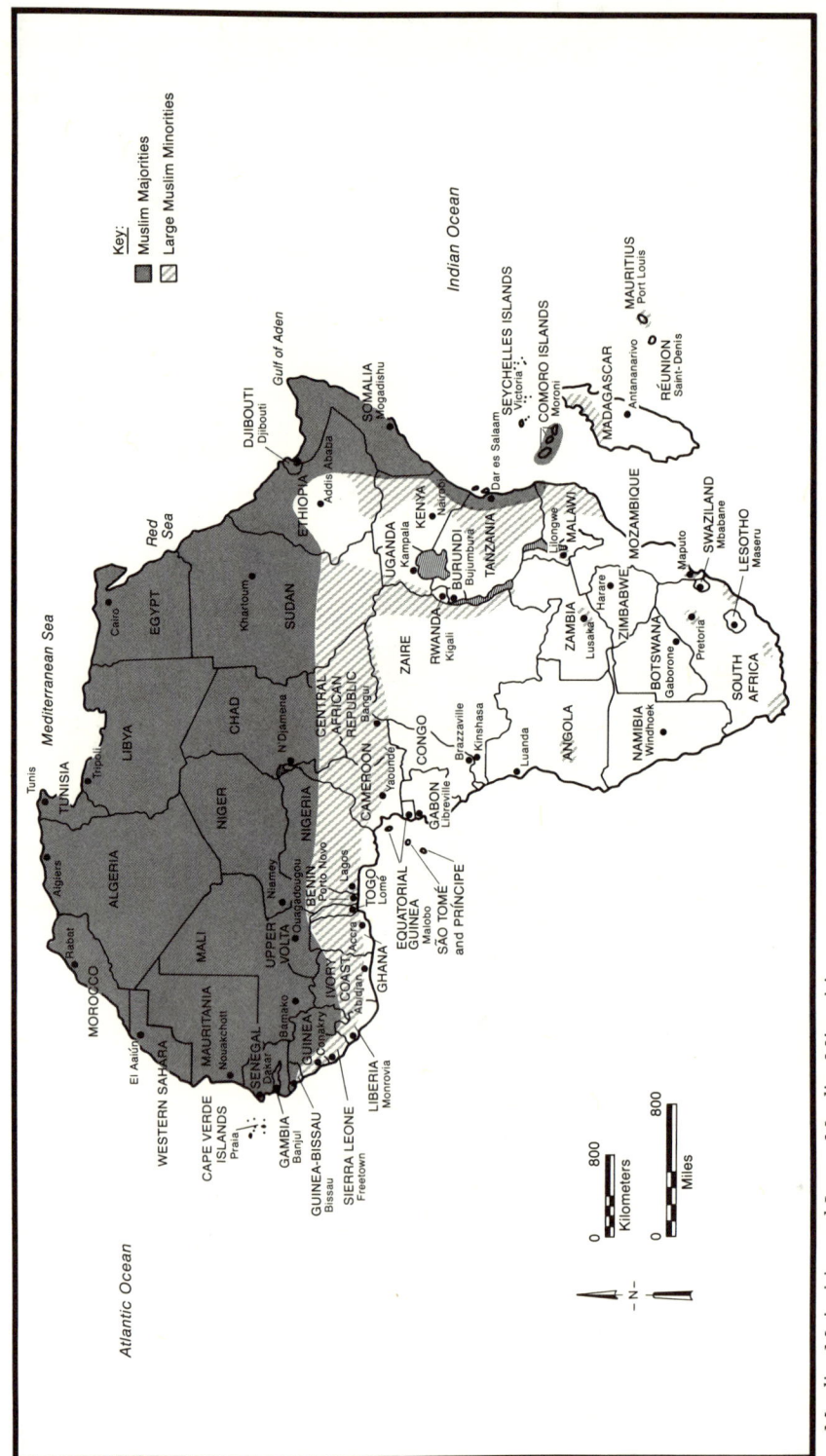

Muslim Majorities and Large Muslim Minorities

Appendix A: Maps

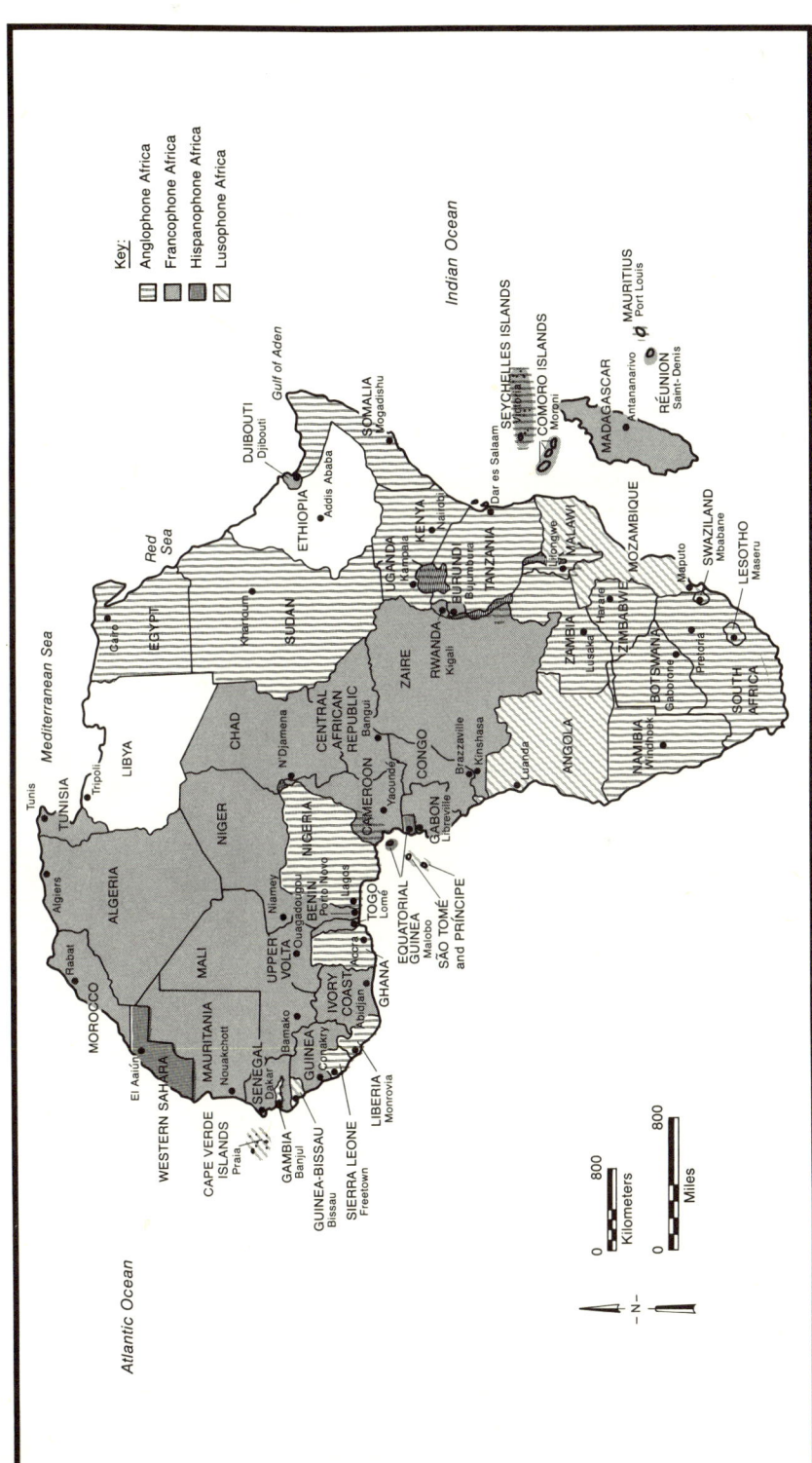

Predominant European-Language Areas of Africa

APPENDIX B: TABLES

B-1 *Gross National Product/Per Capita of the Top 18 Countries*
B-2 *Growth Rates of the Most Populous Countries*
B-3 *Regional and State Populations*
B-4 *Ministries Concerned with Development Administration*
B-5 *Selected Political Data*
B-6 *Political Instability in Independent States*
B-7 *Diplomatic Relations*
B-8 *Communist Technicians and Military Personnel in Sub-Saharan Africa, 1978*

TABLE B-1

GNP/PC of the Top 18 Countries

COUNTRY	GNP/PC	COUNTRY	GNP/PC
Libya	$8,640	Mauritius	$1,060
Réunion	3,830	Nigeria	1,010
Gabon	3,680	Botswana	910
South Africa	2,290	Morocco	860
Algeria	1,920	Swaziland	680
Seychelles	1,770	Cameroon	670
Namibia	1,410	Zimbabwe	630
Tunisia	1,310	Egypt	580
Ivory Coast	1,150	Zambia	560

TABLE B-2

Growth Rates of Most Populous Countries

COUNTRY	PERCENTAGE GROWTH RATE	COUNTRY	PERCENTAGE GROWTH RATE
Kenya	3.9	Ghana	3.1
Algeria	3.2	Sudan	3.0
Morocco	3.2	Zaire	2.8
Nigeria	3.2	Mozambique	2.6
Tanzania	3.2	Ethiopia	2.5
Uganda	3.2	South Africa	2.4
Egypt	3.1		

TABLE B-3

**Regional and State Populations
(In Millions)**

REGION/STATE		REGION/STATE		REGION/STATE	
North Africa	117.0	**Central Africa**	48.9	**Southern Africa**	71.4
Egypt	44.8	Zaire	30.3	South Africa	30.0
Morocco	22.3	Cameroon	8.9	Mozambique	12.7
Algeria	20.1	Chad	4.6	Zimbabwe	8.0
Sudan	19.9	Central African		Angola	6.8
Tunisia	6.7	Republic	2.4	Malawi	6.6
Libya	3.2	Congo	1.6	Zambia	6.0
		Gabon	.7	Lesotho	1.4
West Africa	150.0	Equatorial		Namibia	1.1
Nigeria	82.3	Guinea	.3	Botswana	.9
Ghana	12.4	São Tomé and		Swaziland	.6
Ivory Coast	8.8	Príncipe	.1		
Mali	7.1			**Indian Ocean Area**	11.2
Upper Volta	6.7	**East Africa**	96.9	Madagascar	9.2
Senegal	5.9	Ethiopia	30.5	Mauritius	1.0
Niger	5.8	Tanzania	19.9	Réunion	.5
Guinea	5.3	Kenya	17.9	Comoro	.4
Benin	3.7	Uganda	13.7	Seychelles	.1
Sierra Leone	3.7	Rwanda	5.4		
Togo	2.8	Somalia	4.6		
Liberia	2.0	Burundi	4.4		
Mauritania	1.7	Djibouti	.5		
Guinea-Bissau	.8				
Gambia	.6				
Cape Verde	.3				

TABLE B-4

Ministries Concerned with Development Administration

STATE	NAME OF MINISTRIES
Algeria	Planning; Forests and Agricultural Development
Angola	Planning
Benin	Rural Development; Planning and Statistics
Botswana	Finance and Development Planning
Burundi	Planning; Rural Development
Cameroon	Economy and Planning
Cape Verde	Rural Development; Cooperation and Planning
Central African Republic	Planning and International Cooperation
Chad	Planning
Comoro	Finance, Economy, Planning, and Foreign Trade
Congo	Planning
Egypt	Development; Planning, Finance and Economy
Equatorial Guinea	Transport and Urban Planning
Ethiopia	Planning Commission; Housing and Urban Development; Planning and Development; Natural Resources Development; Government Farming Development; Tea and Coffee Development
Gabon	Planning, Development, and Participation; Commerce, Industrial Development, and Promotion of Small and Medium Enterprise
Gambia	Economic Planning and Industrial Development
Ghana	Finance and Economic Planning; Youth and Rural Development
Guinea	Planning and Statistics; Environment and Town Planning
Guinea-Bissau	Rural Development; Economic Coordination and Planning; Public Works, Construction, and Town Planning
Ivory Coast	Industry and Planning
Kenya	Cooperative Development; Economic Planning; Livestock Development; Water Development
Lesotho	Cooperatives and Rural Development
Liberia	Planning and Economic Affairs; Action for Development and Progress
Libya	Planning
Madagascar	Finance and Planning; Rural Development and Agrarian Reform
Malawi	Housing and Community Development
Mali	Industrial Development and Tourism; Planning; Interior and Town Planning
Mauritania	Rural Development
Mauritius	Economic Planning and Development; Housing, Lands, and Town and Country Planning
Morocco	Equipment and National Development

TABLE B-4—Continued

Ministries Concerned with Development Administration

STATE	NAME OF MINISTRIES
Mozambique	Planning and Agriculture
Niger	Planning; Rural Development
Nigeria	Special Duties (Steel Development); National Planning
Rwanda	Planning
São Tomé and Príncipe	Planning, Labor, and Social Affairs
Senegal	Housing and Urban Development; Planning and Cooperation; Rural Development; Industrial Development and Crafts
Seychelles	Planning and Development; Youth and Community Development
Sierra Leone	Lands, Housing, and Country Planning; Finance, Development, and Economic Planning; Social Welfare and Rural Development
Somalia	National Planning; Mineral Resources and Water Development; Local Government and Rural Development
South Africa	Cooperation and Development
Sudan	National Planning
Tanzania	Economic Affairs and Planning; Manpower Development; Local Government and Rural Development
Togo	Planning and Administrative Reform; Rural Planning; Rural Development; State-Owned Companies and Industrial Development
Tunisia	Planning and Finance
Uganda	Housing and Urban Development; Culture and Community Development; Planning and Economic Development
Upper Volta	Planning and Cooperation; Rural Development; Commerce, Industrial Development, and Mining; Public Works, Transport, and Urban Development
Zaire	Agriculture and Rural Development; Public Works and Territorial Development
Zambia	Agriculture and Water Development; National Commission for Development Planning
Zimbabwe	Manpower, Planning and Development; Lands, Resettlement, and Rural Development; Economic Planning and Development; Industry and Energy Development; Natural Resources and Water Development; Community Development and Women's Affairs

TABLE B-5

Selected Political Data

STATE	COLONIAL RULER	DATE OF INDEPENDENCE	CURRENT FORM OF GOVERNMENT
Algeria	France	July 3, 1962	"One-Party" mobilization machine under the National Liberation Front (FLN), advocating socialism
Angola	Portugal	Nov. 11, 1975	"One-Party" mobilization machine under the Popular Movement for the Liberation of Angola (MPLA), advocating Marxism-Leninism
Benin	France	Aug. 1, 1960	"One-Party" mobilization machine under the Popular Revolutionary Party of Benin (PRPB) advocating Marxism-Leninism
Botswana	Great Britain	Sept. 30, 1966	Democratic, competitive-party system
Burundi	Belgium	July 1, 1962	Military dictatorship under the Unity for National Progress (UPRONA)
Cameroon	France	Jan. 1, 1960	"One-Party" under the National Cameroon Union (UNC), advocating centrist positions
Cape Verde	Portugal	July 5, 1975	"One-Party" system under the African Party for the Independence of Cape Verde (PAICV), advocating "national revolutionary democracy"
Central African Republic	France	Aug. 13, 1960	Military dictatorship
Chad	France	Aug. 11, 1960	Military dictatorship
Comoro Islands	France	July 6, 1975	"One-Party" system of unclear objectives
Congo	France	Aug. 15, 1960	"One-Party" mobilization machine under the Congolese Worker's Party, advocating Marxism-Leninism
Djibouti	France	June 27, 1977	"One-Party" dominant system under the Popular Rally for Progress (RPP), that tolerates a minority party Democratic Front for the Liberation of Djibouti
Egypt	Great Britain	1923	Competitive-party system committed to a mixed economy
Equatorial Guinea	Spain	Oct. 12, 1968	Military dictatorship

TABLE B-5—Continued

Selected Political Data

STATE	COLONIAL RULER	DATE OF INDEPENDENCE	CURRENT FORM OF GOVERNMENT
Ethiopia			"One-Party" mobilization machine under the Commission for Organizing the Party of the Working People of Ethiopia (COPWE), advocating Marxism-Leninism
Gabon	France	Aug. 17, 1960	"One-Party" system under the Gabonese Democratic Party (PDG), committed to free enterprise
Gambia	Great Britain	Feb. 18, 1965	Democratic, competitive-party system
Ghana	Great Britain	Mar. 6, 1957	Military dictatorship under the Provisional National Defense Council
Guinea	France	Oct. 2, 1958	"One-Party" mobilization machine under the Democratic Party of Guinea (PDG), committed to socialism
Guinea-Bissau	Portugal	Sept. 10, 1974	"One-Party" mobilization machine under the African Party for the Independence of Guinea and Cape Verde (PAIGC), committed to socialism
Ivory Coast	France	Aug. 7, 1960	"One-Party" system under the Democratic Party of the Ivory Coast (PDCI), committed to free enterprise
Kenya	Great Britain	Dec. 12, 1963	"One-Party" system under the Kenya African National Union (KANU), committed to free enterprise
Lesotho	Great Britain	Oct. 4, 1966	Dictatorship under the leader of the Basotho National Party (BNP), with unclear objectives
Liberia			Military dictatorship under the People's Redemption Council (PRC), with unclear objectives
Libya	Italy/UN	Dec. 24, 1951	An esoteric dictatorial system committed to socialism and Arab unity
Madagascar	France	June 26, 1960	"One-Party" military dictatorship committed to Marxist socialism
Malawi	Great Britain	July 6, 1964	"One-Party" system under the Malawi Congress Party (MCP), with commitments to capitalism and harsh rule

Continued on next page

TABLE B-5—*Continued*

STATE	COLONIAL RULER	DATE OF INDEPENDENCE	CURRENT FORM OF GOVERNMENT
Mali	France	June 20, 1960	"One-Party" military system under the Democratic Union of Malian People (UDPM), with unclear objectives
Mauritania	France	Nov. 28, 1960	Military dictatorship of unclear objectives
Mauritius	Great Britain	Mar. 12, 1968	Democratic, competitive-party, parliamentary system
Morocco	France	Mar. 2, 1956	Constitutional monarchy with competitive-party system
Mozambique	Portugal	June 25, 1975	"One-Party" mobilization machine committed to Marxism-Leninism
Namibia	South Africa		Colony of South Africa
Niger	France	Aug. 3, 1960	Military dictatorship
Nigeria	Great Britain	Oct. 1, 1960	Democratic multiparty presidential system committed to a mixed economy
Réunion			Department of France
Rwanda	Belgium	July 1, 1962	"One-Party" military system under the National Revolutionary Movement for Development (MRND)
São Tomé and Príncipe	Portugal	July 12, 1975	"One-Party" system under the Movement for the Liberation of São Tomé and Príncipe (MLSTP), committed to vague socialist principles
Senegal	France	June 20, 1960	Democratic, multiparty presidential system
Seychelles	Great Britain	June 29, 1976	"One-Party" system under the Seychelles People's Progressive Front (SPPF), committed to socialism
Sierra Leone	Great Britain	Apr. 12, 1961	"One-Party" system under the All-People's Congress (APC), with unclear objectives
Somalia	Italy/Great Britain/UN	July 1, 1960	"One-Party" system under the Somali Revolutionary Socialist Party (SRSP), committed to socialism and irredentism
South Africa	Great Britain	1910	Democratic, multiparty, parliamentary system for Whites; absolute dictatorship for the non-White majority

TABLE B-5—Continued

STATE	COLONIAL RULER	DATE OF INDEPENDENCE	CURRENT FORM OF GOVERNMENT
Sudan	Great Britain/Egypt	Jan. 1, 1956	"One-Party," quasi-federal system under the Sudanese Socialist Union (SSU), committed to "Sudanese socialism"
Swaziland	Great Britain	Sept. 6, 1968	Traditional monarchy
Tanzania	Great Britain	Dec. 9, 1961 (Tanganyika), Dec. 10, 1963 (Zanzibar)	"One-Party" presidential system under the Chama Cha Mapinduzu (CCM), committed to socialism and self-reliance
Togo	France	Apr. 27, 1960	"One-Party" system under the Rally of Togolese People (RPT), supporting basically a free market
Tunisia	France	Mar. 20, 1956	"One-Party" presidential system under the Socialist Destour Party (PSD), committed to a mixed economy
Uganda	Great Britain	Oct. 9, 1962	Multiparty system of questionable legitimacy
Upper Volta	France	Aug. 5, 1960	Military dictatorship
Western Sahara	Spain		Status in dispute
Zaire	Belgium	June 30, 1960	"One-Party" system under the Popular Movement of the Revolution (MPR)
Zambia	Great Britain	Oct. 24, 1964	"One-Party" system under the United National Independent Party (UNIP)
Zimbabwe	Great Britain	Apr. 18, 1980	Multiparty parliamentary system

TABLE B-6

Political Instability in Independent States[1]

	ELITE INSTABILITY[2]			GENERAL-POPULATION INSTABILITY[3]	
COUNTRY	COUPS D'ETAT[4]	ATTEMPTED COUPS D'ETAT	COUNTRIES	COMMUNAL INSTABILITY[5]	MASS INSTABILITY[6]
Algeria	June 19, 1965		Algeria		
Angola			Angola		
Benin	Oct. 28, 1963 Dec. 22, 1965 Dec. 17, 1967 Dec. 10, 1969 Oct. 26, 1972 Nov. 30, 1972	May 27, 1977 Feb. 23, 1972 Jan. 21, 1975	Benin	Ethnic Violence, March 13, 1964 Rebellion, June 1965	
Botswana			Botswana		
Burundi	July 8, 1966 Nov. 28, 1966 Nov. 1, 1976	Oct. 18, 1965 Apr. 29, 1972	Burundi	Civil War, Oct. 20–Nov. 1965 Hutu Rebellion, May 30, 1972	
Cameroon			Cameroon	Sporadic Rebellion by Bassa and Bamaleke, 1955–1962	
Cape Verde			Cape Verde		
Central African Republic	Dec. 31, 1965 Sep. 20, 1979 Sep. 1, 1981	Apr. 10, 1973 Mar. 3, 1982	Central African Republic		Student Riots, Apr. 1979
Chad	Apr. 13, 1975	Aug. 27, 1971 Apr. 1, 1977 Feb. 13, 1979	Chad	Civil War, 1965–Present	
Comoro	Aug. 3, 1975 May 3, 1978 (Mercenary)	Mar. 3, 1981	Comoro		

Appendix B: Tables

Congo	Aug. 15, 1963 Aug. 3, 1968 Feb. 8, 1979	June 1966 Mar. 22, 1970 Feb. 27, 1972 May 17, 1973 Feb. 15, 1973 Mar. 18, 1977 Aug. 14, 1977	Congo	Ethnic Violence, Feb. 7–11, 1963 Rebellion, Aug. 29, 1968
Djibouti			Djibouti	Afar Rebellion, June 27, 1979
Egypt	July 23, 1952	Apr. 1975	Egypt	
Equatorial Guinea	Aug. 3, 1979	Mar. 1969	Equatorial Guinea	
Ethiopia	June 30–Sep. 12, 1974 Nov. 23, 1974 Feb. 3, 1977	Dec. 14–17, 1960	Ethiopia	Civil War (Eritrea), 1955–present Somali Irredentism, 1960–present
Gabon		Feb. 18–20, 1964	Gabon	
Gambia		July 30, 1981	Gambia	
Ghana	Feb. 24, 1966 Jan. 17, 1972 July 5, 1978 June 4, 1979 Dec. 31, 1981	Apr. 17, 1967 Dec. 1975 May 15, 1979 Nov. 23, 1982	Ghana	Ewe Irredentism, 1957–1963 Dagomba Rebellion, 1979 Konkomba vs. Nanumba clash in north, Apr.–June 1981
Guinea	Nov. 15, 1980		Guinea	Market Women Riots, Aug. 27, 1977
Guinea-Bissau			Guinea-Bissau	
Ivory Coast		Aug. 1, 1982	Ivory Coast	Riots, Dec. 1973–Feb. 1974
Kenya			Kenya	Agni Rebellion, Dec. 1969 Remnants of Mau Mau continue Rebellion, July 1961–1965

Continued on next page

TABLE B-6—Continued

COUNTRY	ELITE INSTABILITY[2]		GENERAL-POPULATION INSTABILITY[3]		
	COUPS D'ETAT[4]	ATTEMPTED COUPS D'ETAT	COUNTRIES	COMMUNAL INSTABILITY[5]	MASS INSTABILITY[6]
Lesotho	Jan. 30, 1970 (Palace coup)		Lesotho		
Liberia	Apr. 12, 1980	June 24, 1955 Aug. 11, 1981	Liberia		Food Riots, Apr. 1979
Libya	Sep. 1, 1969	1975 Mar. 6, 1978 Feb. 1979	Libya		
Madagascar	May 18, 1972 Dec. 31, 1974– Feb. 5, 1975		Madagascar	Southern Revolt, Apr. 1972	Unemployed Riots, May 1978
Malawi			Malawi		Revolt by ex-Ministers and followers Sep. 1964–Oct. 1967
Mali	Nov. 19, 1968	Dec. 31, 1980	Mali	Tuareg Rebellion, Aug. 1963–Aug. 1964	Student/labor union rebellion, Nov. 1979–May 1980
Mauritania	July 10, 1978 Jan. 7, 1980	Dec. 26, 1980 Mar. 16, 1981	Mauritania	Black-White Racial Violence, Jan.–Apr. 1966 Sarakolé versus Haratin Ethnic Clash, May 1967	
Mauritius			Mauritius		
Morocco	July 1971 Aug. 16, 1972		Morocco		
Mozambique			Mozambique		

Appendix B: Tables 211

Namibia		
Niger	Apr. 15, 1974	Exiles Revolt, 1960–1965
Nigeria	Aug. 1975	
	Mar. 15, 1976	
	Feb. 13, 1976	
	Jan. 15, 1966	Tiv Rebellion, 1960, 1964
	July 29, 1966	Anti-Ibo Pogroms, May–Oct. 1966
	July 29, 1975	Civil War (Biafran), May 1967–Jan. 15, 1970
		Kano Religious Riots, Dec. 1980
		Conservative Muslim Riots in Kano, July 10, 1981
Réunion		
Rwanda	July 5, 1973	Civil War (Tutsi), 1963–64, 1966
	Apr. 22, 1980	
São Tomé and Príncipe	Sept. 1979	
Senegal	Dec. 17, 1972	Food Riots, Dec. 1981
Seychelles	June 6, 1977 (Palace coup)	Student Riots, May 1973
	Apr. 30, 1978	
	Nov. 27, 1981	
Sierra Leone	Mar. 21, 1967	Mendé versus Temne Ethnic Violence, Dec. 1968
	Mar. 23, 1967	
	Apr. 18, 1968	
	Mar. 23, 1971	
	July 1974	
Somalia	Oct. 21, 1969	Riots over Prices, Mar. 3, 1980
	Dec. 10, 1961	
South Africa	Apr. 9, 1978	Northern Revolt, Apr.–May 1963
		Sharpville Killings, Mar. 21, 1960
		Soweto Riots, June 1976

Continued on next page

212   The African Political Dictionary

TABLE B-6—Continued

COUNTRY	ELITE INSTABILITY[2]		COUNTRIES	GENERAL-POPULATION INSTABILITY[3]	
	COUPS D'ETAT[4]	ATTEMPTED COUPS D'ETAT		COMMUNAL INSTABILITY[5]	MASS INSTABILITY[6]
Sudan	Nov. 17, 1958 May 25, 1969	May 21, 1959 Nov. 9, 1959 Dec. 18, 1966 July 20, 1971 Sep. 5, 1975 July 2, 1976 Feb. 2, 1977 Mar. 17, 1981	Sudan	Civil War (Black South versus Arab North), 1955–1972 Ansar Muslim Sect Rebellion, Mar. 1970	Judges, Civil Servants, Workers Revolt, Oct. 20–30, 1964 Revolt over Prices, Aug. 1979
Swaziland	Apr. 12, 1973 (Palace coup)		Swaziland		
Tanzania			Tanzania		
Togo	Jan. 13, 1963 Jan. 13, 1967	Nov. 21, 1966	Togo		
Tunisia			Tunisia		
Uganda	Feb. 22, 1966 (Palace coup) Jan. 25, 1971 May 10, 1980	June 20, 1972 Mar. 1974 Nov. 1974	Uganda	Bunyoro versus Buganda Ethnic Violence, Feb. 15–Mar. 30, 1963 Amba and Konjo versus Toro, 1962–1963 Buganda Rebellion, Mar.–July 1966	
Upper Volta	Jan. 3, 1966 Feb. 8, 1974 (Palace coup) Nov. 25, 1980 Nov. 7, 1982		Upper Volta		

Appendix B: Tables

Western Sahara			Western Sahara		
Zaire	Sep. 14, 1960 Nov. 25, 1965	Nov. 19, 1963 June 1975	Zaire	Civil War (Katanga), 1960–1963 Civil War (Bukavu), 1967 Luba versus Lunda Ethnic Violence, May 1963 Shaba Rebellion from Angola, Mar. 1977 Second Shaba Rebellion, May 1978	Socialist Revolt, 1960–1966 Student Riots, Autumn 1968, Feb. 1969, June 1969
Zambia			Zambia		Lumpa Church Revolt, Oct. 1964–Nov. 1967 Kitwe Riots, June 22, 1977
Zimbabwe			Zimbabwe		

[1]Compiled by the author primarily from the following: *Africa News*; *Africa South of the Sahara*, 10th ed., 1980; *Cambridge Encyclopedia of Africa*, 1981; Colin Legum, ed., *Africa Contemporary Record*, Vols. 10 (1979) and 13 (1982); and Donald Morrison, et al., *Black Africa*, 1972.
[2]For the definition of *elite instability*, see pp. 125–126.
[3]Includes only overt action countered by the police or army resulting in deaths, injuries, and/or imprisonment. Does not include alleged plots, conspiracies, strikes, demonstrations, mutinies, or guerrilla warfare.
[4]Military coups unless indicated otherwise. Includes only successful overthrows of governments.
[5]For the definition of *communal instability*, see p. 124.
[6]For the definition of *mass instability*, see p. 129.

TABLE B-7

Diplomatic Relations

COUNTRY	WITH OTHER AFRICAN STATES	WITH FIRST WORLD STATES[1]	WITH SECOND WORLD STATES[2]	WITH THIRD WORLD STATES[3]	TOTALS
Algeria	39	22	14	43	118
Angola	19	17	12	8	56
Benin	21	19	13	10	63
Botswana	14	17	8	6	45
Burundi	21	20	11	9	61
Cameroon	33	21	9	12	75
Cape Verde	19	16	13	4	43
Central African Republic	14	18	8	5	45
Chad	19	15	8	12	54
Comoro	3	11	6	4	24
Congo	22	19	14	6	61
Djibouti	11	13	8	8	40
Egypt	40	25	12	49	126
Equatorial Guinea	5	7	11	3	26
Ethiopia	35	21	17	27	100
Gabon	26	19	9	13	67
Gambia	21	19	11	13	64
Ghana	34	23	12	22	91
Guinea	40	18	15	19	92
Guinea-Bissau	18	16	12	4	50
Ivory Coast	27	20	7	17	71
Kenya	28	23	8	25	84
Lesotho	15	20	8	11	54
Liberia	26	19	8	11	64
Libya	27	19	11	36	93
Madagascar	9	20	13	8	50
Malawi	12	19	1	5	37
Mali	22	18	14	14	68
Mauritania	20	17	14	17	68
Mauritius	12	20	10	13	55
Morocco	22	22	11	35	90
Mozambique	23	17	13	10	63
Niger	24	20	10	13	67
Nigeria	37	24	14	26	106
Rwanda	18	18	12	5	53
São Tomé and Príncipe	8	9	13	1	31
Senegal	28	23	12	29	92
Seychelles	7	17	13	8	45
Sierra Leone	28	19	12	15	74
Somalia	12	18	14	19	63

TABLE B-7—*Continued*

Diplomatic Relations

COUNTRY	WITH OTHER AFRICAN STATES	WITH FIRST WORLD STATES[1]	WITH SECOND WORLD STATES[2]	WITH THIRD WORLD STATES[3]	TOTALS
South Africa	1	24		12	37
Sudan	30	21	13	25	89
Swaziland	14	17		7	38
Tanzania	28	23	15	17	83
Togo	21	19	13	9	62
Tunisia	35	24	12	30	101
Uganda	34	20	12	16	82
Upper Volta	19	21	12	11	63
Zaire	39	20	11	16	86
Zambia	36	22	15	23	96
Zimbabwe	18	18	11	4	51

[1] Includes Western European states, the United States, Canada, Australia, New Zealand, Japan, Turkey, Israel, and the Vatican.

[2] Includes the Soviet Union, Eastern European states, China, Cuba, and People's Democratic Republic of Yemen.

[3] Non-African Third World states.

TABLE B-8

Communist Technicians and Military Personnel in Sub-Saharan Africa, 1978[1]

COUNTRY	SOVIET UNION AND EASTERN EUROPE[2]		CUBA		CHINA	
	TECHNICIANS	MILITARY	TECHNICIANS	MILITARY	TECHNICIANS	MILITARY
Angola	1,400	1,300	8,500	19,000	10	
Equatorial Guinea		40		150		
Ethiopia	650	1,400	500	16,500	250	100
Gabon	10				65	
Gambia					75	
Ghana	95				80	
Guinea	700	100	35	200	300	30
Guinea-Bissau	265	65	85	140	55	
Kenya	25				5	
Liberia	10				200	
Madagascar					200	
Mali	475	180			550	15
Mauritius					15	
Mozambique	750	230	400	800	120	100
Niger	10				150	
Nigeria	1,625				125	
Rwanda	10				50	
São Tomé and Príncipe	20		140		100	
Senegal	100				400	
Sierra Leone	10				300	

Somalia	50				3,000	
Sudan	125				650	
Tanzania	165		200		1,000	
Zambia	125		20		5,500	
Others	1,020	500	1,090	485	5,415	345
Totals	7,640	3,815	10,970	32,275	18,615	590

[1]Compiled by the author from tables in United States Department of State, *Current Policy No. 99; Communism in Africa,* October 18, 1979.
[2]Mainly Soviets, the remainder being mostly East Germans.

SELECTED BIBLIOGRAPHY

References Cited in the Text

Anderson, David. 1982. "America in Africa, 1981," in William P. Bundy, ed. *Foreign Affairs: America and the World 1981.* New York: Pergamon Press.

Bairoch, Paul. 1973. *The Economic Development of the Third World.* Tr. by Lady Cynthia Postan. Berkeley: University of California Press.

Boahen, A. Adu. 1966. *Topics in West African History.* London: Longmans.

Braibanti, Ralph. 1961. "The Relevance of Political Science to the Study of Underdeveloped Areas." In Ralph Braibanti and Joseph J. Spengler, eds. *Tradition, Values, and Socio-Economic Development.* Durham: Duke University Press.

Caiden, Naomi, and Aaron Wildavsky. 1974. *Planning and Budgeting in Poor Countries.* New York: Wiley.

Champmarin, A. 1982. "What did the Paris Conference Achieve?" *The Courier: African-Caribbean-Pacific Community.* Brussels.

Crowder, Michael. 1962. *The Story of Nigeria.* London: Faber and Faber.

Eker, Varda. 1981. "On the Origins of Corruption: Irregular Incentives in Nigeria." *Journal of Modern African Studies.* Vol. 19, No. 1 (March), 173–82.

Ekpo, Monday U., ed. 1979. *Bureaucratic Corruption in Sub-Saharan Africa.* Washington: University Press of America.

Federal Republic of Nigeria. 1976. *Report of the Constitution Drafting Committee Containing the Draft Constitution.* Lagos: Federal Ministry of Information.

Gant, George F. 1979. *Development Administration.* Madison: University of Wisconsin Press.

Hallett, Robin. 1974. *Africa since 1875.* Ann Arbor: Univeristy of Michigan Press.

Huntington, Samuel P. 1968. *Political Order in Changing Societies.* New Haven: Yale University Press.

Larkin, Bruce D. 1981. "China in Africa in 1980." In Colin Legum, ed. *Africa Contemporary Record*, XIII, A153–60.
Legum, Colin, ed. 1968–1981. *Africa Contemporary Record*. Vols. I–XIII. New York: Africana Publishing Co.
Legum, Colin, I. William Zartman, Steven Langdon, and Lynn K. Mytelka. 1979. *Africa in the 1980s: A Continent in Crisis*. New York: Mc-Graw-Hill.
Lerner, Daniel. 1959. *The Human Meaning of the Social Sciences*. New York: Meridian Books.
Mabogunje, Akin L. 1981. *The Development Process: A Spatial Perspective*. New York: Holmes and Meier.
Mazrui, Ali. 1977. *Africa's International Relations*. Boulder, Col.: Westview Press.
McGowan, Patrick J. 1979. "Economic Dependence and Economic Performance in Black Africa," *Journal of Modern African Studies*, Vol. 14, No. 1 (March), 25–40.
Morrison, Donald G., Robert C. Mitchell, John N. Paden, and Hugh M. Stevenson. 1972. *Black Africa*. New York: Free Press.
Murdock, George P. 1959. *Africa: Its Peoples and Their Cultural History*. New York: McGraw-Hill.
Myrdal, Gunnar. 1973. *Against the Stream: Critical Essays on Economics*. New York: Vintage Books.
Oliver, Roland A., and Anthony Atmore. 1981. *Africa Since 1800*. Cambridge: Cambridge University Press.
Olugbemi, Stephen O. 1979. "The Civil Service: An Outsider's View." In Oyelele Oyediran, ed. *Nigerian Government and Politics under Military Rule, 1966–79*. London: Macmillan Press.
Ottaway, David, and Marina Ottaway. 1981. *Afrocommunism*. New York: Africana Publishing Co.
Phillips, Claude S. 1964. *The Development of Nigerian Foreign Policy*. Evanston: Northwestern University Press.
Senghor, Leopold. 1962. "What is Negritude?" *Negro Digest* (April).
Singer, H. W. 1978. "The New International Economic Order," *Journal of Modern African Studies*, Vol. 16, No. 4 (December), 539–48.
Sklar, Richard. 1975. *Corporate Power in an African State*. Berkeley: University of California Press.
Spengler, Joseph J. 1971. "Democratic Political Systems as Vehicles for Economic Development." In Monte Palmer and Larry Stern, eds. *Political Development in Changing Societies*. Lexington, Mass.: Heath Lexington Books.
Stolper, Wolfgang. 1966. *Planning without Facts: Lessons in Resource Allocation from Nigeria's Development*. Cambridge: Harvard University Press.
Stryker, Richard. 1977. "Development Strategies." In Phyllis M. Martin and Patrick O'Meara, eds. *Africa*. Bloomington: Indiana University Press.
Study Commission on U.S. Policy toward Southern Africa. 1981. *South Africa: Time Running Out*. Berkeley: University of California Press.

Thompson, W. Scott. 1978. "A World of Parts." In W. Scott Thompson, ed. *The Third World: Premises of U.S. Policy.* San Francisco: Institute for Contemporary Studies.
Vengroff, Richard. 1977. "Dependency and Underdevelopment in Black Africa: An Empirical Test." *Journal of Modern African Studies,* Vol. 15, No. 4 (December), 613–30.
Zartman, I. William. 1963. "The Sahara—Bridge or Barrier?" *International Conciliation,* No. 541 (January), 1–62.
Zartman, I. William. 1966. *International Relations in the New Africa.* Englewood Cliffs, N.J.: Prentice-Hall.

Recent Works of a General Nature

Africa Research Bulletin. 1981. Vol. 18. Exeter: Africa Research Ltd.
Africa South of the Sahara. 1980. Tenth Edition. London: Europa Publications, Ltd.
Albright, David E., ed. 1980. *Communism in Africa.* Bloomington: Indiana University Press.
Aluko, Olajide, ed. 1977. *The Foreign Policies of African States.* London: Hodder and Stoughton.
Aluko, Olajide. 1981. "African Response to External Intervention in Africa since Angola." *African Affairs.* Vol. 80, No. 319 (April), 159–79.
Amin, Samir. 1977. *Unequal Development: An Essay on the Social Formations of Peripheral Capitalism.* Tr. by Brian Pearce. New York: Monthly Review.
Amnesty International. 1981. *Report 1981.* London: Amnesty International Publications.
Barkan, Joel D., and John J. Okumu. 1979. *Politics and Public Policy in Kenya and Tanzania.* New York: Praeger.
Bates, Robert H. 1981. *Markets and States in Tropical Africa: The Political Basis of Agricultural Policies.* Berkeley: University of California Press.
Bowman, Larry W., and Ian Clark. 1980. *The Indian Ocean in Global Politics.* Boulder, Col.: Westview Press.
Carter, Gwendolen M., and Philip E. Morgan, eds. 1981. *From the Frontline Speeches of Sir Seretse Khama.* Stanford: Hoover Institution Press.
Carter, Gwendolen M., and Patrick O'Meara, eds. 1982. *International Politics in Southern Africa.* Bloomington: Indiana University Press.
Carter, Gwendolen, and Patrick O'Meara, eds. 1982. *Southern Africa: The Continuing Crisis.* 2d ed. Bloomington: Indiana University Press.
Cervenka, Zdenek. 1978. *The Unfinished Quest for Unity: Africa and the OAU.* New York: Holmes & Meier.
Chime, Chimelu. 1978. *Integration and Politics Among African States: Limitations and Horizons of Mid-Term Theorizing.* Uppsala: Scandina-

vian Institute of African Studies.
Clapham, Christopher. 1976. *Liberia and Sierra Leone—An Essay in Comparative Politics.* New York: Cambridge University Press.
Collier, Ruth Berius. 1982. *Regimes in Tropical Africa.* Berkeley: University of California Press.
Crahan, Margaret E., and Franklin W. Knight. 1979. *Africa and the Caribbean: The Legacy of a Link.* Baltimore: Johns Hopkins University Press.
Curtin, Philip, Steven Feierman, Leonard Thompson, and Jan Vansina. 1978. *African History.* Boston: Little, Brown & Co.
Davidson, Basil. 1981. *No Fist Is Big Enough To Hide the Sky: The Liberation of Guinea and Cape Verde.* London: Zed Press.
Decalo, Samuel. 1976. *Coups and Army Rule in Africa: Studies in Military Style.* New Haven, Conn: Yale University Press.
Dunn, John, ed. 1978. *West African States: Failure and Promise.* Cambridge: Cambridge University Press.
Entelis, John. 1980. *Comparative Politics of North Africa.* Syracuse, N.Y.: Syracuse University Press.
Esposito, John, ed. 1980. *Islam and Development: Religion and Socio-Political Change.* Syracuse: N.Y.: Syracuse University Press.
Gann, L. H., and Peter Duignan. 1981. *Africa South of the Sahara: The Challenge to Western Security.* Stanford: Hoover Institution Press.
Harris, Richard, ed. 1975. *The Political Economy of Africa.* Cambridge, Mass.: Schenkman Publishing Co.
Harrison Church, R. J. 1979. *West Africa.* London: Longman.
Henriksen, Thomas H., ed. 1981. *Communist Powers and Sub-Saharan Africa.* Stanford: Hoover Institution Press.
Hull, Galen Spencer. 1982. *Pawns on a Chessboard: The Resource War in Southern Africa.* Washington, D.C.: University Press of America.
Hutchison, Alan. 1976. *China's African Revolution.* Boulder, Col.: Westview Press.
Ibingira, Grace S. 1980. *African Upheavals since Independence.* Boulder, Col.: Westview Press.
Jackson, Henry F. 1982. *From the Congo to Soweto: U.S. Foreign Policy Toward Africa.* New York: William Morrow & Co.
Jackson, Robert H., and Carl G. Rosberg. 1982. *Personal Rule in Black Africa.* Berkeley: University of California Press.
Kaunda, Kenneth David. 1980. *Kaunda on Violence.* Ed. by Colin M. Morris. London: Collins.
Kotecha, Ken C., and Robert W. Adams. 1981. *African Politics: The Corruption of Power.* Washington, D.C.: University Press of America.
Kuper, Hilda. 1978. *Sobhuza II: Ngwenyama and King of Swaziland.* New York: Holmes & Meier.
Legum, Colin, and Bill Lee. 1978. *Conflict in the Horn of Africa.* New York: Holmes & Meier.
LeoGrande, William M. 1980. *Cuba's Policy in Africa, 1959–1980.* Berkeley: Institute of International Studies, University of California.

LeVine, Victor T., and Timothy W. Luke. 1979. *The Arab-African Connection.* Boulder, Col.: Westview Press.
Lloyd, Peter. 1982. *A Third World Proletariat?* Winchester, Mass.: Allen & Unwin, Inc.
Long, David E., and Bernard Reich. 1980. *Government and Politics of the Middle East and North Africa.* Boulder, Col.: Westview Press.
Lowenthal, Richard. 1977. *Model or Ally?: Communist Powers and the Developing Countries.* New York: Oxford University Press.
Lozoya, Jorge A., and Hector Cuadra, eds. 1980. *Africa, the Middle East and NIEO.* Elmsford, N.Y.: Pergamon Press Inc.
Luthuli, Albert. 1969. *Let My People Go.* New York: NAL.
Martin, Phyllis M., and Patrick O'Meara, eds. 1977. *Africa.* Bloomington: Indiana University Press.
Mazrui, Ali A. 1980. *The African Condition.* New York: Cambridge University Press.
Moore, Clement Henry. 1970. *Politics in North Africa.* Boston: Little, Brown & Co.
Oliver, Roland, and Michael Crowder, eds. 1981. *Cambridge Encyclopedia of Africa.* Cambridge: Cambridge University Press.
Olson, Robert K. 1981. *U.S. Foreign Policy and the New International Economic Order.* Boulder, Col: Westview Press.
Ostheimer, J. 1975. *The Politics of the Western Indian Ocean Islands.* New York: Praeger.
Ottaway, Marina. 1978. "Soviet Marxism and African Socialism." *Journal of Modern African Studies.* Vol. 16, No. 3 (September), 477–85.
Paden, John, and Edward W. Soja, eds. 1970. *The African Experience.* Vol. I. *Essays.* Evanston, Ill.: Northwestern University Press.
Potholm, Christian P. 1979. *The Theory and Practice of African Politics.* Englewood Cliffs, N.J.: Prentice-Hall.
Price, Robert M. 1978. *U.S. Foreign Policy in Sub-Saharan Africa: National Interest and Global Strategy.* Berkeley: Institute of International Studies, University of California.
Reubens, Edwin P., ed. 1981. *The Challenge of the New International Economic Order.* Boulder, Col.: Westview Press.
Rosberg, Carl G., and Thomas M. Callaghy, eds. 1979. *Socialism in Sub-Saharan Africa.* Berkeley: Institute of International Studies, University of California.
Samuels, Michael A. 1980. *Africa and the West.* Boulder, Col.: Westview Press.
Scarritt, James R. 1980. *Analyzing Political Change in Africa.* Boulder, Col.: Westview Press.
Shaw, Timothy M., ed. 1981. *Alternative Futures for Africa.* Boulder, Col.: Westview Press.
Slater, Charles C., et al. 1979. *Easing Transition in Southern Africa.* Boulder, Col.: Westview Press.
Stevens, Christopher. 1976. *The Soviet Union and Black Africa.* New York: Holmes & Meier.
Vansina, Jan. 1980. "Bantu in the Crystal Ball, II." *History in Africa: A*

Journal of Methodology. Vol. 7, 293-325.
Weinstein, Warren, and Thomas H. Henriksen, eds. 1980. *Soviet and Chinese Aid to African Nations.* New York: Praeger.
Young, Crawford. 1982. *Ideology and Development in Africa.* New Haven: Yale University Press.

Recent Works on Individual Countries

Adamolekun, Ladipo. 1976. *Sekou Toure's Guinea: An Experiment in Nation Building.* New York: Methuen Inc.
Aluko, Olajide. 1981. *Essays in Nigerian Foreign Policy.* Boston: Allen & Unwin.
Anglin, Douglas G., and Timothy M. Shaw. 1979. *Zambia's Foreign Policy.* Boulder, Col.: Westview Press.
Arnold, Guy. 1981. *Modern Kenya.* London: Longman Group, Inc.
Austin, Dennis, and Robin Luckham, eds. 1977. *Politicians and Soldiers in Ghana.* London: Frank Cass Co.
Baker, Raymond W. 1978. *Egypt's Uncertain Revolution under Nasser and Sadat.* Cambridge, Mass.: Harvard University Press.
Barbour, K. M. 1980. "The Sudan since Independence." *Journal of Modern African Studies.* Vol. 18, No. 1 (March), 73-97.
Bechtold, Peter K. 1978. *Politics in the Sudan.* New York: Praeger.
Beckett, Paul, and James O'Connell. 1978. *Education and Power in Nigeria.* New York: Holmes & Meier.
Bender, Gerald. 1978. *Angola under the Portuguese: The Myth and the Reality.* Berkeley: University of California Press.
Bissell, Richard E., and Chester A. Crocker, eds. 1979. *South Africa into the 1980s.* Boulder, Col.: Westview Press.
Bratton, Michael. 1980. *The Local Politics of Rural Development: Peasant and Party State in Zambia.* Hanover, N.H.: University Press of New England.
Carter, Gwendolen M. 1980. *Which Way Is South Africa Going?* Bloomington: Indiana University Press.
Colclough, Christopher, and Stephen McCarthy. 1980. *The Political Economy of Botswana: A Study of Growth and Distribution.* Oxford: Oxford University Press.
Cox, Thomas S. 1976. *Civil-Military Relations in Sierra Leone: A Case Study of African Soldiers in Politics.* Cambridge, Mass.: Harvard University Press.
Debel, Anne. 1979. *Cameroon Today.* New York: Hippocrene Books.
Decalo, Samuel. 1980. "Regionalism, Political Decay, and Civil Strife in Chad." *Journal of Modern African Studies.* Vol. 18, No. 1 (March), 23-56.
Dudley, Billy J. 1982. *An Introduction to Nigerian Government and Politics.* Bloomington: Indiana University Press.
Diallo, Siradiou. 1979. *Zaire Today.* New York: Hippocrene Books.

El Fathaly, Omar, and Monte Palmer. 1980. *Political Development and Social Change in Libya.* Lexington, Mass.: Lexington Books.

Gann, L. H., and Peter Duignan. 1981. *Why South Africa Will Survive.* New York: St. Martin's Press.

Gellar, Sheldon. 1982. *Senegal.* Boulder, Col.: Westview Press.

Hanf, Theodor, et al. 1981. *South Africa: The Prospects for Peaceful Change.* Bloomington: Indiana University Press.

Hillis, Denis Cecil. 1981. *The Last Days of White Rhodesia.* London: Chatto & Windus.

Houbert, Jean. 1981. "Mauritius: Independence and Dependence." *Journal of Modern African Studies.* Vol. 19, No. 1 (March), 75–105.

Joseph, Richard A. 1977. *Radical Nationalism in Cameroon.* New York: Oxford University Press.

Kirk-Greene, Anthony, and Douglas Rimmer. 1981. *Nigeria since 1970: A Political and Economic Outline.* New York: Holmes & Meier.

Klinghoffer, Arthur Jay. 1980. *The Angolan War: A Study in Soviet Policy in the Third World.* Boulder, Col.: Westview Press.

Kofele-Kale, Ndiva. 1980. *An African Experiment in National Building: The Bilingual Cameroon Republic since Reunification.* Boulder, Col.: Westview Press.

Lawless, Richard I. 1981. *Algeria.* Santa Barbara, Cal.: American Bibliographic Center.

Lewis, I. M. 1980. *A Modern History of Somalia: Nation and State in the Horn of Africa.* New York: Longman.

Leys, Colin. 1975. *Underdevelopment in Kenya: The Political Economy of Neo-Colonialism, 1964–71.* Berkeley: University of California Press.

Liebenow, J. Gus. 1969. *Liberia: The Evolution of Privilege.* Ithaca, N.Y.: Cornell University Press.

Linden, Ian. 1980. *The Catholic Church and the Struggle for Zimbabwe.* New York: Longman.

Lowenkopf, Martin. 1976. *Politics in Liberia: The Conservative Road to Development.* Stanford: Hoover Institution Press.

Martin, David, and Phyllis Johnson. 1981. *The Struggle for Zimbabwe.* Salem, N.H.: Faber & Faber.

McHenry, Dean E., Jr. 1979. *Tanzania's Ujamaa Villages: The Implementation of a Rural Development Strategy.* Berkeley: Institute of International Studies, University of California.

Morrison, Minion K. C. 1981. *Ethnicity and Political Integration: The Case of Ashanti, Ghana.* Syracuse, N.Y.: Foreign and Comparative Studies Program, Syracuse University.

Mwansasu, Bismark, and Cranford Pratt, eds. 1979. *Towards Socialism in Tanzania.* Downsview, Ontario: University of Toronto Press.

Norcliffe, Glen, and Tom Pinfold, eds. 1981. *Planning African Development: The Kenyan Experience.* Boulder, Col.: Westview Press.

Obasanjo, Olusegun. 1981. *My Command: An Account of the Nigerian Civil War, 1967–1970.* London: Heineman.

O'Brien, D. B. C. 1975. *Saints and Politicians: Senegalese Peasant Society.*

New York: Cambridge University Press.
O'Brien, Rita C., ed. 1979. *The Political Economy of Underdevelopment: Dependence in Senegal.* Beverly Hills, Cal.: Sage.
Ottaway, Marina, and David Ottaway. 1978. *Ethiopia: Empire in Revolution.* New York: Holmes & Meier.
Oyediran, Oyelele, ed. 1979. *Nigerian Government and Politics under Military Rule, 1966-1979.* New York: St. Martin's.
Phillips, Claude S. 1980. "Nigeria's New Political Institutions, 1975-9." *Journal of Modern African Studies.* Vol. 18, No. 1 (March), 1-22.
Phillips, Earl. 1974. "State Regulation and Economic Initiative: The South African Case to 1960." *International Journal of African Historical Studies.* Vol. 7, No. 2, 227-54.
Pettman, Jan. 1974. *Zambia: Security and Conflict, 1964-73.* New York: St. Martin's.
Rosberg, Carl G., and Robert M. Price, eds. 1980. *The Apartheid Regime: Political Power and Racial Domination.* Berkeley: Institute of International Studies, University of California.
Rotberg, Robert I., and John Barratt, eds. 1980. *Conflict and Compromise in South Africa.* Lexington, Mass.: Lexington Books.
Saint Veran, Robert. 1981. *Djibouti: Pawn of the Horn of Africa.* Metuchen, N.J.: Scarecrow Press, Inc.
Schatzberg, Michael G. 1980. *Politics and Class in Zaire.* New York: Holmes & Meier.
Sheik-Abdi, Abdi. 1981. "Ideology and Leadership in Somalia." *Journal of Modern African Studies.* Vol. 19, No. 1 (March), 163-72.
Sherman, Richard. 1980. *Eritrea: The Unfinished Revolution.* New York: Praeger.
Simmons, Adele S. 1982. *Modern Mauritius: The Politics of Decolonialization.* Bloomington: Indiana University Press.
Spencer, John H. 1977. *Ethiopia: The Horn of Africa and U.S. Policy.* Cambridge, Mass.: Institute for Foreign Policy Analysis Inc.
Thompson, Virginia, and Richard Adloff. 1981. *Conflict in Chad.* Berkeley: Institute of International Studies, University of California.
Tordoff, William, ed. 1974. *Politics in Zambia.* Berkeley: University of California Press.
Vail, Leroy, and Landeg White. 1981. *Capitalism and Colonialism in Mozambique.* London: Heineman.
Wai, Dunstan M. 1981. *The African-Arab Conflict in the Sudan.* New York: Holmes & Meier.
Warburg, Gabriel. 1978. *Islam, Nationalism and Communism in a Traditional Society: The Case of Sudan.* London: Frank Cass.
Waterbury, John. 1978. *Egypt: Burdens of the Past, Options for the Future.* Bloomington: Indiana University Press.
Williams, T. David. 1978. *Malawi: The Politics of Despair.* Ithaca, N.Y.: Cornell University Press.
Wolpe, Howard. 1974. *Urban Politics: A Study of Port Harcourt.* Berkeley: University of California Press.
Yeager, Rodger. 1982. *Tanzania.* Boulder, Col.: Westview Press.

INDEX

Cross-references to dictionary entries are located in the text at the end of each definition paragraph. Page references in BOLD type indicate dictionary entries. For individual countries, consult the *Guide to Countries* on p. xiii.

Aba Women's Riots, **53**
Aborigenes' Rights Protection Society, 61, 65
Absolute monarchies, 96
Acephalous society, **19–20**
  colonial domination, 32
  democracy, 72
  politics, 81
  Warrant chiefs in, 52
ACP. *See* African-Caribbean-Pacific Community
ADB. *See* African Development Bank
Administration, development, **87–88**
Administration, table of ministries, 202–203
Administrative bodies, 70
Advisors in foreign aid, 116
African and Mauritian Common Organization (OCAM), 153
African-Caribbean-Pacific Community (ACP), 147, 153, **172**
African Charter on Human and People's Rights, 159
African Defense Force, **139–140**
African Development Bank (ADB), **140**, 153, 164, 175
African diplomatic relations, 144
African Economic Community, proposed, 159
African Group, **173**
African independent churches, **54**
Africanization, 92–93
African Liberation Committee (ALC), 134, **142–143**
  ANC and, 122, 143
  FNLA and, 143
  MPLA and, 143
  OAU and, 158
  PAC and, 143
  Polisario and, 143
  support for Mugabe and Nkomo, 143
  SWAPO and, 143
African Methodist Episcopal Church (AME), 55
African National Congress (ANC, South Africa), 61, **121–122**
  ALC and, 143
  banned, 122
  guerrilla warfare, 126
  OAU and, 159
  PAC and, 134
African personality, **67**
African Research Bulletin, 163
African socialism, **67–68**, 83
Africa south of the Sahara. *See* Sub-Saharan Africa
Afrikaans, 35, 40, 42
Afrikaner, **35**, 40
  Boer connection, 39
  cultural nationalism of, 40
  English-speaking Whites and, 50
  Great Trek of, 47
  separate development and, 50
  "ungodly equality," 46
  unmoved by passive resistance, 122
Afro-Arab Summit (1977), 170
Afro-Asiatic languages, 27
Age grade, 20, 53

Age groups, **20**
Age set, 20
Agni, 136
Agricultural collectives (Tanzania), 68–69
Agricultural Revolution, 12, 20–21
Agriculture, 19, **20–21**
　cash crops, 21
　development and, 103
　development islands of, 106
　economic development, 105
　economic viability of, 115
　migration and, 22
　ministries of, 94
　modernization and, 117, 118
　specialization of labor and, 21
　subsistence, 21
　in Sudanic Belt, 16
　New World crops in Africa, 22
Air Afrique, 164
Aksum, 3, 26
ALC. *See* African Liberation Committee
Algeria. *See* Guide to Countries
Alignment, 119
Ali, Muhammad. *See* Muhammad Ali
Al-Mahdi, Muhammad Ahmad. *See* Mahdi, Muhammad Ahmad Al-
Aluko, Olajide, 156
Ambassador, 143
American Revolution, 135
Amin, Idi
　expulsion of Asians, 51
　Israel and, 170
　Julius Nyerere and, 146
　mercenaries and, 129
　rescue at Entebbe, 185
　terrorism and, 84, 145
Amnesty International, 135, 163
ANC. *See* African National Congress
Ancient Ghana, 16, 17, 32
Ancient Mali, 16, 17, 32
Anderson, David, 167
Anglophone Africa, 163, **173–175**
Angola. *See* Guide to Countries
Anticolonialism, 151
Apartheid, **35–36,** 41, 122, 170, 183, 188, 191
　Asians and, 51
　boycott and, 141
　Coloreds and, 42–43
　divestiture and, 180
　Lusaka Manifesto and, 157
　nonaligned nations and, 184
　OAU and, 158
　separate development, 50
　Sullivan principles and, 187
Arab Africans, 175

Arab Bank for Economic Development in Africa (BADEA), 153, **175**
Arab bloc, 184
Arabic, 8, 16
Arabic-speaking Africa, 159, 164, 169
Arab influences, 4
Arab League, 153, 164, 169, 191
Arabs, 8, 59
Arab states, 117, 173
Armed struggle, 128
Arms embargo, 159
Army officers, 131
Art, 21
Arusha Declaration, **68–69**
Asante. *See* Ashanti
Ashantehene (king of the Ashanti), 54–55
Ashanti, 32, 82
Ashanti (Asante) resistance, **54–55**
Ashanti Empire, 17, 55
Ashanti wars, 61
Asian settlers, 13, 35, 39, **50–51**
　Black antagonism and, 51
　expelled from Kenya, 51
Assassination, 134
Assembly of Heads of States and Governments, 158
Assimilado Policy, **36–37**
Assimilation, 37
Association, French colonial policy of. 37
Aswan Dam in Egypt, 186
Atheism, 68
Atlantic slave trade, 17, **21,** 63
Atlas Mountains, 5
Australia, 91
Authoritarianism, 82
Authoritative politics, 81
Autocratic rule, 88
Autonomy vs. independence, 44–45
Awolowo, Obafemi (chief), 78
Axum. *See* Aksum
Azania, 123
Azanian People's Organization (AZAPO), 123
Azikiwe, Nnamdi, 77

BADEA. *See* Arab Bank for Economic Development in Africa
Baganda, 82
Bai Bureh, 64
Bairoch, Paul, 115
Balance of power, 49
Balewa, Abubaker Tafawa, 157
Bambata, 64
Banning, practice of, 122, 124, 134

Bantu Affairs Department (South
    Africa), 39, 149
"Bantu" peoples (South Africa), 149
Bantu-speaking peoples, **22–23**, 27
Bantustans (Homelands in South
    Africa), 43, **149–150**
Baptist church, 57–58
Barth, H., 44
Basutoland. *See* Guide to Countries,
    Lesotho
Bechuanaland. *See* Guide to Countries,
    Botswana
Belgian Congo. *See* Guide to Countries,
    Zaire
Belgian Empire, **37–38**
    independence movement in, 127
    Kimbanguism in, 57–58
    Kitawala Movement and, 58
    Leopold II (King), 37, 64
Belgium
    Berlin Conference of 1884–85 and,
        38
    Shaba invasions and, 165, 166
    Zaire and, 58, 127
Beliefs, 85
Benevolent monarchies, 96
Benin. *See* Guide to Countries
Benin City (Nigeria) and British
    destruction, 64
Benin, precolonial kingdom of, 17, 32
Berbers, 25
Berlin Conference of 1884–85, **38–39**
Biafra, 77, 136, 185
Bicameralism, 94
Biko, Steve, 122
Biology and culture, 23
Bismarck, Otto von, 38
Black Africa, 14, 127, 169
Black Africans, 17, 23, **39**. *See also*
    Blacks
Black African states, 36
    Arabic-speaking states and, 159
    critical of BADEA, 175
    Ethiopian conflicts and, 159
    refugees, 162
    relations with Israel, 159
    Zionism as racism and, 191
Black consciousness, **122–123**
Black Frenchmen, 45
Black Jews, 170
Black majority rule, 149
Black minority governments, 162
Blacks, 35, **39,** 56, 57–58, 165
    ANC and, 121
    boycotts against segregation, 141
    Clark Amendment and, 177
    Coloreds and, 42

denied citizenship in South Africa,
    121
divestiture and, 179, 187
Homelands (South Africa) and, 149,
    150
land ownership denied (South
    Africa), 121
negritude and, 78
pan-Africanism and, 78
resistance to the Central African
    Federation, 55–56
Sharpeville killings, 122
in Sudan's civil war, 123
as victims of terrorism, 84
violations of human rights and, 159
Bloch, Dora, 185
Boahen, A. Adu, 55, 219
Boer doctrine of the "elect," 40
Boers, **39–40,** 46–47
Boer War (1899–1902), **40,** 47
Bokassa, Jean-Bedel, 84, 146
Bongo, Albert-Bernard (Omar), 130
Booth, Joseph, 56
Bophuthatswana (Homeland in South
    Africa), 149
Botswana. *See* Guide to Countries
Boundaries in Africa, 50, 77
Bourgeaud, Gilbert. *See* Bob Denard
Boycott, 56, **141–142**, 163, 164
    Byrd Amendment and, 175, 188
    Luthuli's plea, 179
    Polisario and, 160
Braibanti, Ralph, 88
Brandt, Willy, 110
Brazil, 91
Bridewealth, 25
British Commonwealth, 41
British Empire, **40–41**. *See also* Great
    Britain
British West Africa, 127
Broederbond, **41**
Buganda, 32
Bunyoro, 32
Bureaucracy
    development administration and,
        87–88
    indigenization and, 93
    modernization and, 118
    political development, 112
    public administration, 100–101
Bureaucratic structures, 114
Bureau for the Placement and
    Education of African Refugees,
    163
Burmi, battle of, 57
Burton, R., 44
Burundi. *See* Guide to Countries

230   The African Political Dictionary

Bushman. *See* San
Bushmanoid, 12
Byrd Amendment, **175–176**
Byrd, Harry, 175

Cabinet, 90, 94
Caiden, Naomi, 99
Caillié, René, 44
Calvinism, 39
Cameroon. *See* Guide to Countries
Camp David accords, 171
Canada, 91
  "contact" group, 173, 183
  MNCs and, 118
Cape Colony, 40, 46
Cape Malays, 42
Cape Verde. *See* Guide to Countries
Capitalism, 67, 75, 146
  classes and, 82
  dependency, 104
  economic growth of, 104, 105
  inequality, 104
  neocolonialism and, 107
  parastatals, 98
  planning, 99
  as revolutionary, 136
Carter, Jimmy, 176, 187, 188
Carthage, 26
Casablanca Group, 157, 184
Casely-Hayford, J. R., 65
Castro, Fidel, 178
Catholicism, 48
Caucasoid, 12
CEAO. *See* West African Economic Community
Central Africa, **3,** 13, 16, 163
  Bantu languages, 27
  kingdoms in, 32
  as source of slaves, 21
Central African Federation, **55–56**
Central African Republic. *See* Guide to Countries
Centralization, governmental, 112, 118
Césaire, Aimé, 77
Chad. *See* Guide to Countries
Chagos Archipelago, 8
Champmarin, A., 107
Changamire, 32
Chargé d'affaires, 143
Chief, 31
Chief executives, 94
Chiefs, Warrant, **51–52**
Chilembwe, John, **56**
China
  divestiture in, 178
  FNLA and, 178
  as model for escaping neocolonialism, 108

policy in Africa, 176–177
Robert Mugabe and, 128
Shaba invasions and, 165
Soviet competition and, 128, 186
Chinese policy in Africa, **176–177**
Christianity, 78
  Catholic, 29
  among Coloreds, 42
  communism in, 69
  Coptic, 4, 28, 29
  diffusion into Africa, 114
  education, 29, 48
  imperialism and, 55
  independent churches, 55
  Kimbanguism, 57–58
  Mau Mau, 59–60
  missions and missionaries, 29, 48
  polygyny, 25
  Protestant, 29
  racism and, 55
  slave trade and, 29
  in Sudan, 123
  in Uganda, 64
Christian missions, **48**
Chromium, 16, 175–176
Churches, African independent, **54**
Circumcision, 30
Ciskei (Homeland), 150
Cities, 16, 17
Citizenship, 145
Civil rights (in Marxist states), 76
Civil servants (in military systems), 133
Civil service standards (in parastatals), 98
Civil service systems, 100–101
Civil wars, 91, **123–124,** 135
  in Angola, 178
  in Nigeria, 91, 124, 185
  international war and, 155
Clans, 19
Clapperton, H., 44
Clark Amendment, **177–178**
Class distinctions, 20, 82
Class struggle, 68, 75
Climate, **4**
Clitoridectomy, 30
Cocoa, 21
Coffee, 21
Cold War, 183–184
Collective good, 82
Colonialism
  the African Group and, 173
  African intervention in, 145, 156
  Afro-Arab summit and, 171
  Angola and, 179
  OAU and, 158
  public administration and, 101
  Soviet policy on, 186

Index

Colonialism/Imperialism, **41–42**
  Aba women's riots and, 53
  African independent churches and, 55
  Ashanti resistance, 54–55
  Belgian Empire, 38
  Berlin Conference of 1884–85 and, 38–39
  British Empire, 40–41
  Chilembwe, John, 56
  dependency and, 104
  direct rule and, 43
  education and, 48–49
  French Empire, 45
  Fulani resistance, 57
  German Empire, 46
  independence movements and, 127
  indigenization and, 92
  indirect rule and, 47
  Italian Empire, 48
  Kimbanguist resistance, 57–58
  Kitawala movement, 58
  Maji Maji Rebellion, 59
  Mau Mau and, 59–60
  Muhammad Ali and, 60
  Ndebele-Shona Rebellion, 61
  political culture and, 80
  Portuguese Empire, 49
  proto-nationalism and, 61–62
  Samori Touré, 62–63
  Sanusiyya resistance, 63
  scramble for Africa, 49–50
  Spanish Empire, 52
  superior European weapons and, 65
  Watch Tower Movement and, 66
Colonial possessions, map, 197
Colonizers, 82
Colony, 38, 206
Coloreds, 35, 39, **42–43**
Commerce and finance (ministries of), 94
Commissioner, 95
Commission on refugees, 162
Commonwealth, 41, 143, 153
  member nations, 174
  South Africa and, 40
Communal instability, **124,** 128
Communalism, 67, 68
Communications, 105
Communism, **69–70**
  equalitarian goals, 81
  socialism and, 82–83
Communist party, 70, 112
Communists as ideologues, 73
Communist states, parastatals in, 98
Communist technicians and military personnel, 216–217
Community, French. *See* French Community

Comoro Islands. *See* Guide to Countries
Comparative population growth rate, 11
Competitive candidates, 88–89
Competitive party system, **85–86**
Computer age, 117
Congo. *See* Guide to Countries
Congo Free State, 37, 38
Congo River, 44. *See also* Zaire River
Consciousness, Black, **122–123**
Constitution, 70, **86–87,** 91
Constitutionalism, **70–71**
Constitutional monarchy, 206
Constitution Drafting Committee (Nigeria), 90
Construction, 116
"Contact" groups, 173, 183
Contagion effect, **124–125**
Contract negotiation, 98
Convention People's Party (CPP, Ghana), 127
Coordinating Committee for the Liberation Movements of Africa, **142–143**
Copper, 16, 65
Coptic Christianity, 4
Corruption, 101
Cotton, 21
Council of Ministers. *See* Organization of African Unity (OAU)
Council of State (Ghana), 95
Coup d'etat, 96, 123, **125–126,** 133, 135
Craftsmanship, 21
Credit (foreign aid), 117
Creole languages, 27, 29
Crocker, Chester A., 148, 189
Crowder, Michael, 57
Cuba
  alignment and, 184
  Angola and, 156, 177
  Ethiopia and, 156
  failure of divestiture in, 179
  as model for escaping neocolonialism, 108
  Shaba invasions and, 166
  United States policy on, 188
Cubans in Africa, 139, **178–179**
Cultural evolution, 33
Cultural nationalism, 77
Culture, 20, **23–24,** 33, 114
Customs and Economic Union of Central Africa (UDEAC), 153–154, 164

Dahomey. *See* Guide to Countries, Benin
Dahomey, precolonial kingdom, 17, 32
Danquah, J. B., 68
Dar es Salaam, 142

Dash (corruption), 79
Data and planning, 99
Debt cancellation, 110
Decentralized political structures, 105
Decree, **87**
Defense, ministries of, 94
de Gaulle, Charles, 44, 45
Democracy, **71–73**, 82, 87
    equalitarian goals and, 81
    "one-party" systems and, 68
Democratic Party of Guinea (PDG), 127
Democratic political patterns, 114
Democratic systems
    Botswana, 204
    Egypt, 204
    Gambia, 205
    Mauritius, 206
    Nigeria, 206
    Senegal, 206
    South Africa (for Whites only), 206
    Zimbabwe, 207
Demographic transition, **9**
Denard, Bob, 130
Denmark, 148
Department of France (Réunion), 206
Department of Plural Relations (South Africa), 39
Departments in executive branches, 94
Dependency, 108
Dependency theory, development, **103–104**
Desert
    Kalahari, 6
    Namib, 6
    Sahara, 6
Developed countries, 114
Developing countries, 89, 114
Development, **103**
    dependency theory, **103–104**
    economic, **105–106**
    least developed countries (LLDC), **106–107**
    neocolonialism, **107–109**
    New International Economic Order (NIEO), **109–110**
    North-South dialogue, **110–111**
    political, **111–113**
    social, **113**
    without growth, 105
Development Administration, **87–88**, 94, 99, 101, 202–203
"Development islands," 105–106
Development thesis, militarism, **131–132**
Diamonds, 16
Dictatorship, 68, 70, 86, 98, 205
Diego Garcia Island, 8, 175
Diffusion theory, **114–115**

Diplomatic relations, **143–144**, 154, 214–215
Direct rule, **43**, 59
Disengagement, 104
Distribution of powers, 92
Divestiture in South Africa, **179–180**
Djibouti. *See* Guide to Countries
Doctrinal purity, 128
Domestic affairs, 150–151
Domestic elites, 108
Domestic jurisdiction, **144–146**
Domino thesis, 124–125
Drakensberg Mountains, 5
Droughts, 15
Dutch Reformed Church (South Africa), 35, 40, 41

EAC. *See* East African Community
East Africa, **3**, 16, 163
    age groups in, 20
    Asian settlers in, 50
    Bantu languages, 27
    kingdoms in, 32
    racism in, 13
    slavery, 21
East African Airways, 146
East African Common Services Organization, 146
East African Community (EAC), **146–147**, 164
East Germany. *See* Germany, East
ECA. *See* Economic Commission for Africa
Economic aid to Africa, 190
Economic and Social Council (UN), 173
Economic Commission for Africa (ECA), 140, 152, 159
Economic Community of West Africa (CEAO), 180
Economic Community of West African States (ECOWAS), 116, **147–148**, 154, 164
Economic cooperation vs. political unity, 157
Economic dependency, 104
Economic development, **105–106**, 140
    development administration and, 87
    foreign aid and, 116
    OPEC oil price increase and, 111
    politics and, 88, 112
Economic equality, 110, 115
Economic gap, 106
Economic growth, 105
Economic viability, 12, **115–116**
Economic vs. military aid, 190
ECOWAS. *See* Economic Community of West African States
Education, 48–49, 94, 118

EEC. *See* European Economic Community
Egypt. *See* Guide to Countries
Egypt-Israeli peace treaty, 171
Eker, Varda, 80
Ekpo, Monday U., 80
Elections, 81, **88–89,** 112
Elite instability, 129
Elites, 118, 124
Embargo, 145, **148,** 164, 179
Emergency Committee for African Refugees of the Phelps-Stokes Fund, 162
Emirs, 57
Emperor or supreme king, 31
Empire
  Ashanti, 55
  Belgian, 37–38
  British, 40
  French, 45
  German, 46
  Italian, 48
  Mande, 62
  Portuguese, 49
  Spanish, 52
Energy, 88, 115
Engels, Frederick, 75, 83
English-speaking Africa. *See* Anglophone Africa
Entente Council (Conseil de l'Entente), 154
Entrenched leadership, 112
Entrepreneurial class, 115
Envoy, 143
Equalitarian societies, 81
Equality, 47, 113
Equatorial Guinea. *See* Guide to Countries
Eritrea
  ALC refusal to support, 143, 151
  Ethiopian civil war, 123
  Italian colony, 48
  nationalism, 77
  secession, 136
  supported by Arabic-speaking states, 159
Ethiopia. *See* Guide to Countries
Ethiopian Church, 55
Ethiopian-Somali war, 124, 159
Ethnic fears, 124
Ethnic groups, 33, 77
Ethnicity, **24,** 101
Europe
  balance of power in Africa and, 49
  colonialism in Africa, 63
  explorations of Africa, 44
  MNCs and, 118
  pre-scramble contacts, 48

scramble for Africa, 4
slave trade and, 48
stereotypes of Africans, 67
trade with, 172
varieties of resistance to, 63–65
White settlers from, 51–52
European Economic Community (EEC), 107, 153, 172
European exploration of Africa, **43–44**
European languages, 114
Evolution, social, 135
Ewé, 136, 155
Executive, 70, 87, **89–91**
Executive Council (Benin), 95
Executive Council (South Africa), 95
Executives
  exchange of diplomats and, 143
  legislatures and, 94
  public administration and, 101
Experimentalism, 87–88
Explorers in Africa, **43–44**
Extended families, 25, 68
External factors and economic performance, 108

Family, 19, **24–25**
Fante, 55, 65
FAO. *See* Food and Agricultural Organization
Farming, 13, 15
Fascists, 73
Federal government, **91–92**
Federalism, 55–56
Federal Military Government (Nigeria), 133
First World, 119
Fixed prices, 110
FNLA. *See* National Front for the Liberation of Angola
FNLC. *See* Front for the National Liberation of the Congo
Food, 116
Food and Agricultural Organization (FAO), 152
Ford, Gerald, 188
Foreign affairs, ministries of, 94
Foreign aid, **116–117**
  economic development and, 106, 108–109, 116
  NIEO and, 110
  United States and, 189
Foreign policy, 154
Foreign staffs, 98
Fourth World (LLDC), 106
France
  arms trade with South Africa, 148
  assimilation, 37
  association, 37

Berlin Conference of 1884-85 and, 38
colonial expansion, 63-64
colonial objectives, 37, 127
Community, 44-45
Comoro Islands and, 167
"contact" group, 173, 183
cultural chauvinism, 180
direct rule, 43
Empire, 45
Fourth Republic, 46
Mayotte, 151
mercenaries and, 130
political rights in colonies, 37
resistance to independence movements, 127
Samori Touré and, 62
South Africa and, 159
troops in Africa, 139
Union, 45-46
unitary system, 102
Francophone Africa, 147, 163, **180-181**
Francophonie, 180
Franc Zone, 153
Free market, 105, 189
FRELIMO. *See* Front for the Liberation of Mozambique
French Community, **44-45**
French Equatorial Africa, 3, 45
French Foreign Legion, 165
French in South Africa, 39
French National Assembly, 46
French Revolution, 135
French-speaking Africa, 67. *See also* Francophone Africa
French West Africa, 45, 127
Front for the Liberation of Mozambique (FRELIMO), 127, 142
Front for the National Liberation of the Congo (FNLC), 165
Front-Line States, **149**, 183, 188
Fulani, 12, 26
Fulani Resistance, **57**

Gabon. *See* Guide to Countries
Gambia. *See* Guide to Countries
Gandhi, Mahatma, 142
Gant, George, 98
Gene pool, 12
General Popular Committee (Libya), 95
General Secretariat (OAU), 158
Genocide, 123
Geography
climate, **4**
large land areas, 102
location, **4-5**
representation, 94
size, **5**
topography, **5-6**

German Empire, **46**
Germany
Berlin Conference of 1884-85 and, 38
Boers and, 39
colonies, 41
confrontation with Britain, 38-39, 56
Maji Maji Rebellion and, 59
Ruanda-Urundi and, 38
South West Africa and, 182
World War I and, 46
Germany, East, 166, 186
Germany, West, 173, 183
Ghana. *See* Guide to Countries
Ghana (ancient), 16, 17, 32
GNP/PC. *See* Gross National Product/Per Capita
Gods, 28
Gold, 16
Gold Coast, 54-55, 61, 65. *See also* Guide to Countries, Ghana
Golden stool, 55
Governmental centralization, 112
Government corporations, 98
Grant, J., 44
Grants, 116
Grasslands, 6
Great Britain
Aba Women's Riots and, 53
acephalous societies and, 52
Ashanti resistance, 54-55
Bai Bureh and, 64
Berlin Conference of 1884-85 and, 38
bilateral declaration of independence, 167
Boer War and, 40
Central African Federation and, 55
Chagos Archipelago and, 8
colonial policy, 127
Commonwealth and, 174
confrontation with Germany, 38-39
constitution, 86
constitutionalism and, 70
"contact" group, 173, 183
Diego Garcia Island and, 8
Fante allies, 55, 65
human rights in South Africa, 47
indirect rule, 47
Kenyan railroad, 64
King Ja Ja of Niger Delta, 64
Mahdist resistance in Sudan, 64
Mau Mau and, 59-60
Mauritius and Queen of England, 96
Muhammad Ali and, 60
Northern Nigeria and, 57
OAU and, 151
parliamentary executive, 90
Royal Niger Company, 64

slave trade, 21, 29
South Africa and, 159
Southern Africa and, 15
supremacy of Parliament, 102
tax resistance in Sierra Leone, 64
unilateral declaration of
  independence (Rhodesia), 149, 159
unitary system, 102
Warrant chiefs and, 52, 53
White settlers, 50
World War I and, 56
Zulu resistance of 1906 and, 64
Great Lakes, 5, 44
Great Powers, 36, 38–39
Great Rift Valley, **7**
Great Trek, **46–47**
Greenberg, Joseph H., 27
Griot, 28
Gross national product (GNP), 105
Gross national product/per capita
  (GNP/PC), **10,** 200
Group identification, 68
Group of 77, 110–111
Growth without development, 105
Guardian thesis, militarism, **132–133**
Guerrilla warfare, 36, **126,** 165
  African intervention and, 156
  ANC and, 121, 143
  Maoism, 128
  OAU and, 158
  PAC and, 134, 143
  Polisario and, 160
  refugees and, 163
  in Rhodesia, 56
  Samori Touré and, 62
  in South Africa, 52, 151
  SWAPO and, 183
  UDI and, 167
  in Zimbabwe, 149
Guilds, 82
Guinea. *See* Guide to Countries
Guinea-Bissau. *See* Guide to Countries
Guinea coast, 13, 21

Habré, Hissene, 160
Hallett, Robin, 58, 66
Hassan (King of Morocco), 96
Hausa, 30, 32, 33
Hausa city states, 17
Hausa-Fulani, 82
Headless society. *See* Acephalous society
Head of government, 87, 96
Head of state, 96
Health services, 113
Herding, 16, 21, **25–26**
High commissioner, 143
Higher education, 118
Highlands, 5

Hindi, 27
Hiring and firing in parastatals, 98
Hispanophone Africa, **181**
Historical materialism, 75
Hoare, Mike, 130
Holland (Netherlands), 21
Homelands (South Africa), 43, **149–150**
Homogeneity of population, 103
Horn, The, **7,** 16, 162, 186
Hottentot. *See* Khoi-Khoi
Houphouet-Boigny, Felix, 37, 44, 46,
  72
House of Assembly (Zimbabwe), 94
House of Chiefs (Botswana), 94
House of Representatives (Nigeria), 94
Huguenots, 39
Humanism, 68
Human rights, 146
Human rights, proposed charter on,
  159
Hunting and gathering, 19, **26**
Huntington, Samuel P., 117
Hutu, 84, 146

Ibo. *See* Igbo
IBRD. *See* International Bank for
  Reconstruction and Development
  or World Bank
IDA. *See* International Development
  Association
Ideological parties, 85
Ideologues, 73–74
Ideology, 23, **73–74,** 114
  Cubans in Africa, 179
  modernization and, 117
  "one-party" systems and, 98
  parastatals and, 98
IFC. *See* International Finance
  Corporation
Igbo (Ibo), 19, 30, 33
  as classless society, 82
  Nigerian civil war and, 123, 124
  secessionists, 136
Illiteracy, 105
Imperialism. *See* Colonialism/
  Imperialism
Import restriction, 110
Incarceration, political, 135
Indebtedness, 116
Independence movements, 52, 77, **127,**
  188
Independent Commission of
  International Development Issues,
  110
India, 91, 127, 148
Indian Ocean area, **7,** 163
Indians, 50–51, 64
Indigenization, **92–93,** 101

Indirect rule, **47**
Industrial and Commercial Workers' Union, 65
Industrialization, 68–69, 118
Industrial Revolution, 9, 12, 103, 117
Industries, Science and Technology, Ministry of, 95
Inefficiency, 93, 101
Information and Presidential Affairs, Ministry of, 95
Inheritance of office, 81
Instability, 115, 117
Instability, communal, **124**
Institutions, governmental, 112
Interest aggregation, 97
Interest articulation, 97
Interest-free loans, 110
Interest groups, 94, 99–100
Inter-ethnic violence, 124
Internal Affairs, Ministry of, 94
Internal factors and economic performance, 108
Internally sustained economic growth, 105
International Bank for Reconstruction and Development (IBRD or World Bank), 152
International Court of Justice, 150, 160, 173, 183
International Development Association (IDA), 152
International Finance Corporation (IFC), 152
International law, **150–152**, 154
International organization, **152–154**
International pricing, 99
International relations, **154–155**
International war, **155–156**
Intervention, **156**, 185, 186
Iran, 144
Iraq, 175
Iron use, 22, **26–27**
Irredentism, 124, 155
Islam, 4, 8
   among Coloreds, 42
   diffusion, 16, 29, 78, 114
   in Nigeria, 170
   in North Africa, 14, 16, 169
   regionalism and, 164
   in Sudan, 123
   traditional African law and, 16
Israel
   African Group and, 173
   peace treaty with Egypt, 184
   relations with African states, 117, 170
   relations with South Africa, 191
   rescue at Entebbe, 185
   terrorism and, 83

Italian Empire, **48,** 63
Ivory Coast. *See* Guide to Countries

Ja Ja (King of Niger Delta), 64
Japan, 15, 118
Jefferson, Thomas, 188
Jehovah's Witnesses, 66. *See also* Watch Tower Movement
Johanson, Donald, 7
Johnson, Lyndon, 176, 188
Joint venture, 109
Jonathan, Leabua, 96
Judicial bodies, 70, 101
Jurisdiction disputes, 91
Jurisdiction, domestic, **144–146**
Justice, Ministry of, 94

Kabaka of Baganda (King), 64
Kadalie, Clements, 65
Kalahari Desert, 6, 12
Kamwana, Eliot, 66
Kanem-Bornu, 17, 32
Katanga, 136, 165. *See also* Shaba
Kaunda, Kenneth David, 68
Kennedy, John F., 188
Kenya. *See* Guide to Countries
Kenyatta, Jomo, 77, 146
Kerekou, Mathieu, 130
Khoi-Khoi, 40, 42
Khoisan, 12, 22, 27
Kikuyu, 59–60
Kimbanguism, **57–58,** 66
Kimbangu, Simon, 57–58
King as chief of state, 31
Kinship, 20, 33, 68
Kissinger, Henry, 177
Kitawala Movement, **58,** 66
Kodjo, Edem, 160
Kongo, 32
Kordofanian, 27
Kpelle, 30
Kush, 26
Kuwait, 175
Kwaku Dua III (King of the Ashanti), 54–55

Labor, Ministry of, 94
Labor theory of value, 75
Labor unions, 65, 118
Lagos, 147
Lagos Plan of Action, 159
Lake Chad, 63–64
Lake Victoria, 6, 12, 64
Lander, R., 44
Lands and Natural Resources, Ministry of, 95
Languages, 24, **27**
Larkin, Bruce D., 177

Law, international. *See* International Law
LDC. *See* Less developed countries
Leadership succession, 112
League of Nations mandates, 38, 41, 42, 45, 182
Leakey, Louis B., 7
Leakey, Richard, 7
Least developed countries (LLDC), **106–107**
Lebanon, 51
Legislative acts, 87
Legislative bodies, 70
Legislature, 89–90, **93–94**, 101
Legitimacy, **74**, 89, 94, 112
Legum, Colin, 128, 135, 136, 148, 163, 170, 184
Lenin, V. I., 97
Leninism-Stalinism, 76, 185
Lenshina, Alice, 124
Leopold II (King of Belgium), 37–38, 49
Lerner, Daniel, 117
Lesotho. *See* Guide to Countries
Less developed countries (LDC), 106, 107, 110
Levantine settlers, **51**
Liberalism, 47
Liberia. *See* Guide to Countries
Libya. *See* Guide to Countries
Lifespan, 113
Limann, Hilla, 95
Limpopo River, 56
Lincoln, Abraham, 188
Lingua francas, 27
Literacy, 103, 113
LLDC. *See* Development
Loans, 116
Local entrepreneurs, 93
Local Government and Rural Development, Ministry of, 95
Loi-cadre (French community), 44
Lomé conventions, 153
Lomé I and II, 172
Lozi, 32
Lualaba River, 44
Luba, 32
Lugard, Sir Frederick, 57
Lumpa Church, 124
Lumumba, Patrice, 185
Lunda, 32
Lusaka Manifesto, **156–157**
Lusophone Africa, **181–182**
Luthuli, Albert John, 121, 134, 179

Maasai, 26, 82
Machine guns, 65
Madagascar. *See* Guide to Countries
Maghreb, **8,** 170
Mahdi, Muhammad Ahmad Al-, 64
Mahdists, 64
Maji Maji Rebellion, **59**
Majoritarian democracy, 72
Malagasy Republic. *See* Madagascar
Malan, Dr. D. F., 40
Malawi. *See* Guide to Countries
Malayo-Polynesian languages, 27
Mali. *See* Guide to Countries
Mali (ancient), 16, 17, 32
Malinke (Mande), 62
Management prerogatives, 98
Mandates, 38, 41, 42
Mande (Malinke), 62
Maoism, **128–129**
Mao Tse-tung, 68, 128
Marriage, 25, 30
Marxism, 68, **74–76**, 104, 178, 185
Marxism-Leninism, 69
Marxist mobilizational patterns, 114
Marxists, 70
Marxist states, 98, 118
Marx, Karl, 68, 69, 74–76, 82–83
Mashona chiefs, 94
Mashonaland, 61
Massacre, 134
Mass education, 118
Mass instability, 124, **129**
Mass participation, 89, 112, 118
Matabele chiefs, 94
Matabeleland, 61
Mau Mau, **59–60**
Mauritania. *See* Guide to Countries
Mauritius. *See* Guide to Countries
Maxim guns, 57
Mayotte, 7, 151, 167
Mazrui, Ali, 170
Mboya, Tom, 142
Mbuti, 26
McGowan, Patrick J., 104
Mende-Temne clashes, 124
Mengistu, Haile Miriam, 84
Mercenaries, **129–130**
Middle class, 82
Middle East, 8, 14, 26, 173
Middle East and Africa, **169–172**
Militancy, 121, 134
Militarism, **130–131**
  development thesis, **131–132**
  guardian thesis, **132–133**
Military
  aid, 190
  coup, 124, 125, 195
  defense, 21
  dictatorships, 72, 204–207
  equipment and training, 116
  intervention, 156

officers, 93
regimes, 87, 89, 96
rule, 74, **133–134**
strength, 116
Military Committee for National Salvation (Mauritania), 96, 133
Minerals, 16, 115
Mining, 106
Minister plenipotentiary, 143
Ministries, 88, **94–96**, 202–203
Ministry of Plural Relations (South Africa), 149
Missions and missionaries (Christian), **48–49**
Mixed economic systems, 98
MNC. *See* Multinational Corporation
Mobilization machines, 70, 86, 94, 97
Mobutu Sese Seko, 165
Modernization, 88, **117–118**
Moi, Daniel Arap, 160
Mombasa (Kenya), 64
Monarchy, **96**
Mondale, Walter, 188
Mongoloid, 12
Monogamy, 25
Monrovia Group, 157, 184
Morocco. *See* Guide to Countries
Morocco-Polisario War, 159, 160
Morrison, Donald G., 104, 124, 155
Moshoeshoe II (King of Lesotho), 96
Mount Cameroon, 5
Mount Kenya, 5
Mount Kilimanjaro, 5
Mozambique. *See* Guide to Countries
MPLA. *See* Popular Movement for the Liberation of Angola
Mugabe, Robert, 128, 176, 189
 guerrilla leader, 149
 opposition to competitive party system, 86
 Patriotic Front and, 143
Muhammad Ali, **60**
Multinational Corporation (MNC), **118–119**
 dependency and, 104
 neocolonialism and, 107–108
 NIEO and, 110
Multiracialism, 122
Muslim countries, 196
Muzorewa, Abel, 176
Myrdal, Gunnar, 115

Namib Desert, 6
Namibia. *See* Guide to Countries
Namibia Issue, **182–183**
Napoleon, 60
Nasser, Gamal Abdul, 184, 185
Natal, 40, 51

Nation, 33
National Assembly (Botswana), 94
National Congress of British West Africa, 61, 65
National Executive Council (Zaire), 95
National Front for the Liberation of Angola (FNLA)
 Chinese support for, 128, 176, 178
 civil war in Angola, 177
 independence movement, 127, 142
 South Africa support for, 178
 United States support for, 178
National integration, 113, 118
Nationalism, 61, 65, 74, **76–77**
 education and, 48–49
 Marxism and, 76
 Mau Mau and, 59–60
 pan-Africanism and, 78
 regionalism and, 164
 Zionism as, 190
Nationalists, 188
Nationalization, 98, 109
National Party (South Africa), 35, 40, 41, 50
National planning, 87–88
National self-reliance, 104
National Union for the Total Independence of Angola (UNITA)
 China support, 128, 176
 civil war in Angola, 177
 as independence movement, 127, 142
 mercenaries and, 129
 South African support, 178
 United States support, 178
Natives Land Act (South Africa), 50
Ndebele, 61
Ndebele-Shona Rebellion of 1896–1897, **61**
Negrillo, 12
Negritude, 67, **77–78**
Negro Digest, quoted, 78
Negroid, 12
Nehru, Jawaharlal, 184
Neocolonialism, 104, **107–109**, 184
Neolithic Age, 27
Netherlands, 39, 122
Neto, Agostinho, 143, 178
Neutralism, 119
New International Economic Order (NIEO), **109–110**, 117, 128, 172, 177
New Stone Age, 27
New World crops, 22
New World slavery, 29
Nguema, Francisco, 84
Nguema, Macias, 146
NIEO. *See* New International Economic Order

Niger. *See* Guide to Countries
Niger Basin Authority, 154
Niger-Congo languages, 27
Niger Delta, 64
Nigeria. *See* Guide to Countries
Niger River, 6, 44, 63
Nile River, 6, 44
Nilo-Saharan languages, 27
Nilotes, 12
Nixon, Richard, 188
Nkomo, Joshua, 128, 143, 149, 176
Nkrumah, Kwame
 African Defense Force and, 139
 African personality, 67
 Casablanca Group and, 157
 Convention People's Party and, 127
 Gandhi and, 142
 as ideologue, 73
 independence for Ghana and, 127
 nationalist, 77
 neocolonialism and, 107
 nonalignment and, 184
 pan-Africanism and, 78, 169
 Togo and, 158
Nomads, 15
Non-Aligned Summit (1964), 110
Non-Aligned Summit (1979), 184
Nonalignment, 119, 151, 158, **183-184,** 188
Noncompetitive candidates, 88-89
Non-governmental organization (NGO), 152
Nonideological parties, 85
Nonintervention, 157
Nonviolence, 121
Non-Whites, 40, 41, 43
"No-party" system, **97**
North Africa, **8,** 163
 Afro-Asiatic languages and, 27
 Europe and, 16
 Islam and, 16
 Middle East and, 14, 169-171
Northern Nigeria, 47
Northern Rhodesia. *See* Guide to Countries, Zambia
North-South dialogue, 109, **110-111**
Nuclear cooperation, 148
Nuer, 19, 82
Nuncio, 143
Nutrition, 113
Nyasaland. *See* Guide to Countries, Malawi
Nyerere, Julius
 African Defense Force and, 140
 African socialism, 68
 Arush Declaration and, 68-69
 East African Community and, 164
 failures of agricultural policies and, 68-69
 Idi Amin and, 146
 nationalist, 77
 pan-Africanist, 169
 socialist revolution and, 136

OAPEC. *See* Organization of Arab Petroleum Exporting Countries
OAU. *See* Organization of African Unity
Obote, Milton, 170
OCAM. *See* African and Mauritian Common Organization
Ogaden, 124, 136
Okpara, Michael, 68
Olugbemi, Stephen O., 88
Olympio, Sylvanus, 158
"One-party" system, 72, **97-98,** 100, 205-207
 decrees and, 87
 democracy and, 68
 elections and, 89
 legislatures and, 94
 Marxism and, 76
 membership in, 68-69
 as mobilization machines, 97
 socialist states and, 83
OPEC. *See* Organization of Petroleum Exporting Countries
Oral tradition, **28**
Orange Free State, 40
Orange River, 46
Order of the Seraphim and Cherubim, 55
Organization for Economic Cooperation and Development (OECD), 15
Organization for the Development of the Senegal Basin, 154
Organization, international, **152-154**
Organization of African Unity (OAU), 7, 155, **157-160,** 164
 African Defense Force, 139, 140
 African Group, 173
 African Liberation Committee, 142
 African Liberation Day, 142
 Angola and, 177
 boycotts, 141
 Charter, 157-158
 committees, 158
 Council of Ministers, 95, 158
 divestiture in South Africa, 179
 embargoes on South Africa, 148
 governing principles, 151, 158
 Homelands in South Africa and, 150
 Israel and, 191
 Lusaka Manifesto, 157
 mercenaries and, 130
 MPLA and, 178
 nonalignment, 184

noninterference in internal affairs, 145, 156, 186
OAPEC and, 170
Polisario and, 124, 155, 160
political assassinations and, 151
refugees and, 162, 163
rescue at Entebbe, 185
Sullivan Principles and, 187
United States and, 189
weaknesses, 159, 166
Organization of Arab Petroleum Exporting Countries (OAPEC), 170
Organization of Petroleum Exporting Countries (OPEC), 107, 111, 184
Ottaway, David, 76, 105
Ottaway, Marina, 76, 105
Ottoman Empire, 60
Oyo, precolonial kingdom, 17, 32

PAC. *See* Pan-Africanist Congress
Palace coup, 96, 125
Palestine, 60, 170, 190
Palm oil trade, 64
Pan-Africanism, 77, **78–79**, 157, 164
Pan-Africanist Congress (PAC), 122, 126, **134**, 144, 159
Papal Internuncio, 143
Papal Legate, 143
Parastatal, 68–69, **98–99**, 133
Park, Mungo, 44
Parliament, 94
Parlimentary executive, 89–90
Partition of Africa. *See* Berlin Conference of 1884–85
Pastoral peoples, 15
Patriotic Front, 143, 159
Peace Corps, 188
Peaceful leadership succession, 112
Peasantry, 68, 128
People's Redemption Council (Liberia), 95, 133
Petroleum, development islands of, 106
Phillips, Claude S., 170
Phillips, Earl, 99
Planning, 87–88, 94, **99**
Plural economic activities, 106
Plural Relations, Minister of (South Africa), 149
Police officers, 93
Polisario Front, 8, 155, **160–161**
Morocco and, 124
OAU and, 143, 151, 159
Politburo (Somalia), 96
Political appointees, 95
Political assassinations, 151
Political corruption, **79–80**
Political culture, **80**
Political data, 204–207
Political development, **111–113**

Political elites, 82
Political independence, 108
Political instability, 74, 163, 208–213
Political integration, 27
Political participation, 131
Political parties, **99–100**
demands for independence, 127
legislatures and, 94
militarism and, 131
nationalism and, 77
Political prisoners, 135
Political Security Council, **161–162**
Political stability, 103, 116
Political violence, **134–135**
Politicians, 133
Politics, 21, **81**, 100, 105
Polygyny, 25, 55
Popular Movement for the Liberation of Angola (MPLA)
civil war in Angola, 177
Cuban troops, 178
independence movement, 127, 142
Neto, Agostinho, 178
OAU support, 159
Shaba conflicts, 165
Soviet support, 128, 176, 186
Population
decline, 38, 63
demographic transition, 9
density, 9
explosion, 9
gross national product/per capita (GNP/PC), **10**, 200
growth, **10**, 15, 115, 200
size, **11**, 22, 79, 102, 115, 201
Population Reference Bureau, 10, 11
Population representation, 94
Poro society, 31
Portugal
assimilado policy, 36
Berlin Conference of 1884–85 and, 38
boycott of, 141, 148, 165
claims in Africa, 38
explorations of Africa, 43–44
missionaries from, 48
non-racial policy, 36
resistance to independence movements, 127
scramble for Africa and, 49
slave trade and, 21
ties with former colonies, 182
UDI of Guinea-Bissau and, 167
Portuguese Empire, **49**
Portuguese-speaking Africa. *See* Lusophone Africa
Posts and Communications, Ministry of, 94
Poverty, 104, 116

Powers of government, 86
Praetorianism. *See* Militarism
Praise-poems, 28
Premier, chief executive as, 90
Prempeh I (King of the Ashanti), 54–55
President, chief executive as, 90, 94
Presidential executive, 89–90
Primacy of politics, 81
Prime minister, chief executive as, 90, 94
Privileges and immunities, diplomatic, 143–144
Productivity, problems of, 105
Professors and teachers, 116
Property destruction, 135
Protectorates, 42
Protestants, 48
Proto-Bantu, 22
Proto-nationalism, **61–62**, 65
Provisional Military Administrative Council (Ethiopia), 33
Public administration, **100–101**
  development administration and, 87
  indigenization and, 93
  military rule and, 133
  ministries, 95
  parastatals, 98
  principals of, 100
Public corporations, 98
Public Service Commission, 100–101
Public works, 87–88
Pygmies. *See* Mbuti
Pygmoid, 12

Qaddafy, Muammar, 133
  as ideologue, 73
  OAU host, 160
  PAC and, 134
  revolutionary, 136
Qualified competitive market, 82

Race, **12,** 24
Racial civil war, 36, 122, 143
Racism, **13**
  African Group and, 173
  African National Congress on, 121
  Afro-Arab Summit (1977) and, 171
  Angola and, 179
  Black consciousness, 122
  Byrd Amendment and, 176
  Chilembwe, John, 56
  induces African interventions, 145, 156
  Kitawala movement and, 58
  labor unions and, 65
  Lusaka Manifesto, 157
  mercenaries and, 130
  negritude, 77
  nonalignment and, 184
  OAU and, 151
  in Pan-Africanist Congress, 134
  Soviet policy on, 186
  in United States, 189
  Zionism as, 190
Railroad, 64, 177
Rain forest, 6, **13**
Reagan, Ronald, 148, 178, 183, 188
Rebellion, 53, 124, 135
"Red terror," 84
Referenda, 89
Refugees, 146, **162–163**
Regionalism, **163–164**
Regional populations, 201
Regions of Africa, 194
Regularized elections, 112
Relations, diplomatic, 143
Relations, international, **154–155**
Religion, 21, **28–29**
Religious groups, 73
Republic of South Africa. *See* Guide to Countries, South Africa
Rescue at Entebbe, **185**
Resistance to colonialism, 57, 63–65
Resistance to democracy, 72–73
Resolution 435 (UN Security Council), 183, 188
Respect for territorial boundaries, 157
Restraints on government, 70
Returned slaves, **29**
Réunion. *See* Guide to Countries
Revolt and mass instability, 129
Revolution, 129, **135–136**
Rhodes, Cecil, 61
Rhodesia. *See* Guide to Countries, Zimbabwe
Rhodesia (pre-independence)
  boycotts, 141, 148
  Byrd Amendment and, 176, 188
  OAU sanctions, 165
Right of self-determination, 151, 157
Rights and duties, 86
Riots, 53, 135
Riots, Aba Women's, **53**
Rites of passage, **29–30**
Robben Island (prison), 122, 134
Roberto, Holden, 143
Roman Empire, 9, 117
Roosevelt, Franklin, 188
Royal Niger Company, 64
Ruanda-Urundi, 38
Rubber, 21
Rub of cultures, 24
Rule, military, **133–134**

Rulers, 97
Russian Revolution (1917), 135
Rwanda. *See* Guide to Countries

Sabotage, 134
SADCC. *See* Southern African Development Coordination Conference
SADR. *See* Saharan Arab Democratic Republic
Sahara Desert, 6, **14**, 16, 63
Saharan Arab Democratic Republic (SADR), 160
Sahel, **14**
Sahel Club, 15
Sahelian drought, 162
Sahrawi Republic, 155
Salazar, Antonio de Oliveira, 165
Samori Touré, 61, **62–63**
San, 26, 40, 42
Sanction, **164–165**
Sanctity of inherited boundaries, 151
Sande society, 31
Sanusiyya Resistance, **63**
São Tomé and Príncipe. *See* Guide to Countries
SASO. *See* South African Student Organization
Satellites, 42
Saudi Arabia, 175
Savannah. *See* Sudan
Savings, 105
Science and technology, 87–88, 114
Scientific socialism, 82
Scientific view, 117
Scramble for Africa, **49–50**
Secession, **136–137**
Second World, 119, 144
Secretary, 94
Secret societies, **30–31**
Security Council Resolution 419 (UN), 130
Security Council Resolution 435 (UN), 183
Segregation. *See Apartheid*
Selassie, Haile, 157
Self-determination in Lusaka Manifesto, 157
Self-reliance
 Arusha Declaration and, 68–69
 dependency and, 104
 economic development and, 108–109
 Maoism and, 128
 neocolonialism and, 108
Senate, 94
Senegal. *See* Guide to Countries
Senghor, Leopold, 68, 78
Separate development, **50**

Separation of powers, 94
Settlers
 Asian, **50–51**
 Levantine, **51**
 White (Europeans), **51–52**
Seychelles. *See* Guide to Countries
Shaba conflicts, 136, 159, **165–166**
Shagari, Shehu, 189
Shaka, 64
Sharpeville, 122, 134
Shona, 61
Sierra Leone. *See* Guide to Countries
Sisal, 21
Sklar, Richard, 119
Slavery, **31**, 42, 114, 188
Slave trade, Atlantic, **21–22**, 29, 31, 48, 49
Sobhuza (King of Swaziland), 96
Sobukwe, Robert, 122, 134
Social classes, **81–82**
Social conditions, chaotic, 131
Social development, **113**
Social institutions, 23, 114, 117
Socialism, 67–68, **82–83**
 Arusha Declaration and, 68–69, 147
 dependency and, 104
 diffusion into Africa, 114
 economic development and, 105
 neocolonialism and, 108
 planning and, 99
 as revolutionary, 136
 vanguard of workers and, 97
Socialists, 73
Socialist states, 98
Social mobility, 105
Social welfare, 87–88
Sokoine, Edward, 69
Sokoto (sultan of), 57
Somalia. *See* Guide to Countries
Somali-Ethiopian War, 124, 159
Somalis, 26, 30, 77, 136
Songhai, 16, 17, 32
South Africa. *See* Guide to Countries
South African Student Organization (SASO), 122
Southern Africa, **15**, 16, 163
 Bantu languages in, 27
 kingdoms in, 32
 racism in, 13
Southern African Customs Union, 164
Southern African Development Coordination Conference (SADCC), 164, **166–167**
Southern provinces of Sudan, 123
Southern Rhodesia. *See* Guide to Countries, Zimbabwe
South Korea, 148
South West Africa. *See* Guide to Countries, Namibia

Index

South West African People's Organization (SWAPO), 127, 143, 183
Soviet bloc, 75, 110, 122, 163
Soviet policy in Africa, **185–187**
Soviet Union. *See* Union of Soviet Socialist Republics (USSR)
Soweto, 122
Spain, 38, 160, 181
Spanish Empire, **52**
Spanish Sahara. *See* Guide to Countries, Western Sahara
Spanish-speaking Africa. *See* Hispanophone Africa
Special interest representation, 94
Special presidential advisors (Nigeria), 95
Speke, J., 44
Spengler, Joseph J., 115
Stages of economic development, 105
Stalin, Joseph, 99
Stanley, H. M., 44
State, 19, **31–32**
  agriculture and, 21
  Marxist concept of, 75
  politics and, 81
  socialism and, 82–83
State commissioner, 95
State formation, 62
Stateless society. *See* Acephalous society
State-owned enterprises, 98, 105
States of emergency, 87
Statutes, 87
Statutory authority, 98
Stereotypes of Africans, 67
Stolper, Wolfgang, 99
Strike and run tactics, 126
Strikes, 135
Sub-Saharan Africa, 13, **16,** 27, 29, 170
Subsistence agriculture, 105
Sudan. *See* Guide to Countries
Sudan (region), 6, 16, 27
Sudanic Belt, **16**
Sukarno, 184
Sullivan, Leon, 187
Sullivan Principles, **187**
Supreme Military Council
  Equatorial Guinea, 95
  Ghana, 133
  Niger, 133
Supreme Revolutionary Council (Madagascar), 96, 133
Swahili, 27, 28
SWAPO. *See* South West African People's Organization
Swaziland. *See* Guide to Countries
Sweden, 122
Switzerland, 91
Syria, 51, 60

"Take off" (second stage of economic development), 105
Tallensi, 82
Tambo, Oliver, 122
Tanganyika. *See* Guide to Countries, Tanzania
Tan-Zam (Tazara) railroad, 128
Tanzania. *See* Guide to Countries
Tanzania-Uganda war, 159
Technical experts, 116
Technology, 114, 116, 117
Tembu National Church, 55
Temne-Mende clashes, 124
"Ten percenters" and corruption, 79
Terrorism, 73, **83–84,** 134, 135, 145
Third World, 106–107, 110, 118, **119–120**
Tile, Nehemiah, 55
Timbuctu, 63
Tiriki, 30
Tito, Josip Broz, 184
Tiv, 19, 30
Tobacco, 21
Togo. *See* Guide to Countries
Torture, 134
Touré, Sekou, 44
  Democratic Party of Guinea and, 127
  failure of self-reliance, 109
  as ideologue, 73
  independence movement and, 127
  as nationalist, 77
  Pan-Africanism and, 169
Tourism, 146
Trade and Tourism, Ministry of, 95
Tradition, 81, 117
Traditional monarchy, 207
Traditional values, 131
Transhumance, 25
Transkei, 149
Transnational Corporation (TNC). *See* Multinational Corporation (MNC)
Transvaal, 40
Treaties, 154
Tribalism, 24, **32**
Tribe, **33**
Tropical Africa, **17**
True believers, 97
Trusts (UN), 42
Tswana, 149
Tubman, William V. S., 157
Tunisia. *See* Guide to Countries
Tutsi, 84, 146

UDEAC. *See* Customs and Economic Union of Central Africa
UDI. *See* Unilateral declaration of independence
Uganda. *See* Guide to Countries
Uganda-Tanzania war, 159

Underdevelopment. *See* Development
UNDP. *See* United Nations Development Program
UNESCO. *See* United Nations Educational, Scientific and Cultural Organization
UNHCR. *See* United Nations High Commissioner for Refugees
Unilateral declaration of independence (UDI), 159, **167**
Union, French, **45–46**
Union of South Africa. *See* Guide to Countries, South Africa
Union of Soviet Socialist Republics (USSR)
  aligned with Ethiopia, 184
  Angola and, 177
  arms to Libya, 189
  arms to South Africa, 148
  Aswan Dam, 116
  Byrd Amendment and, 176
  Chinese rivalry with, 176
  constitutionalism and, 70
  Egypt and, 116
  foreign aid and, 109
  influence, 188
  Joshua Nkomo and, 128
  leadership succession, 112
  Marxism-Leninism and, 69
  military presence, 139
  as model for escaping neocolonialism, 108
  MPLA and, 178
  noncompetitive elections, 88
  planning, 99
  policy in Africa, **185–187**
  Polisario and, 161
  Shaba invasions and, 166
  state power and, 76
UNITA. *See* National Union for the Total Independence of Angola
Unitary government, **102**
United Nations (UN), 12, 36, 106
  Africa Group, 158, 173
  boycott of Rhodesia, 141
  Congo (Zaire) crisis (1960–65), 188
  International Court of Justice, 150
  Namibia and, 182
  organizations, 152–153
  principles governing, 150
  Security Council, 130, 148, 150, 173, 183
  threats to peace and, 148
  Trustee system, 182
  Zionism as racism in, 170, 190, 191
United Nations Conference on Trade and Development (UNCTAD), 111
United Nations Development Program (UNDP), 152

United Nations Educational, Scientific and Cultural Organization (UNESCO), 153
United Nations High Commissioner for Refugees (UNHCR), 153
United Nations International Development Organization, 109
United Nations Trusts, 42
United Native African Church, 55
United States
  aid to Africa, 190
  Berlin Conference of 1884–85 and, 38
  "Contact" group and, 173, 183
  credits and, 117
  Diego Garcia Island and, 8
  federal system, 91, 102
  FNLA and, 128, 176, 178
  freed slaves and, 29
  military support for Morocco, 161
  Multinational Corporations (MNC) and, 118
  presidential executive, 90
  refugees and, 163
  trade with South Africa, 148
  UNITA and, 128, 176, 178
  Zaire and, 165
United States Policy in Africa, **187–190**
Universal Declaration of Human Rights, 151
Universalistic international organizations, 152–153
Universalistic values, 118
Upper Volta. *See* Guide to Countries
Uranium, 16
Urbanism, 21, **33**
Urbanization, 118
Urban Revolution, 12
Urundi, 46
USSR. *See* Union of Soviet Socialist Republics

Vaal River, 46
Vanguard of workers, 97
Vansina, Jan, 22
Varieties of African resistance to colonialism, **63–65**
Venda, 149
Vengroff, Richard, 104
Viability, economic, **115–116**
Village, 19
Village cooperatives, 68–69
Violence, 81, 122, 127, 142
Violence, political, **134–135**

Wage disparities, 65
Waldheim, Kurt, 148
War, civil, **123–124**
Warfare, guerrilla, **126**

Index

War, international, 154, **155-156**
Warrant chiefs, **51-52**
Watch Tower Movement, 55, 58, **66**
Wesleyan Methodist Church, 55
West Africa, 16, **17**, 163
  African independent churches and, 55
  Agricultural Revolution in, 21
  Fulani, 26
  great empires of, 16
  griots, 28
  independence movements, 127
  iron use in, 26
  kingdoms, 32
  Levantine settlers, 51
  Niger-Congo languages, 27
  population, 11
  precolonial states and empires, 17
  proto-nationalist movements, 61, 65
  secret societies, 31
  slave trade, 17, 21
  state formations, 62
  urbanization, 33
West African Economic Community (CEAO), 154
West coast of Africa, 106
Western democracies, 100
Western Industrialized Nations, 15
Westernization, 29
Western Sahara. *See* Guide to Countries
Western tastes, 108, 114
Western technology, 60
Western world, 109
West Germany. *See* Germany, West
White electoral roll (Zimbabwe), 94
White-minority governments, 162
Whites, 35
  Black unions and, 65
  Lusaka Manifesto and, 157
  as mercenaries, 129
  as racists, 52
  as settlers, 51-52
  sexual relations with non-Whites (South Africa), 43
  in Shaba conflicts, 165
  in South Africa, 179
  as terrorists in South Africa, 84
  violation of human rights and, 159
  in Zimbabwe, 55-56, 94
White settlers, **51-52**
  John Chilembwe and, 56
  Mau Mau and, 59-60
  resistance to independence movements, 127
  in Southern Africa, 15
  in Zimbabwe, 61
Wildavsky, Aaron, 99
Women's affairs, 88
Workers' vanguard, 97
Works and Housing, Ministry of, 95
World Bank (IBRD), 152
World Health Organization (WHO), 153
World trade and dependency, 104
World War I, 46, 49-50, 56
World War II, 127

Xhosa, 149

Yoruba, 30, 33, 71, 82
Young, Andrew, 188
Youth and Social Welfare, Ministry of, 95

Zaire. *See* Guide to Countries
Zaire River, 6
Zambezi River, 6, 44
Zambia. *See* Guide to Countries
ZANU, 128
Zanzibar. *See* Guide to Countries, Tanzania
Zanzibar Island, 33
  as British colony, 41
ZAPU, 128
Zartman, I. William, 6, 170
Zimbabwe. *See* Guide to Countries
Zionism as racism, 170, 171, 184, 185, **190-191**
Zone of peace, 8
Zulu, 64